ART REBELS

Art Rebels

Race, Class, and Gender in the Art of Miles Davis and Martin Scorsese

Paul Lopes

PRINCETON UNIVERSITY PRESS

PRINCETON AND OXFORD

Copyright © 2019 by Princeton University Press

Published by Princeton University Press
41 William Street, Princeton, New Jersey 08540
6 Oxford Street, Woodstock, Oxfordshire OX20 1TR

press.princeton.edu

All Rights Reserved

Library of Congress Control Number: 2018958699
ISBN 9780691159492

British Library Cataloging-in-Publication Data is available

Editorial: Meagan Levinson and Jacqueline Delaney
Production Editorial: Mark Bellis
Jacket Design: Layla Mac Rory
Jacket Credit: (*top*) Martin Scorsese, courtesy of Steve Schapiro;
(*bottom*) Miles Davis © Sony Music
Production: Erin Suydam
Publicity: Tayler Lord and Katie Lewis
Copyeditor: Dawn Hall

This book has been composed in Adobe Text Pro and Gotham

Printed on acid-free paper. ∞

Printed in the United States of America

10 9 8 7 6 5 4 3 2 1

CONTENTS

Introduction. American Rebels: The Heroic Age
of American Art   1

PART I: REBELS MAKING ART

Interlude   27

1   Miles Davis: Jazz, Race, and Negotiating the Popular   31

2   Martin Scorsese: Rival Narratives of Autonomy
in American Film   70

PART II: THE BIOGRAPHICAL LEGENDS OF REBELS

Interlude   105

3   Miles Davis: The Unreconstructed Black Man in Modern Jazz   109

4   Martin Scorsese: A Sojourn from Italian American to White
Ethnic American   146

Conclusion. American Rebels: Redux   176

Acknowledgments   199

Notes   201

Index   223

ART REBELS

American Rebels

THE HEROIC AGE OF AMERICAN ART

MILDRED: Hey Johnny, what are you rebelling against?
JOHNNY STRABLER: What do you got?
—THE WILD ONE (1953)[1]

Clad in a black leather jacket and slanted cap, astride a Triumph Thunderbird GT motorcycle, Marlon Brando's Johnny Strabler in *The Wild One* (1953) quickly became an iconic symbol of postwar rebellion. The real rebel, however, was not on the silver screen. Stanley Kramer was the producer behind this Hollywood studio film when he took an ill-advised two-year stint at Columbia Pictures in the middle of what was a legendary career as an *independent* producer and director in American film. Here is a list of some of his more famous independent films: *The Champion* (1949), *Home of the Brave* (1949), *Cyrano de Bergerac* (1950), *High Noon* (1952), *The Defiant Ones* (1958), *On the Beach* (1959), *Inherit the Wind* (1960), *Judgment at Nuremburg* (1961), and *Guess Who's Coming to Dinner* (1967). It was a heady time in Hollywood when Kramer began his career as an independent producer. The Hollywood studio system was collapsing and anyone and everyone were striking out on their own. It was the beginning of a long revolution in American film from the most pulp to the most avant-garde films. And Kramer was there at the beginning, personifying what *New York Times* columnist Peter Bart called the "the *enfant terrible*, the *wunderkind*, the tough-minded young operator who could work within the lethargic Hollywood system, yet produce films that defied its very precept."[2]

But it turns out that in the 1950s American rebels were popping up across the arts in film, music, dance, literature, poetry, and even pulp comic books. Marlon Brando's Johnny Strabler was actually not expressing a directionless ennui in answering Mildred's question about what he was rebelling against. He was expressing a general no-holds-barred attitude seemingly permeating American culture. Yet such a generalization is misleading, because this also was the Cold War era of suburban homes, anticommunist hysteria, investigative congressional hearings, censorship, book burnings, white citizen's councils, and foreign interventionist wars. America seemed to be split into warring factions: Martin Luther King Jr. vs. Senator Joe McCarthy, Chuck Berry vs. Pat Boone, Marlon Brando vs. Ozzie Nelson, Stokely Carmichael vs. George Wallace, Abbie Hoffman vs. Robert McNamara, and Gloria Steinem vs. Hugh Hefner. Sound familiar?

Of course, I am a sociologist. We live for generalizations. But generalizations based on empirical evidence, systematic analysis, and a penchant for cramming the messy things of social life into neat theoretical or conceptual boxes. We seek patterns and trends from the minutiae of everyday life and the various events of history. And I have a historical generalization to share with you about art in the United States. Building from the work of French sociologist Pierre Bourdieu, I call the roughly three decades following World War II the Heroic Age of American Art.[3] The American arts during this period would experience a general rebellion against the institutional structures that had constrained artists and others in creating their art and reaching potential audiences, or worse, exploited their talents to reap the benefits from commercial markets or cultural institutions. While the terms *avant-garde* and *independent* existed in the field of arts and entertainment before this period, they remained quite marginal, especially in the public discourse about art and entertainment. There was a brief moment in the Jazz Age of the 1920s when the first modernist urges of artistic rebellion or entrepreneurial efforts at independent production expressed themselves. But the Great Depression, and then World War II, put a damper on such aspirations. It was only in the late 1940s that the American avant-garde and American independents began to make major strides against cultural orthodoxy and institutional power.

This book approaches the Heroic Age of American Art through music and film and two iconic artists in these fields, Miles Davis and Martin Scorsese. I look at the careers and what I call the *public stories* of two artists who came to define major rebellions in music and film during the Heroic Age: modern jazz and New Hollywood film. I chose Davis and Scorsese not only because they were highly celebrated icons of their respective rebellions, but also because no other artists from their generation of rebels remained as independent, innovative, outspoken, and successful over their extended careers. The public stories about music and film, and about Davis and Scorsese, were the narratives in sound, image, and text about these art fields, artists, and their artwork. These public stories were fashioned in live performances, records, films, books, television, radio, journals, magazines, newspapers, and live events. These stories were told by various storytellers, including critics and journalists and the artists themselves. So, these public stories were *collective* narratives told and experienced over time. Such public stories were also told through what Boris Tomaševskij calls an artist's *biographical legend*: the linking of personal biography with an artist's career and art.[4] For both Davis and Scorsese, personal biography played an important role in their public stories. This book asks what do the public stories and biographical legends of Miles Davis and Martin Scorsese tell us about the Heroic Age of American Art in the last half of the twentieth century?

I also examine how the social identities of Miles Davis and Martin Scorsese informed their rebellions, careers, and public stories: Davis as a middle-class, male, African American musician and Scorsese as a working-class, male, Italian American filmmaker. I initially began this analysis with no preconceived notion of what I would find outside of the basic context of the importance of race, ethnicity, and gender in American art and society. What I found was quite remarkable and startling. As you will see, the *public stories, biographical legends*, and *art* of Davis and Scorsese speak just as powerfully about race, ethnicity, and gender in the last half of the twentieth century as they do to the rebellion in American arts. So, these artists provide compelling accounts not only of the conflicts over autonomy, creativity, and status in American art since the mid-twentieth century but also compelling accounts of the powerful and dynamic forces of race, ethnicity, and gender in American art and society during this period. This is because Davis's and Scorsese's social identities were integral, as well as inescapable, elements of their rebellious and autonomous art as well as their public stories. From the race consciousness and masculinity expressed and inscribed in Davis's music and public story to the ethnic consciousness and masculinity expressed and inscribed in Scorsese's films and public story, we will discover how artists, critics, producers, audiences, and others in art fields have circulated, contested, and rearticulated racial, ethnic, and gender ideology not only in their art but also in the public stories they tell about this art and its artists.

This introduction, however, will begin with a discussion of the work of Pierre Bourdieu and my analysis of the Heroic Age of American Art. I will paint a generalized picture of this rebellion in arts and entertainment. I will look at the contours of this rebellion in terms of how certain distinct paths appeared in this rebellion often called highbrow, middlebrow, and lowbrow art. I will look at how autonomy and independence became valued norms during this period. I will also write about art fields, especially music and film, in which we can imagine the positions taken by artists, producers, critics, and audiences in terms of these paths, the ideas active in these fields, and the quest for one important, yet often elusive, idea called autonomy. And again, sociologists generalize not because the world is so clearly structured with all the pieces fitting precisely in the categories and positions of an art field, but because such generalization helps us understand what I call *structured meaningful activity* in art. As sociologist Ron Eyerman argues, structured meanings inform, in part, the actions, interpretations, appreciations, and emotions of those active in an art field.[5] And such structured meanings are the product of a historical and collective process even as individuals engage, and possibly transform, such meanings. But such structured meaningful activity is improvisational and always happening in an unpredictable world. And meanings themselves are not necessarily crystal clear. But yet, people act on ideas, or as sociologists like to say, human activity is embedded in symbolic interaction in which we act on ideas and interpret others' actions, and of course, their art, with these ideas.

Before I move to the Heroic Age of American Art, I think one quick example of how structured meaningful activity works in an art field will be helpful. In this book, I look at "independent" film. In the art field that people call *independent film*, and an art field in which people *act* with independent film in mind, defining what constitutes an independent film is often a contentious or tenuous affair. Yet "independent film" festivals and organizations dot the North American landscape for something most everyone agrees cannot be easily defined. But as we will see, this conundrum is less about independent film than about Hollywood. It is about the resentment in independent film toward the vast power and resources of Hollywood that marginalize independent film in the commercial film market, or worse, the constant fear in this art field of Hollywood's co-optation of independent film, and therefore, its killing of the spirit of independent film. The perpetual quest for independent film, and its often-elusive nature, is an actual act of positioning oneself as someone committed to the *idea* of independent film and against the *idea* of Hollywood film. And, as will we see, part of the elusive nature of independent film is people come to define these ideas differently. So, I do not use the public stories that inform this book to definitively define, affirm, or reject the ideas expressed by Miles Davis, Martin Scorsese, and others about independence, autonomy, creativity, innovation, race, ethnicity, or gender. My intention is to show how such ideas in these public stories constituted the *structured meanings* that oriented the making and reception of music and film as well as the articulation of various social identities and cultural politics that informed American art since the first rumblings of heroic rebellion in the 1940s.

The Heroic Age of American Art

I borrow the term "heroic age" from the French sociologist Pierre Bourdieu.[6] Bourdieu argues that France underwent such an age in the last half of the nineteenth century in literature and the arts. In terms of Western art history, this is the moment when modernism and the avant-garde transformed the meaning and practice of Western art. It is the moment when modern ideas like autonomy, innovation, progress, and rebellion motivated artists and others. It is the moment when "avant-garde" art became a permanent part of Western modern art. In Bourdieu's terms, avant-garde art became a permanent position in the structured meaningful activities of artists and others in the field of modern art in France. Individuals acted from a position of being part of an avant-garde movement. And they acted on the various ideas associated with the avant-garde such as autonomy, independence, bohemian, or rebel. And more crucial in Bourdieu's analysis is how this position became permanent. For Bourdieu, the Heroic Age of French Art created a permanent position of avant-garde artist and art that set in motion a perpetual cycle of heresy for each new generation of modern artist.

In Western art history, the permanent position of the avant-garde and its perpetual rebellion of heresy since the late nineteenth century can be seen in the series of art movements—impressionism, postimpressionism, cubism, futurism, surrealism, and such—that present modern art as a world in constant flux, if not in constant progress forward, although postmodernism more or less killed the idea of progress in literature and art. I argue that a similar "heroic age" occurred in American art, but a century later than in France. As mentioned previously, a modernist burst did occur in American art in the 1920s. But the avant-garde at that time was mostly an imported one. A Heroic Age is about the generation of permanent domestic avant-garde or independent art positions within a national field of art. At the same time, not all arts followed the same path. American literature, for example, did advance earlier in establishing a domestic modernist position. But the postwar period was, in a sense, a perfect storm of changes in American art and society that led to a general burst of domestic rebellion and innovation across the arts that truly transformed how Americans viewed the nature of art and entertainment.

The chart below gives you a quick sense of this major transformation in American art. It shows how the national flagship newspaper the *New York Times*, located in the most important center for art and entertainment in the United States, covered "avant-garde" art from the 1920s to the first decade of the twenty-first century. The Heroic Age of American Art is clearly evident in this coverage. We see its initial burst in the late 1940s and then see it hit its stride in the following two decades of the 1950s and 1960s. Then the coverage shows how avant-garde art found a permanent, institutional position in American art during the 1970s that has remained up to the present. Again, what defines the Heroic Age of American Art is the moment when the position of *avant-garde* or *independent* art became a permanent objective and subjective element of the American art field. My own work on American avant-garde and independent art, especially in music and film, also points to the Heroic Age of American Art spanning roughly from the late 1940s through the 1970s.[7] By the 1980s, avant-garde and independent art had become permanent and institutionalized positions in American art. That is, the *taken-for-granted idea* of avant-garde or independent art today, whether applauding this art's vibrant state or lamenting its marginal standing, is both a product and defining feature of the Heroic Age. For some time now, "avant-garde" and "independent" have been important motivating and interpretive ideas in the structured meaningful activities in American art and entertainment.

Sociologists have pointed to several factors that can account for this comparatively late arrival of a Heroic Age of American Art. One major factor is the later institutionalization of high art in America compared to France. Vera L. Zolberg draws attention to a combination of social, economic, and political changes that led to a flourishing of the high arts in the mid-twentieth century.[8] Judith R. Blau argues that a similar group of factors led to this "historical epic" in American high art. She emphasizes a rise in the size of an American middle class, a rise in educational attainment, and a

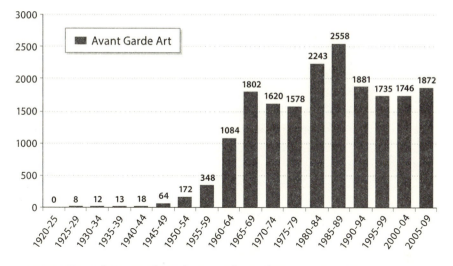

FIGURE 1. *New York Times* articles with avant-garde art reference, 1920 to 2009
Data for this graph was generated from ProQuest Historical Newspapers: New York Times

rise in government and institutional support for the arts in generating a renaissance in cultural creativity and institutionalization across the high arts.[9]
And according to Paul DiMaggio, social-structural changes in the United
States supported this institutionalization of high art across the visual, musical, theater, and dance arts into the mid-twentieth century.[10] It was not
until the middle of the twentieth century that America had the type of
social structure and mature art fields to create the social context necessary
to generate a domestic avant-garde art in high art—a social context similar
to the Heroic Age of French Art. Without mature and institutionalized
high art fields, it was hard to find an orthodoxy to actually rebel against, or
a population of artists large enough to generate artistic heresies. So, it was
in the 1940s and '50s that a wave of domestic avant-garde genres and movements in high art appeared, such as abstract expressionism, experimental
music, and experimental film.

This historical epic, however, also included changes in the middlebrow
and lowbrow popular arts.[11] In the postwar period, the culture industry attained its most concentrated control over film, radio, and music, only to
then suffer a large setback. Artists entered a postwar period in which a select
number of cultural intermediaries had centralized power over film, radio,
and music. Such intermediaries acted more like bureaucratic functionaries
than as enablers of artistic autonomy or innovation.[12] These decision makers
in the industrial oligopoly determined what became popular art. Changes in

technology and law in popular art and mass media in the 1950s undermined this concentrated power in film, broadcast, and recording.[13] Not only did the Hollywood studio system collapse, but the oligopolies of the major radio networks and major record companies collapsed as well. This crisis in the culture industry unlocked film, broadcast, and recording to *independent* artists and *independent* entrepreneurs. Major corporations also adjusted to the new chaos and competition by using *entrepreneurial* producers within their organizations.[14] Suddenly new approaches and new markets appeared in popular art. Popular art, therefore, was able to respond to changes in the tastes and dispositions of artists and audiences in a more dynamic social class structure in the United States in the postwar period. The perfect storm of autonomy, independence, and rebellion at midcentury in the United States, therefore, occurred in both the high and popular arts. The potential for significant changes in the positioning of artists and their works—what Paul DiMaggio calls the "opportunity space" in art fields——unlocked American art for radical realignment.[15]

The struggles for autonomy, innovation, and legitimacy in the Heroic Age of American Art took more diverse directions compared to the paths Bourdieu originally outlined.[16] Bourdieu only focused on the high arts in his model of the avant-garde in the Heroic Age of French Art. I argue that in the Heroic Age of American Art, the struggle between autonomy and the demands of markets, institutions, and industries expressed itself not just in high art but also in middlebrow art and lowbrow art. Forms of rebellion and innovation led to the structuring of genres, works, artists, intermediaries, and audiences along a continuum from high art to popular art with artistic genre communities developing into divergent struggles over autonomy and innovation. The struggle between new generations of heretical artists and older generations of orthodox artists fell along this continuum of high and popular art. And one of the defining distinctions in these rebellions was the relation and distance an avant-garde or independent art genre and its artistic community—a genre community—had to popular aesthetics and popular audiences served by the culture industries. These rebellions, in other words, would include genres wedded to the most abstract of formalist aesthetics consumed by small, mostly well-educated, upper- and upper-middle-class audiences to the most concrete of pulp aesthetics consumed by large, educated, and not-so-educated, middle- and working-class audiences. And at particular moments, different avant-garde or independent art movements would articulate conflicting and contentious meanings and practices over what constituted truly autonomous and innovative art.

American Music and Film

American music and film experienced heroic ages that had a breadth of rebellion and innovation from the most abstract avant-garde experimentalism to the most popular independent pulp. While various genre communities—artistic communities dedicated to a particular style of art called a genre ideal—forged distinct paths of avant-garde or independent music and film, there were moments of connection and interaction between these communities.[17] This was especially the case because a number of these genre communities commonly shared the same urban bohemian spaces or entertainment scenes such as Greenwich Village in New York City or North Beach in San Francisco. In the 1960s, for example, a number of rebel genres in music and film shared a more open social space of an "underground" bohemian art scene in New York City where "happenings" included avant-garde Fluxus artists to modern jazz Loft artists to rock groups like the Velvet Underground. This is the messiness I mentioned earlier in terms of generalizing "distinct" paths of rebellion or innovation. Genre communities, however, oriented artists and others to specific genre ideals in music and film regardless of the interaction between communities or individuals who participated in more than one community. Genre communities also worked on what sociologists call "boundary maintenance," that is, not allowing their genre ideals to be contaminated by other genres. Genre communities, therefore, reveal the distinctions in meaning and practice in music and film that artists and others navigated in their own unique and messy way. Lou Reed of the Velvet Underground is an example of an artist who navigated between the most avant-garde tendencies and most popular tendencies in American music. Miles Davis and Martin Scorsese also navigated between different aesthetic tendencies in their music and film. And it's exceptional artists like Reed, Davis, and Scorsese that bring to light the often contentious or contradictory genre community boundaries and ideals that appeared during the Heroic Age of American Music and Film.

Experimental music and *experimental film* both represent the high art road of rebellion in American music and film during the Heroic Age. Both experimental music composers and filmmakers associated themselves and their art with the broader community of high art avant-garde artists. The high-art American avant-garde, therefore, tended to share certain genre ideals that crossed the different arts as they collaborated in various artistic circles such as the circle of artists and architects who at one time attended or taught at Black Mountain College, North Carolina, in the 1940s and 1950s.

A major genre ideal in experimental film and music was a preference for abstractions or deconstructions of conventional forms of visual or literary representation or abstractions and deconstructions of conventional forms of harmony, melody, and meter. In music, this was evident in John Cage's use of nontraditional modes of sound making—including simply the ambient sound of an outdoor concert stage—and the minimalist repetitive compositions of Steve Reich. In film, this was evident in the structural, nonnarrative films of Stan Brakhage to the minimalist, single continuous-shot films of Andy Warhol that lasted five or more hours. Susan Sontag's 1966 *Against Interpretation*, an important manifesto of the American avant-garde, speaks to the tendencies in avant-garde art to break from commonly held conventions. Such breaks work to make their art unfamiliar and counter to conventional interpretations.[18] Overall, most, although not all, experimental film and music demanded a level of cultural taste and knowledge that limited their accessibility to a large public. Both genre communities struggled in the 1940s, '50s and '60s, but by the 1970s eventually found institutional homes, not surprisingly, in higher education and high art organizations.

Many in the American avant-garde, however, openly rejected the snobbery of the old high art establishment. Both experimental music and film had genre ideals that emphasized a populist appreciation for amateur, folk, and/or popular arts. As Susan Sontag argued, "Because the new sensibility demands less 'content' in art, and is more open to the pleasures of 'form' and style, it is also less snobbish, less moralistic. . . . The fact that many of the most serious American painters, for example, are also fans of 'the new sound' in popular music is *not* the result of the search for new diversions or relaxation. . . . It reflects a new, more open way of looking at the world and at things in the world, our world."[19] So many avant-gardists certainly embraced the popular. What they rejected was the commercial and industrial products manufactured by the culture industry. As Sontag wrote, "It does not mean a renunciation of all standards: there is plenty of stupid popular music, as well as inferior and pretentious 'avant-garde' paintings."[20] The problem, however, for avant-garde artists and other rebel artists was discerning authentic, smart popular culture from commercial, stupid popular culture. And avant-gardists also could not easily separate popular art and popular audiences from the commercial mass market and the culture industries that served them. Then avant-gardists finally had the problem that popular audiences—the American folk—liked to easily interpret and enjoy their art.

Rock 'n' roll and *exploitation film* represent roads of rebellion that pursued more popular-oriented genre ideals during the Heroic Age. Both emerged in the mid-1950s as independent record labels and film production companies served a teen market that the culture industry had no interest in serving, unless with manufactured Pat Boone pop music or moralistic film tales of rebels without a cause. Teenagers, however, preferred Little Richard's *Tutti-Frutti* (1955) on the independent label Specialty or Roger Corman's women-prison exploitation film *Swamp Women* (1955) produced by independent Allied Artists. Both genre communities were looking to capture the mass market in popular music and film. So, a major genre ideal for these communities was commercial and popular appeal—the polar opposite of avant-garde rebels. But both rock 'n' roll music and exploitation films came from the margins of the mass markets dominated by the major record labels and major film studios. Rock 'n' roll came from the marginal race and country markets, and exploitation film came out of the Poverty Row film market of B-reel films. But both also succeeded in breaking into the mass market with local radio airplay and independent record distribution for rock 'n' roll and an exploding drive-in market for exploitation film. Both represented how the Heroic Age in popular art would set in motion a perpetual cycle of rebellion and innovation in popular mass appeal art between subcultures of marginal popular art and the mass market: whether cycles of pop music rebellions from rock to funk to punk to rap to grunge, or cycles of independent exploitation films from George Romero's *Night of the Living Dead* (1968), to John Carpenter's *Halloween* (1978), to Wes Craven's *A Nightmare on Elm Street* (1984), to James Wan's *Saw* (2004).

What is important in recognizing the rock 'n' roll and exploitation film rebellions is not that they represent some actual continuity between various popular art rebellions from the 1950s up to the present, but that they point to the rise of a *permanent* position of "indie" or "alternative" or "underground" or "subcultural" popular art that informs the structured meaningful activities of popular artists and others outside the "mainstream." The structured meaningful activities around "alternative rock" in the 1980s and 1990s, or "underground hip-hop" in the 1990s and 2000s, show the continued orientation of heresy versus orthodoxy that defines even the most popular music. It also explains how James Wan can view his *Saw* franchise as an act of rebellion of an independent spirit even as this franchise has grossed nearly one billion dollars. But this position in American art is not simply about commerce. It is more about a genre ideal wedded to the popular aesthetics reflected in the cultural dispositions and tastes of the individuals who make and consume this art. Within these popular aesthetics other genre ideals can exist, from the anticraftsman and radical ideals of punk to the craftsman and radical ideals of hip-hop. Even exploitation films can incorporate other ideals, as in the late 1960s and 1970s with Dennis Hopper's counterculture *Easy Rider* (1968), Melvin Van Peebles's black-power *Sweet Sweetback's Baadasssss Song* (1971), Martin Scorsese's counterculture *Boxcar Bertha* (1972), and George Romero's anticonsumerist *Dawn of the Dead* (1978).

Modern jazz and *independent film* fall between the high art position taking of avant-garde experimental art and the lowbrow popular sensibilities of rock 'n' roll and exploitation film. Both genre communities saw their rise to prominence in the 1950s. These are middlebrow popular arts that have borrowed from the avant-garde as well as the popular, but also held a genre ideal similar to the avant-garde in terms of creating art and not entertainment. These genre communities would grapple with questions of authenticity, independence, and co-optation in relation to the culture industry and the popular mass markets in music and film. Unlike experimental music and film, modern jazz and independent film continually grappled with the conflicts and contradictions of genre communities with seemingly incompatible genre ideals of art for art's sake and commercial appeal. Such tensions also reflected how both genre communities, like experimental music and film, struggled to establish institutions to support them; institutions that would allow these communities to be free from the demands of the culture industry and also fight the lack of respect for their genre ideals in established high art institutions.

Both modern jazz and independent film also articulated strong genre ideals around the cultural, social, and political currents of their times. The other new rebel genres also would articulate these same currents, but for modern jazz and independent film these currents would fundamentally shape the meaning and practice of their art. Independent film began with a number of "message filmmakers" like Stanley Kramer who produced *Champion* (1949), a tale of the rise and tragic death of an unscrupulous Irish working-class boxer, and *Home of the Brave* (1949), a tale of a black soldier's psychological struggle with the ravages of war and racism.[21] Later independent film articulated the politics of the 1950s civil rights movement, the 1960s New Left, and the post-1960s identity politics of race, gender, and sexuality. Modern jazz would grapple with the rising radicalism of the civil rights movement from the 1950s to the early 1970s as black cultural and political consciousness motivated black jazz musicians in a variety of ways. The rising radicalism of black jazz musicians would force the jazz art world to finally grapple with the long-running co-optation of black jazz music by white musicians, critics, entrepreneurs, and white-run corporations. Modern jazz also would involve a broader continuum between avant-garde tendencies and popular tendencies because it was an art subfield artistically dominated by black musicians blocked from the legitimate position of classical music and the rebellious position of experimental music. There is a reason jazz musicians and critics often call jazz America's classical music.

Miles Davis and Martin Scorsese were iconic artists in the two middle-brow genre communities of modern jazz and independent film; so these will be the communities central to the chapters that follow this introduction. I purposely chose these genre communities because of how their liminal "in-between" state—the constant balancing between the tendencies of the high art avant-garde and the mass-appeal popular—brings to focus important distinctions that shaped the structured meaningful activity of rebellion and innovation during the Heroic Age. I chose Davis and Scorsese because in their respective genre communities no other artists during the Heroic Age, and continuing throughout their careers, consistently created their art, remained central to their genre communities, and also remained financially successful popular artists. The public stories of these genre communities, and of Davis and Scorsese, reveal the contradictions faced in these rebellions in terms of questions and conflicts dealing with aesthetics, autonomy, innovation, authenticity, and commercialism. In particular, we will see how the "popular" existed both as an ideal and as a threat in modern jazz and independent film, just as the "avant-garde" constantly challenged whether modern jazz or independent film were truly innovative and rebellious genres. But amid the various positioning around ideas about art, autonomy, and innovation were other ideas and contradictions in the Heroic Age generated by the racial and gender formations in the United States. The Heroic Age, in other words, did not simply open the American art field to aesthetic rebellions that created over time a more diverse array of art, but it also invited an opening for a cultural politics where race, ethnicity, and gender were integral parts of these rebellions as well as in the art and public stories of Davis and Scorsese.

The Racial Formation

Sociologists Michael Omi and Howard Winant in their classic 1986 work, *The Racial Formation in the United States*, presented a comprehensive analysis of how race serves as a fundamental foundation of American society.[22] The concept of a *racial formation* remains such a powerful critical tool in looking at American society because it unmasks the workings of race and racism from the most micro of everyday practices, what Omi and Winant originally called the "racial etiquette" of everyday life, to the macro structures of social institutions, what sociologists call "institutional racism."[23] And for Omi and Winant, interwoven through the micro and macro structures of the American racial order is the ideological rationalization of this order and the cultural subordination of the racial other. By recognizing the United States as a racial formation, I place race front and center as a defining feature of American society, and therefore, a defining feature of American art. Race, therefore, was an inescapable part of the Heroic Age of American Art. And the public stories of Miles Davis and Martin Scorsese reveal how race played a part from the everyday to the institutional, from the practice of art making to the interpretations of artists and their art, to finally the biographical legends that defined rebel artists.

The various analyses and critiques of "color-blind" ideologies are another important line of argument on the American racial formation. As Omi and Winant originally argued, the greatest power of the racial formation is its ability to refashion itself to fit contemporary social, cultural, economic, and political realities. Color-blind ideology as a mainstream ideology first emerged during the eras of the New Deal and civil rights movement as ideological support for racial equality.[24] Sociologist Eduardo Bonilla-Silva, however, argues that the post–civil rights era has seen the rise of a "color-blind racism" that works to reproduce the racial formation in the United States.[25] Color-blind ideology in the post–civil rights era works to delegitimize the supposed identity politics of African Americans and other minorities as irrelevant, or even worse, provocative and self-interested. This ideology sees an America in which racists and racial prejudice might still exist, but racial discrimination supposedly no longer exists as an institutional, or systemic, obstacle to minorities. The true path to equality in this ideology is a world where an individual is "not judged by the color of their skin but by the content of their character."[26] It is an ideology that expresses itself in both conservative and liberal politics.[27]

Post-civil-rights-era color-blind ideology, in both its conservative and liberal forms, also coincided with the rise of what Michelle Alexander calls the New Jim Crow. Alexander sees a new American racial formation where mass incarceration and the marginalization of African Americans as felons led to a new racial caste system as oppressive as Old Jim Crow America.[28] The racial biases in the justice system and war on drugs has led to a vast criminalization of African Americans in the United States. Therefore, beginning in the 1980s, being labeled a "felon" acted over time, like the color of one's skin in the Old Jim Crow, to place African Americans once again as second-class citizens facing barriers to voting, jury duty, employment, housing, welfare, health care, and education as well as the everyday burden of being stigmatized as a felon.[29] By 2010, it was calculated that over 25 percent of African

American adults were ex-felons.[30] Both Miles Davis's and Martin Scorsese's careers and public stories show how the power of color-blind ideology during both the days of the Old Jim Crow and the days of the New Jim Crow not only affected American politics and society but also significantly affected American art in strikingly complex and diverse ways.

A final line of argument on the American racial formation provides further insights into the ideological and cultural currents of our racial order and American art. The broad scholarship on what has come to be called "whiteness studies" provides a critical lens to understanding the power of white privilege and white identity.[31] Color-blind ideology obviously is one way white privilege is swept under the rug in America. But whiteness studies also points to how the construction of whiteness and white identity has been part of the racial formation since the colonial period in America. As we will see, white identity during the Heroic Age of American Art would express itself in its inescapable relation to "blackness" or the "other." On the other hand, we will see how in conjunction with the rise of color-blind ideology was the construction of a European American white racial identity as a supposedly distinct community with a shared history and culture. Less discussed in whiteness studies, however, was the ongoing recuperation of blackness and black identity in the African American community in the twentieth century. As sociologist Herman Gray argues, blackness has acted as a crucial site not only of white construction of the other but also as a site where African Americans have contested and negotiated the representations of their community to itself and to mainstream institutions and audiences.[32] While whiteness is an ongoing process of reimagining, so blackness is an ongoing process of reimaging as well. As we will see, however, unlike whiteness, blackness was an ongoing process of reimaging where the white racial lens and white privilege constantly worked against efforts on the part of African Americans to construct a self-defined, full-dimensional social identity.

> Race lives on in the house of music because music is so saturated with racial stuff; it inhabits the semiotic site supporting what Wahneema Lubiano calls "The House That Race Built." As a key signifier of difference, music for America—in its wonder, in its transcendence, in its affective danger—historically conjures racial meaning.
>
> **—RONALD RADANO AND PHILIP V. BOHLMAN, MUSIC AND THE RACIAL IMAGINATION (2000)[33]**

Musicologists Ronald Radano and Philip V. Bohlman point to the central role the American racial imagination has played in American music. And in referring to *The House That Race Built*, a 1997 anthology on the American racial order leading into the twenty-first century, Radano and Bohlman point to the unique role music has played in the ideological and cultural conjuring and reproduction of the American racial formation. Since black-faced minstrelsy in the early 1800s, American music has remained a site where the "imagination of race not only informs perceptions of musical practice but is at once constituted within and projected into the social through sound."[34] For Radano and Bohlman, music becomes a "sound-text" in which individuals and their imaginations negotiate the racial contours of the American racial formation. But since the black-faced Irish minstrels of the early 1800s, music has been a site of intimate as well as fraught dynamics of interracial hybridity.[35] "Music thus occupies a domain at once *between* race but has the potential of embodying—*becoming*—different racial significations," while continuing to reproduce the racial imagination of the American racial order.[36]

In terms of modern jazz, jazz studies scholars over the last twenty years have explored the central role of the racial imagination in this genre community.[37] This exploration involves both the white and black racial imaginations and the contentious and conflicting relations of such imaginations in what many white musicians, critics, and fans considered a liberal color-blind art field. The significance of this scholarship is how it shows a complex, multifaceted dynamic of race relations ranging from the white construction of blackness and black masculinity, to black jazz musicians' navigation of this dynamic as they fashioned their own sense of black identity and masculinity, to the battles over the meaning and practice of jazz music. My own previous work on the jazz art world argued that the rise of modern jazz was an expression of the long history of race and racism as a major ideological and structural force in American music. I also looked at how black musicians during the twentieth century worked to construct a race music to redefine the status, and express the culture and history, of the African American community.[38]

Modern jazz, due to the unique *intimacy* and *social distance* that defined this interracial art world, also provides a unique view of the complex dynamics of *blackness* not only as representation but as lived experience and selfhood. All these dynamics of the racial imagination, blackness, and the racial order expressed themselves in modern jazz during the Heroic Age and the career of Miles Davis. Davis's public story allows us to see blackness, as Herman Gray argues, as "shifting cultural fields and social relations and the material circumstances in which black people operate . . . the discursive work—cultural practices, social meanings, and cultural identifications—that

black people use to negotiate and construct meaningful lives."[39] Davis's public story will show how his expression and negotiation of blackness moved
from the everyday dynamics of racial etiquette and social distance that
shaped his reception and appreciation as an iconic jazz musician to his creation and contestation over the meaning and practices of race music in the
last half of the twentieth century.

The field of film reflected the more common dynamic of race in American
art and entertainment. Outside of the field of music, African Americans were
marginalized to the point of either invisibility or brief moments of caricature. African Americans were excluded in the film industry as producers of
popular Hollywood film and limited to small, stereotypical roles. Even as
black actors, like James Edwards and Sidney Poitier, saw small openings as
actors in Hollywood film beginning in the 1950s and 1960s, they were portrayed through the white lens of those creating and producing these films
like Edwards in *Home of the Brave* (1949) and Poitier in *The Defiant Ones*
(1958), both produced by "message filmmaker" Stanley Kramer, who also
directed the second film.[40] During the Heroic Age of American Art this is
most obvious in the marginalization of black filmmakers during this period.
The now celebrated blaxploitation film, a hugely successful crossover genre
in the early 1970s, emerged from a separate circle of artists than those active in the dominant exploitation genre community. And when this circle of
black artists demonstrated the financial rewards blaxploitation could generate both in and outside the African American community, Hollywood and
independent exploitation studios quickly co-opted this genre and placed it
in the hands of white producers and white filmmakers. And once Hollywood
found alternative genres to fill its coffers, it dumped blaxploitation film and
the genre disappeared by the end of the 1970s. The hopes of a "Black Hollywood" were quickly dashed.[41]

The public story of Martin Scorsese resonates with work on the racial
order and whiteness as his biographical legend refracted the evolution of
white identity in the post–civil rights era. Sociologists have analyzed an
ethnic revival beginning in the late 1960s that generated a cultural flowering
of symbolic ethnic identity among European ethnic communities such as
the Italian American community of Martin Scorsese. Sociologists then discovered how once distinct European ethnic identities gradually melded into
a white ethnic racial identity by the last decade of the twentieth century.[42]
Part of this transformation was the rise of a new hyphen-nationalism that
reconstructed white ethnics' historical memories of the American experience. Moving from a Plymouth Rock myth to an Ellis Island myth, white

ethnics viewed their history as immigrants as the foundation of modern America.[43] As we will see, Martin Scorsese's public story will miraculously follow this very transformation as he moved from being an unmeltable Italian American to a cheerleading white ethnic American at the start of the twenty-first century.

Hypermasculinity in Art and Entertainment

Just as race and ethnicity were integral to the art and public stories of Miles Davis and Martin Scorsese, their gender identities were equally important. This should not be surprising given that gender, like race, has been a fundamental social structure of American society. The sociologist Barbara J. Risman has provided a comprehensive framework for understanding the American gender formation similar to what Omi and Winant have done for the American racial order.[44] She focused on socialization and gender identity, everyday social interaction and gendered scripts, and social institutions and institutionalized gender inequality. And interwoven between these elements of the gender formation was a gender ideology and dominant culture that perpetuated this gender order. Risman would return to her original theory in 2005 to reaffirm its validity, address the persistence of gender inequality, and discuss how the gender formation must be understood in light of the intersectionality of race, class, sexuality, and other forms of structured inequality.[45] During the Heroic Age of American Art, the major impact of the gender order was, first, the continued marginalization of women in the dominant cultural institutions and culture industries in the United States, and second, the power of hegemonic masculinity within certain genre communities and their art. Women have always played major roles as singers, songwriters, and actresses in American music and film, but instrumental musicianship and film auteurship, especially at the level of professional music and film, was a masculinized practice. The marginalization of women persisted in the various rebellions during this age, although a number of genre communities afforded women more opportunities as artists and producers. Given my focus on Miles Davis and Martin Scorsese, however, it is the role of gender identity and gender ideology in the masculinity and misogyny permeating music and film that emerges as a striking aspect of the lives, careers, and public stories of these iconic rebel artists.

More recent work in men's studies has focused on the role of hegemonic masculinity and the rise of hypermasculinity as crucial to understanding the gender order. R. W. Connell's classic 1995 *Masculinities* introduced the term "hegemonic masculinity" as a critique of gender role theory that failed to consider power and patriarchy in gender identity and gender ideology.[46] In its original conceptualization, Connell recognized multiple masculinities but placed them in a hierarchy in which hegemonic masculinity acted to subordinate women through objectification and violence as well as to marginalize alternative masculinities. While many critiques followed Connell's original conception of hegemonic masculinity, she argued in 2005 that hegemonic masculinity as a concept and a reality remains crucial to understanding gender formations.[47] But Connell also acknowledged how one must recognize the multifaceted expression of this hegemony; its less powerful hold on other masculinities; the intersectionality of alternative and hegemonic masculinities; women's agency within the hegemonic regime of masculinity; and finally, the *difference* in its articulation in actual individual gender identities, in actual individual and group gendered behavior, and as a cultural signifier in art, entertainment, and sport. Given these important contributions complicating the process of hegemonic masculinity, I find this concept remains extremely relevant to understanding the gender formation in America. This is especially true in dealing with music and film, both art forms central to hegemonic masculinity as a cultural signifier. In music and film, hypermasculinity has played a major role in the performance and presentation of masculinity, and the *normalization* of hegemonic masculinity made such exaggerated gender markings unquestioned in these fields of art and entertainment.

Like music and film, sports has been central to hegemonic masculinity as both a site of enactment and a cultural signifier of gender identity. Michael A. Messner has looked extensively at sports as a cultural phenomenon and social institution in which hegemonic masculinity plays a vital role.[48] His work is especially relevant as he looks at hegemonic masculinity from the microlevel of everyday interaction to the macrolevel of sports institutions. The worlds of music and film, especially in their more popular genre communities, exhibit a similar dynamic of hegemonic masculinity. Messner also points to how "leaders" in sports teams, and the sports world more generally, exhibit, and are compelled to exhibit, hegemonic masculinity in the world of sports. We can extend this analysis to how "stars" in the world of music and film feel compelled to perform hegemonic masculinity on and off stage and on and off screen. Both Miles Davis's and Martin Scorsese's public stories attest in uncontestable ways to the power of hypermasculinity during the Heroic Age of American Art. Miles Davis as a performer and a black jazz artist embodied and expressed this hypermasculinity in his public story to the ultimate undermining of his legacy as a celebrated icon of the African American community. Martin Scorsese has had a career-long obsession with hypermasculinity intimately tied to his ethnic and racial identities. Male violence also would play itself out in both these public stories in frightening ways that speak to such issues that continue to haunt America today.

The Public Stories and Biographical Legends of Miles Davis and Martin Scorsese

My study is based on what I call the *public stories* of Miles Davis, Martin Scorsese, and their art fields. I interpret the "stories" in sound, image, and text about these artists, their artworks, and their art fields. These public stories were found in newspapers, magazines, journals, books, film, television, radio, press releases, conferences, exhibitions, and award ceremonies. These public stories also included the live music performances, recorded music, and films of Davis and Scorsese. They were public in two senses. They were stories told by a wide set of authors and open to a wide set of audiences. Public stories are *collective* renditions of art worlds, artists, and their art. Michael Ryan and Douglas Kellner argue that the *ideological power* of media texts involves understanding them as discursively "transcoding" different discursive fields such as the interpretive schemes found in everyday social life or social institutions.[49] I interpret public stories in this sense. I look at public stories as discursive fields that exist between artworks and the interpretive schemes individuals use in their everyday lives and social institutions. This includes the interpretive schemes used by artists, producers, critics, and others in what John Thornton Caldwell calls the *production cultures* of art fields.[50] Public stories are the collective transcoding of art fields, art, and artists and their cultural, social, and political significance. Looking at public stories is significant because they are expressive spaces where individuals construct and negotiate various narratives and meanings spanning various discursive fields. They reveal not only the *structured meaningful activity* in the making and reception of art but also the interaction of different *structured meanings* from other discursive fields and ideological formations. Public stories are cultural politics enacted and experienced beyond just the making of art, the content of art, and the reception of art. They represent the collective, public conversation *about* art and artists that makes up a crucial part of the cultural politics of art, media, and society.

I also look at the biographical legends of Miles Davis and Martin Scorsese. These legends were one part of their public stories. They spoke to their art, careers, personalities, attitudes, behaviors, and lives in general. The sociologist and film studies scholar Robert E. Kapsis adopted this term from the literary critic Boris Tomaševskij to look at how Alfred Hitchcock and others constructed a biography that transformed this director's reputation in the United States from an insignificant director to a celebrated auteur.[51] Tomaševskij and Kapsis use the term *legend* to emphasize how such biographies are socially constructed and how they act to establish an artist's reputation. While my work addresses the reputations of Davis and Scorsese, it also expands the social significance of biographical legends in the public stories of artists and art fields. Just as France Winddance Twine and Charles A. Gallagher argue that personal biographies act as powerful articulations and personally felt validations of larger ideological formations,[52] biographical legends of artists also become powerful *collective* expressions in public stories where ideological formations are articulated, contested, and rearticulated in the biographical imaginings of artists, storytellers, and audiences. And given how the biographies and social identities of Davis and Scorsese became so prominent in their public stories, these stories were an especially powerful public expressive space where questions of autonomy, creativity, art making, race, ethnicity, class, and gender were linked to the personal and artistic as well as to the social and political. As we will see, the public stories of Davis and Scorsese not only elicited their biographies and social identities, but equally interpolated the biographies and social identities of those who told these stories and those who read them.

To capture these public stories, I made an extensive collection of documents covering a period from the mid-1940s up to the present. I decided to collect the core of my documents from the first public stories of Davis and Scorsese through their long careers. Davis performed and recorded until his death in 1991, so the core documents related to jazz and Davis go from 1946 to 1992. The core documents related to film and Scorsese, who continues as a filmmaker today, go from 1964 up to the present. This involved analyzing magazine and newspaper articles, reviews, criticism, and news from the general press as well as jazz, music, film, art, and industry publications. This material, from over seventy newspapers, 125 magazines, twenty-three jazz and music journals, and nineteen film magazines, was indexed in a database of over three thousand documents that included other miscellaneous material such as press releases. I created a similar database in my earlier research on the rise of a jazz art world.[53] I also used this earlier database for this project. Both these databases were indexed by date, publication, author, coded subject, and individuals referenced in the document. In addition to these collections, I collected trade books, including jazz and film histories, jazz and film criticism, and books related to Davis and Scorsese. I also reviewed film, television, and radio documentaries and interviews related to these artists. Finally, while my analytical focus was on the stories told about Davis, Scorsese, and their artwork and art fields, I consider their art works as part of their public stories. So, I listened to the recordings of Miles Davis from his early recordings in the mid-1940s to his last studio recording *Doo-Bop* (1992) as well as watched videos of live performances. And I viewed Scorsese's films from his first films as a student at NYU to his most recent feature film before the completion of my work, *Silence* (2016). This broad array of material provided a rich empirical foundation for an examination based on an open coded and inductive content analysis of the material.

How to Read This Book and Why

In this introduction, I tried to present the basic themes, questions, and art fields in which I would look at the careers and public stories of Miles Davis and Martin Scorsese. This included some shared distinctions and contradictions in the Heroic Age of American Art that these two artists would encounter in music and film. I then introduced important themes related to the expression of their social identities in their public stories connected to their racial, ethnic, and gender identities. I have broken this book into two parts. Part one, "Rebels Making Art," looks at how public stories in music and film have pointed to the complex interplay of the structured meaningful activities of art making in important genre communities during the Heroic Age and in the artistic trajectories of Davis and Scorsese. It seeks to find the contours of the distinctions and contradictions that defined each field and informed the art making of these two iconic artists and other artists as well. Part two, "The Biographical Legends of Rebels," looks at how the social identities and biographical legends of Davis and Scorsese have informed their public stories and their art. This second part seeks to find how both artists defined their biographical presence as artists and how others also defined these legends in their public stories. The main question is how Davis's and Scorsese's social identities shaped their biographical legends as iconic artists in American music and film.

I wanted my analysis of Miles Davis and Martin Scorsese to reflect as much as possible what emerged from their public stories. I let their public stories do the work in "Rebels Making Art" and "The Biographical Legends of Rebels." This leads to four chapters that touch on an array of issues and themes. On one hand, each chapter provides a different perspective on the art and public stories of Davis and Scorsese. On the other hand, in these four chapters we also find a number of overarching themes and important connections that provide a broader understanding of the Heroic Age of American Art. The goal of this book is less about presenting, and even less so, judging the artists Davis and Scorsese, although I provide a detailed account of their public stories. My intention is to use the public stories of Davis and Scorsese to explore the structured meanings that informed American art around questions of autonomy, rebellion, race, ethnicity, class, and gender. What the four chapters make clear is how the opening of the American art field and the rise of avant-garde and independent art was an invitation for a more vigorous, open, and at times, combative cultural politics. As Davis and Scorsese negotiated the contentious and contradictory nature of autonomy and creativity in their fields, their rebelliousness was intimately tied by them and others to their race, ethnicity, and class. In both cases, it was the expression of their social identities as an African American and Italian American that most significantly defined their authenticity as rebel artists. At the same time, these four chapters show how race, and racism, led to distinctly different aesthetic agendas, and equally distinct receptions of these agendas, for Davis and Scorsese. Furthermore, the dynamics of gender and masculinity as played out in their racial and ethnic rebelliousness would come to problematize their positions as American rebel artists. These artists' rebellions against the culture industries, commercial conventions, and their racial, ethnic, and class marginalization ultimately were intertwined with destructive and controversial expressions of hypermasculinity.

But I am not simply discussing Davis's and Scorsese's art or the remarks they made in their public stories. I am presenting a collective public storytelling in which the invitation to engage in cultural politics was enacted across art fields. These public stories became discursive fields that transcoded structured meanings about autonomy, creativity, commercialism, race, ethnicity, class, and gender as well as politics and American society. The significance of these four chapters is how the public stories of Davis, Scorsese, and others reveal that the Heroic Age of American Art opened up an expressive space in which everyone engaged, contested, negotiated, transformed, and reaffirmed various structured meanings and ideological formations. These public stories were special expressive spaces where individuals directly and collectively confronted the cultural, social, and institutional politics of the last half of the twentieth century into the beginning of the twenty-first century. My work also shows how the conflicts, contradictions, and power of the ideological formations of race and gender interpolated these public stories not only in new, rebellious, and progressive ways, but also in problematic and retrogressive ways that contributed to the reproduction of these formations in the United States.

My work presents a number of significant contributions not only to sociology but to other disciplines as well. My initial research agenda was to apply Pierre Bourdieu's analysis of the Heroic Age of French Art to the United States.[54] No other scholar has actually attempted a similar analysis to another national art field. So, my first contribution is to present a comparative study of a heroic age that reveals a far more complex dynamic of autonomy and cultural politics than in Bourdieu's analysis, and does it in a detailed analysis of the actual structured meanings at play in defining and contesting autonomy and rebellion. Also, while Bourdieu and other scholars like Priscilla Parkhurst Ferguson and Shyon Baumann have looked at the role of criticism in legitimizing genres of art and constructing hierarchies of aesthetics and tastes in art fields, they and other cultural sociologists have not addressed how critics also participate in public stories where cultural politics beyond artistic legitimacy and status take place.[55] My work also expands the understanding of cultural politics found in the work of Herman Gray, Sherrie A. Inness, Ron Becker, and other scholars in cultural and media studies, that focus on the politics of representation and aesthetics in art works.[56] Following Tricia Rose's more recent work on hip-hop music, and expanding Michael Ryan and Douglas Kellner's concept of transcoding, I show how public stories—the collective discourses about art fields—are special expressive spaces that transcode, and therefore, bridge a large range of discursive fields and ideological formations.[57] Following France Winddance Twine and Charles A. Gallagher, I also show how public stories bridge the microlevel of personal biography and art making to the macrolevel of ideological formations and social structure.[58] Thus, this work opens up a remarkable window into how public stories about art commingle the most micro and the most macro, not simply in the making and reception of American art, but in the collective rendition of everyday lives, biographies, careers, aesthetics, art, social identities, politics, and the nature of the American experience.

PART I

Rebels Making Art

Interlude

"Rebels Making Art" is about how Miles Davis and Martin Scorsese made their art and established themselves as iconic American artists. If the artistic career of an artist is the product of structured meaningful activity, it is also a product of the collective generation of ideas in an art field that inform these activities as well as the activities of other artists. I introduced *genre community* as a way to define artistic circles or movements that share a common genre ideal—set of ideas—that structure their art making. Davis and Scorsese were certainly products of such genre communities. And these genre communities continued to shape their art making throughout their careers. Davis was the product of the bebop and modern jazz genre communities and Scorsese was the product of the New American Cinema and New Hollywood genre communities. Part one is also about the Heroic Age of American Art in which various genre communities and their ideals shaped a collective conversation in music and film over what constituted authentic, critical, relevant, and autonomous art. So, to understand Davis or Scorsese one must not only situate them within their own world of art making and their genre communities but also situate them in relation to other genre communities who, in their quest for autonomy, addressed similar questions and oriented themselves to similar concepts in distinct ways. What is striking about both Davis and Scorsese is how they negotiated between competing genre communities and their ideals. Their successful navigation of the opposing or contradictory forces in their art fields, in part, made them such iconic artists.

For bebop and the modern jazz rebellion, the key question among African American musicians was that of forging a "race-music." The ideal of race-conscious music making was the defining pathway of rebellion, innovation, and autonomy central to the evolution of modern jazz. The very birth of modern jazz was rooted in a half-century-long mission on the part of black musicians to create a race music that would legitimate and celebrate the culture and lives of African Americans. Bebop and the birth of modern jazz also was a moment in which African American musicians reclaimed a black music—jazz—they believed white musicians, critics, and fans had culturally appropriated and commercially exploited in the 1920s and 1930s. How Davis and other black musicians positioned themselves in relation to race music and the genre ideals of their artistic communities was the driving force in both their art and the public stories told about them and their music. Davis's quest for autonomy was inseparable from this defining mission of African American jazz musicians. His career highlights the competing claims over race music by various genre communities and their attempts at defining the jazz tradition as a true African American art music.

For New American Cinema and New Hollywood, rebellion, innovation, and autonomy were defined in terms of the personal vision of a filmmaker and the genres' relationship to the power and commercial aesthetic of Hollywood film. The overarching questions for Scorsese and many other filmmakers was what constituted true independence in the field of American film, and thus, how did they position themselves in terms of their personal visions and aesthetic choices in relation to Hollywood. Because, regardless of the various rebellions in American film during the Heroic Age, Hollywood maintained a powerful hold on the commercial market of film. Any filmmaker interested in film in some fashion grappled with the power of Hollywood, if not simply by abandoning the commercial market in which its power held sway. The term *auteur* in the 1960s came to define one such positioning in the field of American film, and it was this genre ideal of filmmaking that has defined Scorsese's work up to the present. Scorsese epitomized the true outsider-insider auteur, as he negotiated his independent "spirit" with the commercial concerns of the Hollywood studio system. But again, to understand Scorsese's career as the iconic auteur director in American film it is necessary to situate him in relation to the competing and contradictory claims of various genre communities over what constituted the art of film and true independence. It is in this broader context, and Scorsese's position within the central questions defining the field, that we better understand the Heroic Age of American Film.

Set against these two distinct core ideals of race music and independent film in the careers of Miles Davis and Martin Scorsese, however, was a shared negotiation between a commitment to music and film as *Art* and its relationship to the aesthetics, markets, and audiences of the *Popular*. Both modern jazz and independent film's rebellions during the Heroic Age were defined in relation to the popular. Jazz musicians were popular musicians who refashioned a popular music—swing—into what they and jazz connoisseurs considered Art worthy of respectful appreciation. Auteur independent filmmakers rebelled in a film field dominated by Hollywood and its view of film as simply well-crafted entertainment. Auteurs viewed film as not simply entertainment but also as Art. Both rebellions also found viable positions in the commercial markets of music and film. In fact, these rebellions were only made possible because of the opportunities that opened up in the music and film markets in the postwar period. So, both the *popular* and the *commercial* would become inescapable questions in the art and public stories of Davis and Scorsese, two artists who embraced what for some constituted two opposing positions of *art* and the *popular* in their art fields. Their unique positions via the *popular* speak volumes to this central and contradictory distinction in the various rebel genre communities that emerged during the Heroic Age of American Art.

1

Miles Davis

JAZZ, RACE, AND NEGOTIATING THE POPULAR

What matters most about Miles Davis is that, in the course of a career
that lasted almost a half-century, he was responsible for at least
five revolutions in the concept and performance of jazz. This made
him arguably the most influential figure in this art form since Duke
Ellington. . . . The fifth and final break-through was a move in 1969
from acoustic into the world of jazz-rock, electronics, and funk. . . . His
musical values would never be the same. . . . If he alienated many of his
older fans, it was a fair exchange, because he acquired a new audience
that enabled him to command up to five or even six figures for a one-
night stand.

—LEONARD FEATHER, LOS ANGELES TIMES (1991)[1]

White critic Leonard Feather and trumpeter Miles Davis knew each other
since the late 1940s. At that time Davis was playing with Charlie Parker in
the final years of the bebop revolution. Feather was an early supporter of
this "modern jazz" revolution. If anyone was familiar with the long career
of Davis, it would be Feather. In remembering the trumpeter after his unexpected death on September 29, 1991, Feather set out two major tropes in
Davis's public story as the iconic genius of modern jazz. The first trope was

Davis as a visionary leader behind most of the stylistic innovations in modern jazz over four and a half decades. And the second trope was how Davis was the most commercially adroit and successful of all modern jazz musicians. Davis only lost his place as the critically and commercially successful messiah of jazz in the 1980s to an equally gifted and visionary black trumpeter named Wynton Marsalis.

> Mr. Marsalis, 29, has been both media darling and critical pariah.... He's acted as a lightning rod, attracting fresh energy to rejuvenate a rigorous, straight-ahead form that had withered during the fusion-addled '70s. He rescued traditional jazz from the museum mantel and supplied an accessible alternative to both pop-styled sap and the pointless virtuoso noodling that passed for jazz in the eye of a non-cognoscenti public.... Yet, for some critics, his insistence on unwavering reverence for jazz tradition suggested that he was a musical Luddite—irreversibly resistant to the creative evolutions necessary to keep the music viable and breathing.
> **—STEVE DOLLAR, ATLANTA JOURNAL AND CONSTITUTION (1991)[2]**

Wynton Marsalis, like Davis, was a revolutionary figure. But more as a counterrevolutionary traditionalist than as a revolutionary innovator. His meteoric rise signaled the end of a modern jazz era that was marked by a commitment to constant musical innovations in jazz practices. Critics would call Marsalis's revolution neoclassical, traditionalist, or neoconservative. And unfortunately for Davis, Marsalis viewed the move to fusion jazz rock, electronic instrumentation, and pop idioms Davis made in 1969 as one of the greatest disasters in the history of jazz. Davis, ironically, represented to Marsalis all the major threats to the jazz tradition in one neat package: avant-gardism, pop music philandering, crass commercialism, and decadent posturing. The era of traditionalist neoclassicism had arrived. The ramparts would be drawn to preserve the jazz tradition against the onslaught of rampant avant-gardism and the commercial decadence of popular music. Davis's death was a symbolic moment for the jazz art world as the icon of avant-garde modern jazz passed the torch to the icon of neoclassical modern jazz.

Of course, since the first modern jazz rebellion of bebop challenged swing in the 1940s, the jazz art world had plenty of firebrand musicians stoking various fires of contention and controversy. In fact, a ratcheting up of contention and controversy seemed to occur with each successive wave of innovation in modern jazz all the way to 1970s fusion jazz. So, Marsalis's articulation of the *modern* jazz tradition, ironically, included his strongly held views, his willingness to share them with anyone, and his messianic leadership. He was merely following in the footsteps of the equally controversial firebrand Miles Davis. One can argue that the era of innovation in modern jazz from the 1940s to the 1970s was one long avant-garde movement of innovation and exploration that defined a set of distinctions that equally defined the neoclassical era. Marsalis and his generation of "Young Lions" simply refashioned these distinctions in jujitsu fashion, flipping over a vision of radical innovation and outward exploration to one of committed conservation and exploration within a bounded tradition.

Questions of innovation versus traditionalism, artistic autonomy versus crass commercialism, and aesthetic vision versus popular appeal, were not the only distinctions that defined modern jazz in both its avant-garde and neoclassical eras. The history of jazz was also a history of the quest by black musicians to fashion a race music—a music that expressed the culture and lives of African Americans and defined a legitimate place of African Americans in American culture. Race-conscious music making defined black music since the first decades of the twentieth century when the craze for black musicals and social dance created both a lucrative market and cultural legitimacy for black musicians. This race-conscious ethos would go on to define jazz beginning with the jazz craze of the 1920s.[3] This ethos was not a clearly delineated aesthetic practice or artistic vision, but a general orientation in which each generation of black musicians, and each individual black musician, would explore what would define the race music of their time. Following the clarion calls made by bandleader James Reese Europe in the second decade of the twentieth century, virtually all black visionary leaders in American music for the rest of the century would look to create a distinct and celebrated "Negro Music."[4] This chapter looks at what sociologist Herman Gray calls the "cultural moves" of these artists over race music and blackness—the strategies and clashes in their structured meaningful activity—in modern jazz and the career of Miles Davis.[5]

Miles Davis is so compelling as a rebel artist during the Heroic Age of American Art and the modern jazz revolution in how he seemed to transverse, transgress, or hover over the distinctions that obsessed the jazz art world during his career. He constantly revealed the contradictions and ideological cul-de-sacs generated by these distinctions. He was a radical innovator who seemed to routinely return to the blues tradition as he moved modern jazz in new aesthetic directions. He was a self-proclaimed, and universally acknowledged, independent jazz musician who cared not one iota what critics or audiences thought of his music or on-stage persona, but he was an astute artist who was unquestionably the most commercially successful modern jazz musician of his time. And as a visionary of modern jazz who eventually incorporated the most radical of jazz practices, he also had a hold on the pulse of popular music practices. And finally, he was a race-conscious jazz musician committed to making race music who still worked with white musicians and incorporated elements of music making common among white musicians in jazz, rock, and classical music. What is remarkable is how Miles Davis brought these supposedly irreconcilable distinctions and irresolvable contradictions into a career in music making that created a coherent artistic repertoire possibly unmatched by any other American musician.

This chapter focuses on the public story of modern jazz and the unique role Miles Davis played in the turbulent period of this art world from the 1940s until his death in 1991. There were certainly moments of calm, even moments of popularity and commercial success, but modern jazz from its avant-garde era into the first decade of the neoclassical era was definitely a roller-coaster ride in terms of jazz music, jazz discourse, social conflicts, and economic booms and busts. A central grievance among musicians, critics, and fans in the jazz art world was how this roller-coaster ride was due in part to jazz as an American *art* never finding patrons and institutions that other high arts found for creating a foundation of cultural and economic viability. And many in this art world also acknowledged that this insecurity resulted from jazz being the invention of African American musicians, and therefore, an African American *art*, in a Jim Crow America. A final sad irony is that the same year Davis died, the Lincoln Center in New York City announced a permanent jazz program, eventually to become Jazz at Lincoln Center, led by a young Marsalis. Davis died at a moment when jazz was attaining greater cultural legitimation.[6]

Young Man with a Horn

"We're not just imitating our idols," Miles makes clear. "We dig what's happening that's all." What is happening with these musicians is a remarkable transformation of jazz. They're not just imitators of their idols. . . . Their equipment and their experience are not sufficient yet to mark them as entirely identifiable individuals. . . . You can't miss Miles' relentless interest in new music, in fresh figures, in arresting handling of bebop. . . . These are the emerging jazz heroes.

—BARRY ULANOV, "MILES AND LEO," METRONOME (1947)[7]

The eighteen-year-old Miles Davis arrived in New York City in fall 1944. He was ostensibly in the city to attend the Juilliard School of Music, but in reality, he hooked up with Charlie Parker and other beboppers to begin his apprenticeship in this new style of modern jazz. Davis quickly became part of the core of this community. He played on Parker's first recordings in 1946. White critic Barry Ulanov in *Metronome* in 1947 presented a theme that would form a major part of Davis's public story. Davis would find his own voice on trumpet, a radical new voice that would quickly capture the imagination of musicians, critics, and audiences. As critic Leonard Feather proclaimed in *Metronome Jazz 1950*, "Miles Davis has one of the freshest and most fertile minds of the new trumpet school."[8]

Feather was assessing Davis as a jazz musician at the moment when the trumpeter was moving away from bebop. Davis had just finished leading a group of black and white musicians in two recording dates for Capitol Records. These recordings became the inspiration for the next innovative style in modern jazz, called cool jazz. After only five years in New York City as a young bopper, Davis already was moving in a new direction musically. This direction reflected the modernist progressive jazz of the time that looked to classical music for inspiration. But Davis did not pursue this style of modern jazz after these recordings. Instead, he returned to extending the innovations of bebop and the use of black music idioms. But his leadership and playing prowess were decidedly weakened as Davis fell into a five-year period of heroin addiction. Once a promising young jazz artist, he fell more or less out of the limelight even though he continued performing and recording. As if by some miracle, however, Davis broke his addiction in 1954, just when modern jazz enjoyed a booming market and national recognition. And when he returned fresh and focused to the jazz scene, the jazz cognoscenti rediscovered the young trumpeter.

> After a time of confusion and what appeared to be a whirlpool of troubles, Miles Davis is moving rapidly again toward the forefront of the modern jazz scene. . . . Miles already had shown clearly this year how important a jazz voice he still is by his July performance at the Newport Festival, a performance that caused Jack Tracy to write: "Miles played thrillingly and indicated that his comeback is in full stride." . . . So, Miles is now in the most advantageous position of his career thus far.
>
> —NAT HENTOFF, DOWN BEAT (1955)[9]

Davis's comeback was more or less universally acclaimed as a star-making success. It also became a major event in the extensive public story of this modern jazz icon. As always seemed to be the case whenever Davis made a significant stylistic change, musicians and critics noticed. So, when he performed "'Round Midnight" at the Newport Jazz Festival in July 1955, he was quickly dubbed, as white critic Nat Hentoff pointed out in *Down Beat* a few months later, a resurgent leader in the jazz art world. This time Davis was a leader in the new modern jazz movement hard bop. By the end of the 1950s, while Davis had already been recognized as a member of the first bebop revolution, he was now viewed as the leader in modern jazz responsible for two revolutions that defined the decade. As white critic Ralph Gleason wrote in his 1958 review of Miles Davis's postbop career:

> With the possible exception of the Louis Armstrong "Hot Five" and the Benny Goodman trio, the two Davis groups—the one that recorded for Capitol in 1948 and the quintet that has played and recorded together for the last two years—have been the most important small groups in jazz history. Davis' series of LPs during the last two years for Prestige and Columbia have been among the most important recordings of the decade and will continue to rank, I believe, among the top jazz recordings of all time.
>
> —RALPH GLEASON, MILWAUKEE JOURNAL (1958)[10]

Davis attracted positive coverage in the jazz press for another decade. His stature in the jazz art world remained undiminished as he gained unbridled acclaim among critics, musicians, and fans for his recordings and live performances. And Davis continued to gain praise for his constant search for new avenues in music making. Even before the 1950s ended he moved in two other directions. First, he returned to the cool compositional style he performed in his 1949–50 Capitol recordings. Joining Gil Evans, who composed for these earlier recordings, Davis recorded three critically acclaimed albums: *Miles Ahead* (1957), *Porgy and Bess* (1959), and *Sketches of Spain* (1960). In 1959, Davis went one step further, he introduced another new style of modern jazz, modal jazz, in his album *Kind of Blue* (1959). White critic Martin Williams in the *Saturday Review* was impressed with the trumpeter's continued commitment to innovation. "Acclaim of course invites complacency, but for 'Kind of Blue,' a most remarkable LP, Miles Davis resisted the temptation to make formulas of his successes and repeat himself."[11]

In the 1960s, Davis formed what most jazz historians, and even Wynton Marsalis, consider one of his greatest jazz ensembles in recorded and live performance. From 1964 to 1968, Davis and his ensemble stretched both his hard bop and modal innovations, influenced by the free-jazz playing of more avant-garde jazz players, to what many viewed as the logical endpoint of these stylistic innovations. Wynton Marsalis actually considered this Davis Quintet as the pinnacle in the evolution of the great jazz tradition. But what struck critics, musicians, and fans was not only the stylistic innovations Davis accomplished with each new generation of young jazz musicians but also how he would further develop his own trumpet techniques in each phase of transformation in his music making, while still retaining his distinct lyrical, middle-range sound. In the beginning of 1969, just before Davis's controversial turn to fusion jazz, white producer and critic Ross Russell, who recorded the first records of Parker and Davis, celebrated the astounding success of Miles Davis as the leading voice of jazz for two decades: "Miles Davis . . . is easily the most consistently creative spirit in the reluctant art since the Gotterdammerung of the bop movement. . . . Miles has reached a wider audience, both serious listeners and younger musicians, than Thelonious Monk or Ornette Coleman. The only comparable group in point of continuity, prestige and achievement is the Modern Jazz Quartet and Miles is a more restless spirit."[12]

Davis during the first two-and-a-half-decades of his career was notorious for avoiding jazz critics and interviews.[13] And when interviewed, he was taciturn in his answers. Davis also preferred to be interviewed by non-jazz journalists or the few jazz critics he trusted. Most of his interviews were in non-jazz magazines and focused on his biography, the music industry, or American society, not about his music making. His reticence might in part stem from the response he received from his first extensive interview with *Down Beat* magazine in 1955. He praised some musicians, but harshly criticized others, including claiming that the white jazz musicians Dave Brubeck and Paul Desmond could not swing.[14] Black jazz musician Charles Mingus wrote an open letter in *Down Beat* condemning Davis for his comments.[15] Davis also stoked controversy in his comments in the popular *Down Beat* column, "Blindfold Test," where jazz critic Leonard Feather asked musicians to comment on recordings by unidentified jazz musicians.[16] But Davis during this period contributed very little to his public story on his approach to music making. One of the most famous quotes from Miles Davis during this period speaks to both his preference not to talk about his music and his disdain for jazz critics, a disdain held by a majority of top jazz musicians.[17] "There's nothing to say about the music. Don't write about the music. The music speaks for itself."[18] As Nat Hentoff pointed out in 1960, Davis disliked written analysis of jazz, "I'd rather *hear* it."[19] The *word* meant little to Davis in interpreting or explaining his music. This stood in stark contrast to other, more outspoken, black musicians during the avant-garde and neoclassical periods of modern jazz from Max Roach to Archie Shepp to Wynton Marsalis.

Since this chapter is on Miles Davis's career trajectory and music making, I am leaving out quite a lot of the dynamics in the jazz art world of this time. For example, bebop remained for many critics in the 1950s a controversial turn in the jazz art world. Progressive and bop critics called these conservative antimodern critics and fans "moldy figs."[20] And part of this resistance was a Dixieland revival led by white musicians to revitalize the jazz tradition being destroyed by modern jazz musicians who adopted the avant-garde ethos of constant evolution in jazz music. And while Davis was attaining such critical acclaim, other musicians were playing not only Dixieland but also swing, bop, cool, hard bop, modal, and what would be called free jazz. But what is important is how Davis up to 1969 established himself as one of the most acclaimed innovators in modern jazz. He was acclaimed in advancing the jazz tradition in a positive and sophisticated direction as a serious, uncompromising modern jazz musician.

> More has been written about Miles Davis than almost any other jazz performer with the exception of Duke Ellington and possibly Louis Armstrong. Not only have music critics dissected his style and his contributions to jazz, but Davis seems to have transcended the confines of the jazz performer label and become a charismatic personality. . . . Davis, who has played his way through this near-deification with a wry silence, seems to be made of the stuff of which legends are produced.
>
> —"LEGENDARY MILES AT MONTEREY,"
> SACRAMENTO OBSERVER (1969)[21]

As the black newspaper *Sacramento Observer* pointed out in 1969, Davis was a *popular* jazz musician who attracted a large audience of record buyers, club patrons, and concert goers. Davis was the most commercially successful modern jazz musician over the first two and half decades of his career. Five years after signing with Columbia Records in 1956, where he remained for thirty years, Davis earned ten times more per club date than other popular black jazz artists like Cannonball Adderley and John Coltrane and boasted having an annual income of $150,000.[22] And by 1960, articles also focused on his celebrity, expensive fashions, and elaborate lifestyle, including Lamborghinis and Ferraris. Modern jazz had a strong anticommercial ethic since the bebop revolution. At the same time, jazz critics would celebrate the success of modern jazz musicians in the record and live performance markets. It was difficult to separate "success" from "commercial," since jazz musicians and others in the jazz art world wanted to make this art form viable for musicians to earn a decent livelihood. Most jazz musicians, modern or nonmodern, struggled financially throughout the history of modern jazz from its avant-garde to neoclassical eras. During his first two-and-a-half decades as a jazz musician, however, Davis's commercial success was never seen as a negative trait indicating a diluting of the art of jazz, or a wavering commitment to innovation, in order to attract clueless popular audiences. His commercial success was seen as an indication of how he was spreading modern jazz to a broader audience.

> The fact that he is now, like Picasso and a very few other artists, a great commercial success in his own lifetime is a tribute to his courage and his sanity and his basic good sense . . . a rare symbol to all artists everywhere of the complete triumph of uncompromising art.
> —RALPH GLEASON, MILES DAVIS IN PERSON—FRIDAY NIGHT
> AT THE BLACKHAWK (1961)[23]

Critic Ralph Gleason was not alone in admiring the brilliant genius of Davis even as he made music that was commercially successful. Obviously during this prefusion period in Davis's career, critics and fans preferred different styles, but Davis somehow seemed to remain above the fray. Except possibly for those strident fans of Dixieland, Davis seemed to be a "cross-over" within the jazz art world—a modern, innovative jazz musician whose music was appreciated by audiences, critics, and musicians from mainstream to free jazz. He was a musician who dabbled in all the various directions found in modern jazz, from the more classical-music oriented progressive jazz and cool jazz to the race music of bebop, hard bop and his final innovations in modal and free jazz. Davis by the end of the 1960s was truly an icon of modern jazz. As white critic Joe Goldberg wrote in 1965, "Davis, at the peak of his career, is in an unassailable position. 'Miles could spit into his horn,' one A & R man said, 'and get five stars in *Down Beat.*'"[24]

Hard Bop and the Resurgence of Race Music

> But much, even most of jazz was concerned with bop, or as we dubbed it, neo-bop; a music which had been accepted, codified and, finally, combined with a hard swing that reached back into the early days of jazz. . . . But the neo-boppers dominated the field and they, in turn,

were dominated by leaders like drummers Art Blakey and Max Roach, saxophonists Sonny Stitt and Sonny Rollins, pianist Horace Silver, and trumpeter Miles Davis. It was a music that was hard and virile in contrast to some music that we had had during the cool ages.
—BILL COSS, METRONOME JAZZ 57 (1957)[25]

Miles Davis's return to the limelight in 1955 was at a time when black jazz musicians once again reasserted their central role in jazz and their commitment to race music. The bebop rebellion had seen its good fortune in the late 1940s quickly dissipate. First, a downturn in the jazz market at the end of the decade left boppers with few opportunities. And then, when the jazz market rebounded in the early 1950s, a movement of predominantly white cool jazz and progressive jazz musicians captured most of the critical attention and financial rewards. Davis was a leader in this new musical revolt, called hard bop or soul jazz. His 1954 recording of "Walkin'" was a perfect rendition of what critics and musicians referred to as the soul and funk elements in hard bop. Reviewing the year 1956, white *Metronome* editor Bill Coss noted how hard bop ("neobop") was rising in the jazz scene leaving cool jazz as a backdrop to an emerging new style and movement led by Davis and other black musicians. Black musicians were performing a new race music in the jazz art world in an effort to regain their rightful ownership of the jazz tradition.

Race music has always been a part of the agenda of black professional musicians in the twentieth century. What Guthrie P. Ramsey Jr. calls the "Afro-modernism" of postwar urban black musicians—these musicians' refashioning of vernacular or popular idioms into "modern" race music—had its roots in earlier urban black musicians and their cultivation of vernacular jazz into swing music.[26] The foundations of the jazz art world were built on the cultural appropriation of this race music by white musicians, critics, and fans. And while jazz criticism by the 1940s had recognized that the foundations of jazz were built on race music, these initial seeds of the jazz art world set up an inescapable conflict between those who pursued a race-conscious black music and resented the white appropriation, co-optation, and defining of race music and the white musicians, critics, and fans who only saw a white admiration, emulation, and critical appreciation of black music informed by a liberal color-blind ideology. Such a conflict also was exacerbated by how black musicians as *black organic intellectuals* during the avant-garde era of modern jazz continually responded to events and transformations in the African American community that evolved toward a more radical black political and cultural agenda in this community.

The contradictory foundations of the jazz art world—black national-ism versus cultural appropriation—were compounded in two fundamental ways by a white racial imagination and a racial order that dominated this art world.[27] First, while black musicians were celebrated as the driving force of jazz, they continually saw contemporary jazz dominated both in the market and press by white musicians, with white critics and others heralding con-temporary white musicians as the next great white hope to carry jazz into the future. The heyday of bebop as *the* modern movement and future of jazz was actually quite short and seemed more to confirm the continued racial order in jazz when its fortunes faded away in the late 1940s. The second fundamen-tal way a white racial imagination and racial order exacerbated the jazz art world is how most white musicians, critics, and fans did not truly understand or empathize with the meaning and practice of race music to black musicians or African Americans. Such misunderstandings of race music began as early as the 1930s, for example, when leftist, antiracist, white jazz enthusiast John Hammond ridiculed and criticized Duke Ellington for his Afro-modernist extended composition *Reminiscing in Tempo* (1935). Hammond accused Ellington of abandoning jazz as an authentic black musical expression for a middle-class pretention toward classical music.[28] Such *lost in translation* responses to the race music of black musicians would continue to erupt in the jazz art world during the avant-garde era of modern jazz.

> In a somewhat belated back-to-the-earth movement, an increasing num-ber of Negro jazzmen are talking, thinking, and playing "soul" music. Indeed, the word *soul* itself has become synonymous with truth, honesty, and yes, even social justice among Negro musicians. . . . This is reflective, of course, of the ever-sharpening battle for a broader scope of civil rights for the Negro people. It is, too, a manifestation of a spirit of nationalism among Negroes. But the handmaiden of nationalism often is bigotry, and if the extreme example of this is the anti-white Muslim movement, it may also be found (to a much lesser degree) in the subtlety of this "soul society" attitude among Negro musicians.
>
> —JOHN TYNAN, DOWN BEAT (1960)[29]

White critic John Tynan, and other white critics and musicians, felt threatened by the hard bop resurgence among black musicians. Hard bop by the end of the decade successfully established a major standing in the jazz art world. With the fall of bebop to white dominated cool and progressive jazz, it was not surprising that hard-boppers emphasized black music idioms like soul, gospel, blues, and what musicians and critics called "funk." Black musicians explicitly laid claim to a *cultural* ownership over hard bop or soul jazz—not simply a bopper's adeptness at performing modern jazz, but an adeptness at applying various black music idioms to modern jazz. It was an ownership white musicians could not claim.[30] The Jazz Messengers was one of the most successful hard bop groups. According to critic Nat Hentoff, the Messengers were "a blazing band of evangelists" whose ownership of hard bop was reflected in their belief "that jazzmen advance most surely when their roots in the jazz tradition are deepest."[31] Black musicians' intimate ownership of hard bop meant it was a music white musicians supposedly could not copy. As hard bop musician Nat Adderley remarked in 1961, "I don't think anybody is better qualified in the medium solely because of race. However, I *do* find certain inherent qualities that seem to be more natural to Negroes than white-musicians."[32] Black musicians were doubling down on the *blackness* of hard bop and soul jazz. The emphasis on popular black idioms, which ran parallel to the advances in complex harmonic improvisation found in hard bop, set this movement squarely in what Ramsey calls Afro-modernism. And it was the Afro-modernism of harp bop that made it distinctly different from the more abstract modernism found in cool and progressive jazz.

> America is deeply rooted in Negro culture; its colloquialisms, its humor, its music. How ironic that the Negro, who more than any other people can claim America's culture as his own, is being persecuted and repressed, that the Negro, who has exemplified the humanities in his very existence, is being rewarded with inhumanity.
>
> —SONNY ROLLINS, FREEDOM SUITE (1958)[33]

The hard bop saxophonist Sonny Rollins recorded one of the first explicitly political compositions and albums emerging out of an even more radicalized community of old beboppers and young hard-boppers. On the album cover of *Freedom Suite*, he also expressed the first rumbling of a black art ideology that more explicitly linked black musicians' music making to the social, cultural, and political life of African Americans. Critic Nat Hentoff in *The Reporter* in 1961 pointed to this trend toward black nationalist cultural and political music: "A number of jazz composers meanwhile are writing pieces about Africa such as Randy Weston's *Uhuru Africa* and Mr. Roach's own militant *Freedom Now Suite*. Some white jazz critic has put it, 'We have entered an era of Negro Zionism.'"[34] One of the more political jazz musicians moving into the 1960s was Max Roach. Roach played extensively with Sonny Rollins in the late 1950s, and beginning in 1960 he made several politically explicit albums including the "militant" *We Insist! Freedom Now Suite* (1960). As Roach said on a following album, *Percussion Bitter Sweet* (1961), "The artist should reflect the tempo of his time. He should also endeavor to bring about changes where possible. The newspapers are filled with cries for freedom from every corner of the world. It is impossible for a man to escape the world; there are no more ivory towers."[35]

The music you are about to hear may shock you with its naked transmittal of outrage, desire, hopefulness, arrogance, demanding and tenderness. The voicing of the chords, the contours of the melodies, the drive and opposition of rhythms are astonishingly successful in conveying to all who listen the picture that is being painted. The music is all the more potent for the cause it involves. The more deeply a man feels about an issue, the more vivid his expression is likely to be. The fact that the issue is *freedom* allows each listener to relate in his own way.
—MARGO GURYAN, MAX ROACH: PERCUSSION BITTER SWEET (1961)[36]

The hard bop movement's *blackness* as a race music was about more than just the jazz art world and jazz as a musical expression of black musicians. It was also about jazz and race music as an expression of the African American community. As Ingrid Monson argues, jazz musicians constantly engaged in some fashion with the rising political clamor for social, economic, and political justice for African Americans and Africans in the 1950s and '60s.[37] And as Robin D. G. Kelley argues, jazz musicians also were part of a larger black Bohemia of artists and allies who collectively engaged in imagining an Afro-modernism in African American art.[38] This engagement ranged from activities in support of civil rights or black power organizations to the articulation of African American politics, culture, and society in their music making. Race music in the twentieth century always articulated a cultural politics of expressing the *culture* or *history* of African American or African or Afro-Cuban cultures. But as white musician Margo Guryan's liner notes for Max Roach's album *Percussion Bitter Sweet* show, Roach, Sonny Rollins, Abbey Lincoln, and other black musicians in the late 1950s were articulating a music making they argued incorporated the struggles for freedom and survival in the United States and Africa in the music itself. Hard bop not only expressed the honky-tonk, the barrelhouse, and the black church, but black life in general, and the African American and African revolutionary struggles for social justice and freedom. Such intertwining of music making, aesthetics, politics, and culture would become even greater among black musicians as they embraced free jazz and radical black nationalism in the 1960s and '70s.

The New Thing and Black Music

> Some walked in and out before they could finish a drink, some sat mesmerized by the sound, others talked constantly to their neighbors at the table, or argued with drink in hand at the bar. It was, for all this, the largest collection of VIPs the jazz world has seen in many a year.
>
> This special preview for the press brought mixed-up comments.... "He'll change the entire course of jazz." "He's a fake." "He's a genius." "I can't say. I'll have to hear him a lot more times." "He has no form." "He swings like HELL." "I'm going home to listen to my Benny Goodman trio and quartets." "He's out, real far out." "I like him, but I don't have any idea what he is doing."
>
> —GEORGE HOEFER, "ORNETTE COLEMAN," DOWN BEAT (1960)[39]

The Ornette Coleman Quartet made its New York City debut at the Five Spot jazz club on November 17, 1959. What was originally a two-week engagement was quickly extended to a ten-week engagement as the quartet became the talk of the town in jazz circles. Their live performance at the Five Spot coincided with the release of their third album, *The Shape of Jazz to Come*, on the major independent label Atlantic. As the white jazz critic George Hoefer pointed out in his review of the quartet, these young "free jazz" musicians were eliciting every reaction possible, from anger, to befuddlement, to curiosity, to exuberant praise. Major jazz critics quickly hailed, others quickly derided, the arrival of the "New Thing" in jazz. Little did they realize that this musician with the plastic alto saxophone would become a major father figure for a broad movement of free jazz and black music. This movement would rattle the jazz art world in ways far beyond the initial rumblings made by the hard bop pioneers in the late 1950s.

The experimentalism found in free jazz already was part of the jazz art world in the 1950s in the music making of black and white progressive jazz musicians.[40] Progressive jazz musicians borrowed from innovations found in modern classical-music. These musicians experimented with tonal rows, fixed scales, atonality, and free form. While such experimental music caught the attention of modernist jazz critics, it did not attract a significant audience except the big band progressive jazz of Stan Kenton. In fact, the other successful progressive jazz musicians adopted premodern classical forms, like Dave Brubeck, or adopted the race music of hard bop, like Charles Mingus, or both, like John Lewis and his Modern Jazz Quartet. In the 1960s, progressive jazz lost its place at the forefront of experimentalism to free jazz, and "The New Thing" melded the atonal, free-form, and rhythmic experimentalism of progressive jazz with the modal and improvisational experimentalism and race consciousness of hard bop.[41] In 1961, black critic LeRoi Jones informed readers of *Metronome* of this new movement in jazz. "There is definitely an 'avant-garde' in jazz today. A burgeoning group of young men who are beginning to utilize not only the most important ideas in 'formal' contemporary music, but more important, young musicians who have started to utilize the most important ideas contained in that startling music called Bebop."[42] This melding of free jazz and hard bop would be exemplified in the original hard-bopper John Coltrane becoming the icon of the Black Music movement before his death in 1967 at the age of forty.

> Since the end of the 1950's the dominant approach to improvising music has been that of "The New Thing." The generation of players sired by Ornette Coleman and Cecil Taylor has successfully asserted the right of the artist to abandon metrical form and fixed tempi, to dispense with the restrictions of tonality, and to play notes which have no place in the European scale.
>
> —VICTOR SCHONFELD, LINER NOTES, RUFUS (1963)[43]

Rufus (1963) was an album of free jazz that included two young leaders in an emerging Black Music movement, Archie Shepp and John Tchicai. British critic Victor Schonfeld pointed to a common refrain in the public story of this new movement: free jazz musicians Ornette Coleman and Cecil Taylor as its inspirational fathers. Schonfeld also expressed the basic tenets of free jazz in this movement. Black Music adherents in adopting free jazz abandoned standard metrical, rhythmic, chordal, and tonal conventions in jazz. As fellow Black Music advocate Marion Brown argued, "there is possibly more freedom of expression in this music. It should lead to a broader palette of expression because of the theoretical basis on which our music is played. There is total responsibility on these musicians to create their own harmonies, melodies and rhythmic patterns within a given context. In other words, the way is not laid out in advance to be adhered to by all musicians, we have to pave our own way."[44] For Black Music artists, improvisation, the fundamental basis of jazz, was finally finding its full potential as the former structural conventions in jazz fell away to allow the full freedom of instrumentalists to compose their music instantaneously and collectively.

> Here then is the music of a new breed of musicians. We might call them "The Beautiful Warriors" or witch doctors and juju men . . . astroscientists, and magicians of the soul. When they play they perform an exorcism on the soul, the mind. If you're not ready for the lands of Dada-Surreal a la Harlem, South Philly and dark Georgia nights after sundown, nighttime Mau-Mau attacks, shadowy figures out of flying saucers and music of the spheres, you might not survive the experience of listening to John Coltrane, Archie Shepp or Albert Ayler. . . . This music, at the same time it contains pain and anger and hope, contains a vision of a better world yet beyond the present and is some of the most beautiful ever to come out of men's souls or out of that form of expression called jazz.
>
> —STEVE YOUNG, THE NEW WAVE IN JAZZ: NEW BLACK MUSIC (1965)[45]

Impulse Records under Bob Thiele was a major label for free jazz with top artists like John Coltrane and Yusef Lateef. In 1965, it released *The New Wave in Jazz* that announced to the world a new Black Music movement. Black arts activist Steve Young's celebration of the movement expressed important elements of this movement from its Afro-centrism to black nationalism to black aesthetic. More generally, Black Music artists claimed that their music making in meaning and practice reflected the history, culture, and contemporary social, economic, and political realities of the African American community. As critic Nat Hentoff told readers of the *New York Times* in 1966, "As black jazzmen took themselves and their art more seriously, they increasingly utilized their music to tell what they felt about life in America and, in particular, about their experiences as Negros in America. . . . Also on the ascendance was their pride in being black. In the jazz of the nineteen sixties, black consciousness has reached new levels of concentration and intensity . . . an attempt to underline their sense of collective identity with black people." Or as Black Music artist Albert Ayler told Hentoff, "Why should I hold back the feeling of my life, of being raised in the ghetto of America?"[46]

Eric Porter, in his extensive review of the Black Music movement, shows how the artistic directions and aesthetic philosophies of artists in this movement were in many ways quite diverse. What Black Music artists called "creative music" or "new music" was a radical opening of the possibilities of the meaning and practice of race music.[47] The core of the aesthetic was an emphasis on nonwestern music idioms, instrumentation, and traditions, especially African and African American. A review of Roscoe Mitchell in 1967 celebrated the breadth of possibilities envisioned by the Black Music movement. "Gone are the restricting modal methods, chord progressions, uniform tempos; and gone also is the need to reject these traditional techniques. Everything the musicians recalls—non-western music, street cries, rock-and-roll, marches, traffic noises—is there if the music needs it."[48] As white reviewer Terry Martin suggests, a major ideological step for many Black Music advocates was to reject in their eyes the various generic boundaries that separated, and then defined, various nonwestern music, especially black music. They argued that such white-constructed boundaries acted to control and marginalize nonwestern and black music as well as limit their potential toward greater actualization as aesthetic expressions of nonwestern, including African American, peoples. These artists argued that the return to the African and nonwestern idioms in their music making promoted a unique black aesthetic.

One way of defining the new black aesthetic was to reject the term *jazz* as defining black music. As Archie Shepp told *Down Beat* readers in 1965, "I address myself to the chauvinists—the greater part of the white intelligentsia—and the insensitive, with whom the former have this in common, the uneasy awareness that 'Jass' is an ofay's word for a nigger's music."[49] Or as Black Music artists Albert and Donald Ayler told the *National Observer* that same year, "Jazz is Jim Crow. It belongs to another era, another time, another place. We're playing free music."[50] The rejection of the word *jazz* signified more than just the rejection of the historical derision heaped on black music and black musicians. It was a neat and compact way to express several fundamental views among black jazz musicians about the history of black music. The rejection of jazz was also a denunciation of the cultural appropriation of black music under the term *jazz*. At other times, this rejection expressed the condemnation of commercial genre terms like *jazz*, *soul*, or *funk* as attempts to not only exploit black musicians but also limit their ability to create a truly authentic black music. The rejection of jazz was also linked to a theme in the Black Music movement of rejecting all generic musical boundaries created by the West to reassert a new universalist black aesthetic based on nonwestern traditions with a special emphasis on African musical traditions.

Many Black Music artists eventually rejected the term *avant-garde* as an ideologically imposed barrier between Black Music and popular black audiences. Black Music artists claimed their music to be a populist music in line with the long tradition of black music making. As LeRoi Jones argued in his 1967 book, *Black Music*, "The differences between rhythm and blues and the so-called new music or art jazz, the different places, are artificial, or they are merely indicative of the different placements of spirit. . . . That what will come to be called a *Unity Music*. The Black Music which is jazz and blues, religious and secular. Which is New Thing and Rhythm and Blues. . . . That is, the New Black Music and R&B are the same family looking at different things. Or looking at things differently."[51] Such unity music for Archie Shepp meant that "the new Black Music played by himself and the late John Coltrane, Pharoah Sanders, Miles Davis, and a host of other equally well-known Black musicians is the music of liberation, a reflection of the times and the feelings of the Black Community today."[52]

Such aesthetic and populist claims, unfortunately, ran against a black community that did not seem to have an interest in the Black Music of free jazz musicians. This problem emerged quite early in the movement and continued to perplex Black Music artists into the 1970s. As Black Music advocate A. B. Spellman lamented in 1968, "politically conscious African-American musicians despair of seeing only white faces before them every time they pick up their horns. At a time when so many voices are calling on creative black people to apply their talents in the ghetto, the musician can't help wondering if art for art's sake isn't a luxury he can't afford."[53] The struggle *commercially* of the Black Music movement into the 1970s led to familiar defenses as well as belated admission of the lack of appeal of this music to black audiences. Cecil Taylor in 1975 repeated the early critique that the music industry's generic labeling divided what would otherwise be a universal black music. "Hey, the bulk of the black population loves James Brown or Aretha Franklin or whatever, now if you separate it and say hey, that's soul, everybody needs soul . . . understand that's part of the division that is perhaps desirable from those people that control. They're not interested in Milford Graves or Cecil Taylor."[54] Only a year later in the same jazz magazine *Coda*, however, Milford Graves admitted that "the music in the Black community is the foot-patting and snapping the fingers thing. And you must realize this."[55] So, the constant battle to find *large* black audiences for Black Music led many artists to admit that their more free jazz music making was not really reflective of a popular aesthetic. They were still trapped in an avant-garde ethos of modern jazz that created a real breach between Black Music and popular tastes and expectations. As Archie Shepp told *Jazz and Pop*, "We *should* know how to play mass music, popular music. And when we play it we should believe in it. If we don't, we're bourgeois snobs."[56]

The struggle of the Black Music movement was not only in attracting large black audiences in the 1960s and '70s, but also in convincing club owners and other white entrepreneurs that their music was commercially viable in the jazz market. In the early 1960s, regardless of the critical recognition free jazz had attained, a strong contingent of critics, musicians, and fans also considered it "antijazz," a further pressure to make white entrepreneurs reluctant to book free jazz groups.[57] While a Jazz Loft scene of coffeehouses, small theaters, art galleries, churches, bookstores, and other locations appeared in New York City for free jazz, all free jazz musicians struggled to survive.[58] The Jazz Loft circle in 1964 mounted an "October Revolution in Jazz," a four-day event sponsored by the free jazz collective Jazz Composers Guild that featured a wide number of black and white free jazz musicians. Their attempt to garner more critical attention and a broader audience failed. John Tchicai told *Down Beat* in 1964, "The new way to other forms has been shown very clearly by such important persons as Cecil Taylor and Ornette Coleman, and the fact that these two artists— undoubtedly the most important since Bird—still remain disregarded and have so few possibilities of being heard shows us that the whole jazz scene is in a very bad shape."[59]

But the Black Music movement never gave up on their populist agenda and reaching out to the black community. Steve Young, who wrote the liner notes for *The New Wave in Jazz: New Black Music*, was music-art coordinator of a new Black Arts Repertory Theater/School in Harlem. The album was a recording of a benefit for the new arts center performed by free jazz musicians. The Black Music movement would establish such community-based organizations in major cities in the United States from Los Angeles to Detroit to Saint Louis to Chicago. The most important community-based Black Music collective was the Association for the Advancement of Creative Musicians (AACM) in Chicago. It was established in 1965 and remains active today. Many of the most acclaimed and successful Black Music artists came not only from the AACM but also from other artist collectives. These collectives played a vital role, and still do today, in nourishing this movement of black music through rough times.

They've got what they wanted: recording contracts with mass distributed record labels, access to more lucrative nightclub and concert work, and recognition as innovators in a new, "scientific" jazz avant-garde. They follow an international circuit that takes them to Europe once or twice a year (and often to Japan) and into a constantly expanding network of

small clubs, college coffee houses, and musician-supported performance
spaces across the United States.

—ROBERT PALMER, SATURDAY REVIEW (1979)[60]

The struggles of Black Music artists by the late 1960s led them to seek
better financial rewards in Europe. This exodus was spurred on by a general
collapse in the jazz market at the time. In other words, all jazz musicians
faced bleak times as the New Jazz Age heralded in 1954 seemed to have
come to an end. Many of these Black Music artists returned to the United
States as the jazz market began to rebound in the early 1970s. While white
critic Robert Palmer noted that Black Music artists had more opportunities
than in the 1960s, they continued to struggle financially, even as they gained
far greater critical recognition in the jazz press. Part of the history of modern jazz is how most musicians even with critical acclaim and clear cultural
impact struggled financially. Miles Davis until the early 1970s was virtually
alone as a *modern* jazz musician who attained such a high level of financial
remuneration and mass popularity. So, the struggle for economic viability
and large audiences in jazz was not limited to just the Black Music movement, nor did it reflect some failure on the part of this movement to have a
major impact on the jazz art world. The lack of commercial success also did
not reflect the movement's impact on the larger black community. *Ebony*
magazine began a black music Readers' Poll in 1974. It provided readers with
thirteen artists, playing a variety of styles, for their vote for "Most Worthy of
Wider Recognition." The top two winners were major Black Music groups:
the Collective Black Artists and the Art Ensemble of Chicago.[61] So, while
the Black Music movement lamented not reaching a *mass* black audience,
it clearly had garnered the awareness and respect nationally of a significant
number of members of the black community as well as a significant number
of jazz critics and jazz audiences.

Fusion Jazz and the Return of the Popular

The commanding position taken by rock with young audiences no longer
can be shrugged off; nor can the inescapable reality of the decision on
the part of many jazz instrumentalists and composers, that if you can't
beat 'em, you join 'em. . . . A more constructive answer may have been
found in the Miles Davis phenomenon. Here we have all the freedoms of
the various avant-garde jazz movements. . . . The enormous audience he
has found with "Bitches Brew" indicates that a turning point has been

reached, perhaps as auspicious as the Gillespie-Parker revolution of the mid-1940s or the Coleman-Coltrane innovations circa 1960s.
—LEONARD FEATHER, MELODY MAKER (1970)[62]

Jazz is not, and was never intended to be, a mass-appeal music; yet promoters, record men, club owners, festival organizers, and even jazz musicians themselves are frequently heard to lament that jazz doesn't seem to be reaching the kids. . . . perhaps a more sinister conspiracy currently is that which seeks to bring about a fusion between jazz and rock or pop.
—MIKE HENNESSEY, JAZZ AND POP (1970)[63]

By 1970, Miles Davis had established himself once again as a leader of a new style in jazz. And Leonard Feather, once again, heralded Davis as a leader of a new movement. For Feather, this movement of jazz-rock fusion held a potential as significant as bebop and free jazz. What came to be called fusion jazz—the mixing of jazz, rock, funk, third world, and electronic avant-garde music—not only helped resuscitate the jazz market but also provided the jazz art world with a whole new battleground of warring factions. As white critic Mike Hennessey decried in *Jazz and Pop,* fusion jazz for many critics was the new "antijazz" threat on the horizon. Along with fusion jazz, crossover jazz reintroduced soul jazz with even greater pop elements to also help reinvigorate the jazz market with equal exclamations of dismay from many critics, musicians, and fans. It seemed for some that fusion jazz and crossover jazz were undermining the jazz tradition with either seductive smooth sounds, irresistible funk rhythms, or blasting potential audiences *to* jazz with incomprehensible electronic noise.

Davis could not, and did not do it alone. But, like so many great artists in other fields, he did act both as a catalyst and a finalizer, one who assembles and activates various elements in an environment in a way that makes the total greater than the sum of the parts. . . . He took the enormously varied tonal palette of avant-garde jazz and applied its brilliant hues to the repetitive rhythms of rock . . . but at its roots it was highly original and surprisingly viable way of bringing two kinds of music—jazz and an offshoot of jazz—that had often seemed totally antithetical. And it did so in a way—unlike some of the more commercially popular fusions—that managed to preserve the aesthetic integrity of both.
—DON HECKMAN, STEREO REVIEW (1974)[64]

The melding of radical innovation and popular sensibility Davis demonstrated for most of his career once again led the jazz art world into another period of change in 1970. As white critic Heckman informed *Stereo Review* readers in 1974, Davis seemed to have done the miraculous in combining the music making of free jazz with the popular electronic and rhythmic elements of rock in his album *Bitches Brew* (1970). This album was the biggest selling album to date for both the jazz art world and Davis, with sales of over 400,000 in its first year.[65] Heckman also noted, "the irony is that the revolutionary musical devices of the avant-garde jazz of the Sixties took such a circuitous route to find a wider audience."[66] The greater irony is how Davis criticized free jazz musicians in the early 1960s, famously saying about free jazz saxophonist Eric Dolphy, "nobody else could sound that bad! The next time I see him I'm going to step on his foot."[67] But leading into his self-imposed sabbatical from music in 1976, Davis continued his commitment to melding free jazz with popular idioms. And while critics noted how his post-1970 albums did not reach the same level of sales as *Bitches Brew*, his other 1970s albums continued to do well, reaching into the Top 200 Albums Chart in *Billboard*, a rarity for jazz musicians except for top fusion and crossover artists at the time like Weather Report and The Crusaders.[68] He also continued to enjoy success in live performances in the United States and abroad. In the early 1970s, top fusion groups like Weather Report pursued a similar melding of free jazz and pop, but other fusion players' efforts were less successful, such as Herbie Hancock's *Mwandishi*. Hancock, along with most other fusion jazz groups, found greater success in either mining popular idioms like funk with Hancock's *Headhunters* (1973) or Chick Corea's *Light as a Feather* (1973) that emphasized a more smooth jazz pop sensibility found in crossover jazz.

> A new Jazz Age has dawned again in America. . . . In the early '70s, jazz, with its capacity for self-renewal, began to use the best of rock. Trumpeter Miles Davis launched the era of jazz rock with an LP album, *Bitches Brew*, that combined his avant-garde jazz style with rock's electronic sounds and driving rhythms. Davis' daring not only kindled a new form but also reawakened audiences. Jazz had arrived once more, its scope more eclectic than ever. . . . Given musical riches of such diversity and dimension, the future of jazz seems more promising than ever.
>
> —"A FLOURISH OF JAZZ," TIME (1976)[69]

In 1976, *Time* credited Miles Davis and fusion jazz for a boom in records, festivals, clubs, and college-campus performances that heralded a New Jazz

Age. The resurgence in jazz also was spurred on by crossover jazz musicians in the pop market like The Crusaders, George Benson, and Grover Washington Jr. As *Billboard* noted in 1973, in reference to The Crusaders and other crossover jazz stars, "Probably the most important jazz success story this year (or this decade) is the emergence of sophisticated jazz instrumentals as formidable pop chart contenders. . . . Performers like those mentioned so far are making the most obvious jazz inroads into popular acceptance."[70] In his *Stereo Review* article in 1974, Don Heckman also noted that "jazz in the mid-Seventies is very much alive. . . . Jazz groups, playing music that ranges from Dixieland to bop to modern eclectic, seem to be springing up at every neighborhood night spot, and major events like the Newport Jazz Festival are having their greatest success ever."[71]

> In 1970, Miles Davis bowed to corporate pressures, swapped formulas, and recorded a singular album, "Bitches Brew," which sold phenomenally, transiently bought him a new audience, and became quite a pacesetter in the circles of insipid fuzzy-free-funk. Ever since, his recordings have come from the same stand-pat cook book for electric ghetto Muzak. . . . Davis is well-protected by his enthusiastically dedicated crew of professional yes-men . . . because no matter what kind of gibberish he embeds on vinyl, they simply do their verbal magic, and (more likely than not) you will buy it.
>
> —BARRY TEPPERMAN, CODA (1976)[72]

Post-1969 Miles Davis divided the jazz art world as many jazz musicians, critics, and fans felt he had abandoned jazz for the Mammon of pop celebrity. White critic Tepperman was not alone in his vociferous ridicule of the new post-1969 Miles. Unfortunately, accusations of capitulation to commercial demands would haunt Davis until his death in 1991. And while harsh criticism was plentiful, Davis actually received mostly positive reviews of his records and live concerts. As Dan Morgenstern, editor of *Down Beat*, wrote in 1970, "Miles Davis, however, has that rare gift of being able to give birth and life to new things that, no matter how startling, always seem natural and logical, and open up new roads for others to travel after he has moved on. . . . It's pure speculation, of course, but if he were still among us, I have a feeling that Coltrane, that restless seeker, might well once again feel very much at home with Miles."[73] Davis had such wide respect that some criticisms of his turn to fusion remained diplomatic, like the criticism of his longtime friend, trumpeter Clark Terry. "The way he's been ostracized and criticized—and probably rightfully so in many instances—but I suppose in his case he's a man who likes to stay abreast of things, and many times stay ahead of things, and maybe he foresees something that we don't see."[74] Terry, of course, was correct that Davis had indeed discovered a new path in jazz music making and jazz commercial success. But the war over fusion continued across the decade.

> The second fiddle Trumpeter Miles Davis is playing to Johnny-come-lately white rock groups in recent concerts where he has fronted a combo that is far from Black. . . . Most outspoken criticism of Miles has come from "electrified" saxophonist Eddie Harris, who put down Miles' new "white image" in a New York press conference, adding that these same non-Black musicians currently playing with Miles soon will be cutting Black brothers our of gigs they should have.
>
> —"PEOPLE ARE TALKING ABOUT," JET (1970)[75]

For Miles Davis, more important than the negative views of white critics were accusations that the trumpeter was abandoning his commitment to race music with his new fusion jazz groups and performances. The *Jet* article in 1970 revealed how some black musicians and fans felt that Davis had clearly and visibly abandoned his central role in race music. Davis certainly was once again using white musicians in his groups. And Davis had been criticized by black musicians and fans for his use of white musicians earlier in his career. But now the criticism was more glaring as Davis performed before huge white rock audiences at such famous venues as the Fillmore East, Fillmore West, and the Isle of Wight Festival. White critic Leonard Feather, a longtime acquaintance, quickly came to Davis's defense in *Down Beat*. "Nobody who has ever known Miles Davis, has read his acidulous comments through the years, is aware of his constructive militancy and his basically humanistic, non-racist attitude, can possibly believe such scurrilous absurdities. For Eddie Harris or *Jet* or anyone else to level charges of this nature with any justification, positive evidence would have to be adduced that there was a sinister motive in hiring of these musicians."[76]

> You know, some guys are still playing all that shit we did years ago . . . they're still using those clichés and calling it jazz. Black guys as well as white guys. I hear it over and over again—shit that I've even forgotten . . . in general there isn't much happening that I want to hear. All the groups are trying to play like somebody I know. I don't want to hear clichés. I don't want to get back into the past. What's important is what's

happening now, the new music, and the music of the future. . . . I haven't heard anything coming from the white kids with the long hair and shit. I like to hear the Motown Sound and James Brown, them funky singers.
—MILES DAVIS WITH LEONARD FEATHER, PENTHOUSE (1972)[77]

As the quote from *Penthouse* suggests, post-1969 Miles Davis was now a man of his *word*. In seeming anticipation of possible reactions to his transition into fusion jazz with his albums *In a Silent Way* (1969) and *Bitches Brew* (1970), Miles's words about music making were appearing in the jazz and general press in the United States as well as Britain. In his words, Davis confronted two fundamental challenges to his turn to fusion jazz. The first challenge was that Davis was no longer an independent, creative force in jazz, but was a commercial- and celebrity-obsessed musician seeking to retain his iconic status and high earnings. The other challenge was how he was catering to white rock audiences by playing rock-infused music and including white musicians in his bands. Both challenges clearly upset Davis, whose self-conception was based on his iconic status as a renowned African American musical innovator of race music. What Davis told Feather in 1972 was quite clear, that those playing past styles of jazz were uncreative, cliché-ridden artists who were not ready to take risks in their music making by creating music that reflected the contemporary setting of American music. And he was equally clear that long-haired white rock musicians had nothing to do with his new fusion jazz, his fusion jazz was race music like the Motown Sound and James Brown.

The new post-1969 Davis was very vocal about his views on his music and the world of jazz and popular music more generally. In terms of his abandoning jazz and losing his creative edge, he told *Melody Maker* in 1973, "I mean when a guy who calls himself a jazz fan comes up to me and says I'm not playing jazz anymore, it puzzles me. I never set out to play any one type of music because I've never thought of music being divided into different categories. What is a jazz fan anyway? Is he someone who wants to hear the same old clichés over and over again?"[78] But Davis was most concerned about his relation to race music. Davis picked up more than just free jazz musical practices from the Black Music movement. Like many black musicians, Davis rejected the term *jazz* as defining his music past or present. As early as 1969, Davis told *Rolling Stone*, "But I don't like the word rock and roll and all that shit. Jazz is an Uncle Tom word. It's a white folks's word."[79] He told *Melody Maker* in 1970, "I don't' want to be a white man. Rock is a white man's word. . . . Blues is a white man's word. Jazz is a white man's word."[80]

To reemphasize his music as race music, Davis also constantly reminded journalists of the influence of popular black musicians in his music. White critic Don DeMichael in *Rolling Stone* wrote, "Like all great creative artists, he has big ears. He is the first major jazz artist I know of to seriously listen to Jimi Hendrix and Sly Stone."[81] Frederick Murphy in 1975 told *Encore* readers that "the general consensus was that Davis was either playing White rock or had tripped out beyond his own genius."[82] Davis told Murphy, "I don't play rock. Rock is a white word. And I don't like the word jazz because jazz is a nigger word that white folks dropped on us. We just play *Black*."[83]

Miles Davis also returned to his provocative comments on white musicians' inability to play like black musicians. He told *Melody Maker* in 1973, "I don't think you have any musicians who can play. . . . I don't reckon Clapton or any of your guitarists. They keep copying Hendrix and B. B. King."[84] While constantly commenting on how white rock musicians were terrible, once claiming he could instantly create the greatest rock band of all time, Davis did admit he was not reaching the black audiences he was hoping for. In his album *On the Corner* in 1972, he integrated additional black popular idioms into his music making in an effort to attract a larger black audience. As he told *Down Beat* in 1974, "Like with *Bitches Brew*—well, we don't play that shit no more. If I were white and had blonde hair, you know what I mean, then it would be a different thing—but I'm a black, man . . . I don't feel like I'm doing anything, I mean, so what, so I play music, but my race don't get it."[85] But after *On the Corner*, Davis returned to his more free jazz work in his studio albums. It was only on his return to the music scene in 1981 that Davis made a major move back to black popular idioms.

The criticisms against Miles Davis seem disingenuous, although they certainly reflected how many critics and fans felt about post-1969 Davis. Ironically, the "antijazz" claims against Davis and his popular fusion music merely repeated the claims against earlier avant-garde free jazz, although with the added sin of Davis going electric and reaching huge new rock audiences with his music. The power of the modern jazz ethos against the popularization of jazz undermined the obvious truth that Miles Davis led the charge that revitalized jazz in the 1970s. In terms of the second challenge, *all* jazz musicians were performing for predominantly white audiences, except, ironically, fusion jazz artists like Herbie Hancock and crossover artists like The Crusaders. And Davis actually remained popular among black audiences, he simply now performed to sold-out rock concerts as well as jazz festivals, concert halls, and clubs. Davis won the first two *Ebony* Readers' Polls in the category of "Most Innovative Artist or Group" in 1974 and 1975, and only lost out to Herbie Hancock in 1976. The 1976 *Ebony* Readers' Poll showed that black audiences preferred both crossover jazz and fusion jazz over other styles of jazz, with three crossover artists—Grover Washington Jr., Ramsey Lewis, and Cannonball Adderley—wining for best album, and three fusion artists—Herbie Hancock, Miles Davis, and Weather Report— winning for most innovative artists.[86]

> It's hard, man, when you see cats out there making a whole bunch of money playin' <u>shit</u> while you're trying to elevate the music and by elevating the music elevate yourself. . . . I have to be true to myself and play the music that I feel I'm supposed to play. . . . IF the cats that are doing it feel that's where they belong, then I've got no criticism of them. But a lot of it's more business and greed than anything else.
>
> —DON PULLEN WITH VERNON FRAZIER, CODA (1976)[87]

Regardless of the tastes of *Ebony*'s black readers, Black Music artists were not happy about the crass commercialization of fusion jazz musicians. Black Music artist Don Pullen was pretty clear about his view of fusion jazz musicians. Black Music artist Lester Bowie that same year was equally upset with the pop fusion being made by black musicians like Herbie Hancock. "Whoever it was, they're full of shit. What they've done is taken the lower level of the music and turned the whole scene upside down. That's what's happening now. . . . These cats don't know if they're going to be jazz or fusion or funk or disco. They're just tryin' to make some money, you hear that."[88] Black Music advocate Bill Cole's 1974 biography of Miles Davis, one of the first published on the trumpeter, was clear, like his fellow Black Music artists he viewed the once great leader of race music as having abandoned the cause in his move to fusion. "There will always be a Miles Davis, a person whose strength and uncompromising musical position encourages other struggling musicians trying to play the music of African-American people without sacrifice to the pressures of money. To expect the compromise not to happen is naive, but when it does, especially to a person who has resisted as long as Miles had, it pulls the plug on one's fantasies. . . . Miles moved away from the mainstream of African-American music."[89] Regardless of the better times for Black Music in the 1970s, seeing fusion jazz and crossover jazz artists gaining 200,000 to 1 million in album sales, and selling out large concert halls and outdoor amphitheaters, Black Music artists once again felt that the commercial demands of the music industry were undermining the artistic value and autonomy of black music.[90]

Indeed, one of the first things that strikes you about fusion jazz is how little jazz it contains. . . . Fusion refuses to treat any music as the basic style because every music is regarded simply as just another ingredient in the mix . . . jazz is invoked as a public relations tactic to connote, ironically, depth and integrity—precisely those virtues least characteristic of fusion. . . . The music that emerges from this symphony of synthetics is on about the same plane as a James Bond film or a black-exploitation flick. Slick, fluent, full of calculated effects (often spooky or sinister) as full of fake folksiness as a soul commercial for enlistment in the Army or the overture to the latest hoe buttered cornpone musical on Broadway, fusion could be spelled J-I-V-E.

—ALBERT GOLDMAN, ESQUIRE (1977)[91]

As the decade ended, antifusion rhetoric increased more as critics and fans felt that fusion jazz had either gone the way of pop pablum or smooth jazz. White music critic and biographer Albert Goldman expressed the continued disdain for fusion jazz, and the popular more generally, in the jazz art world. The continued split in the jazz art world was most evident in the mixed reception of the most popular fusion jazz group of the decade, Weather Report. White record reviewer David Less trashed their album *Mr. Gone* in 1979. "While Weather Report was innovative and pivotal in its first experiments . . . Weather Report's status has shifted over the years from a combo of premier jazz-rock innovators to a super-hip rock band with jazz overtones."[92] Another reviewer described this album as made of "predominantly pompous preenings and cerebrally sterilized goose-step struttings."[93] White critic Neil Tesser, however, saw their previous album, *Heavy Weather* (1977), as "a glittering pendant anchoring the string of pearls of fusion music, Weather Report . . . have had so enormous an impact on the way many of us listen to music."[94] *Down Beat* readers agreed, voting Weather Report top jazz combo, later small acoustic group or electric group, from 1972 to 1984 with Miles Davis topping this category just before and just after Weather Report's thirteen-year run. White critic Bob Rosenthal, in reviewing the polls for the 1970s in all categories, concluded in 1981, "On the strength of these results, it wouldn't be far-fetched to label Weather Report the 'Group of the '70s.'"[95]

For more than a decade saxophonist Grover Washington Jr. has reigned as the most commercially successful recording artist in jazz. Gold status (sales of 500,000 or more) applies to five of his 14 albums and his double-Grammy winning *Winelight* was certified platinum (a million-plus in sales). At any given time, his recordings are topping the charts in the trades various categories (pop, r&b, jazz). . . . And he's done it all without having won a single poll for his instrumental or compositional abilities. Nor has he had the majority of the jazz press, most of which has had a field day savaging his efforts—smoothly homogenous blends of pop and r&b and jazz—and who often perversely believe success as being everything antithetical to jazz.

—A. JAMES LISKA, DOWN BEAT (1983)[96]

Leading into the 1980s, fusion jazz and crossover jazz still remained the commercial juggernauts of the jazz art world. In fact, jazz had never been this popular since the swing era. One could argue that this was the *popular* moment in modern jazz. As white critic A. James Liska's introduction to his interview with top crossover jazz star Grover Washington Jr. shows, however, crossover jazz musicians found their records regularly panned and their music making basically ignored by the jazz press and jazz fans. Top fusion jazz musicians, however, did receive mostly positive record reviews, expository essays, and interviews. And they did very well in the jazz polls as well. An overview of the top jazz magazines, especially the mainstream and highest circulating jazz magazine *Down Beat*, shows that for the decade of the 1970s the attention of critics in terms of what was of *contemporary* importance to the jazz art world were weirdly avant-garde Black Music and popular fusion jazz. Jazz critics' polls, however, indicated a strong preference still among the critical establishment for mainstream jazz. So, underlying the popularity and dominance of fusion jazz and the critical recognition of Black Music was a current of dissatisfaction as the *mainstream* jazz tradition seemed to be playing second trumpet to the likes of Miles Davis and Black Music trumpeter Lester Bowie. So, when a young, talented, opinionated jazz trumpeter named Wynton Marsalis appeared on the scene in 1982 decrying the miserable state of the jazz tradition, it was not surprising that he received such strong support from critics as a counterrevolution of traditionalists led modern jazz into a new era of neoclassical jazz.

Another Young Man with a Horn and Attitude

WM: . . . The problem with some of the stuff that all the critics think is innovative is that it sounds like European music—European avant-garde, classical 20th century static rhythm music with blues licks in it. All these cats can say for themselves is "We don't sound like anybody else." That doesn't mean shit. . . . Music has a tradition that you have to understand before you can move to the next step.

WM: . . . Anything is jazz, everything is jazz. Quincy Jones' shit is jazz. David Sanborn . . . that's not to cut down Quincy or David. l love funk, its hip. No problem to it.

—WYNTON MARSALIS WITH A. JAMES LISKA, DOWN BEAT (1982)[97]

When Wynton Marsalis released his first album in 1982, he took the jazz art world by storm with a dazzling horn as well as a strong opinion on the state of jazz in America. The same month Marsalis talked with A. James Liska, the trumpeter had won best trumpet, album, and artist of the year in the *Down Beat* Readers' Poll. Not since Archie Shepp and his Black Music declarations of the early 1960s had the jazz art world witnessed such a young messianic spokesperson coupled with such a brilliant talent. A major difference between the two revolutionary artists, however, was Marsalis's clear revolutionary mission to take back and resuscitate the mainstream jazz tradition. His first task was to expose the world to *real* jazz as a musician and as a spokesperson for the jazz art world. His second task was to educate the world, and misguided critics, musicians, and fans in the jazz art world, about how free jazz, fusion jazz, and crossover jazz were not *real* jazz and were undermining this great tradition. The jazz art world witnessed the beginnings of a traditionalist revolution that would forge a new path toward a neoclassical era in modern jazz. And many critics quickly lauded the appearance of this new messiah. As Chris Albertson wrote in *Stereo Review* in 1982, "I predict that Marsalis' contribution to jazz will go far beyond his own music, for he will surely inspire other young players to consider the jazz route. And who knows? He might even inspire some integrity in older defectors."[98]

Before he's fully into his 20s, Marsalis has been hailed as a messiah, lauded as the next trumpet genius and dubbed as a symbol of the 1980s. . . .

"The thing that's really painful to me about jazz is that some of the greatest musicians have sold out at a point in their careers when it wasn't necessary for them to sell out," he said in a hammering staccato voice. "And what that has done is fucked up the music. . . . The cats that have fucked up are mad because they don't want to see anybody expose them for being bullshit ass charlatans. A lot of avant-garde cats are charlatans anyway. They sound like Europeans."

Who's sold out? "Ornette Coleman, Sonny Rollins, a whole bunch of cats. I don't even have to name them. They know who they are. When you see a cat walk out on the stand with a skirt on, robes and shit, you know who they are. We know what's happening."

—WYNTON MARSALIS WITH HOLLIE I. WEST, JAZZ TIMES (1983)[99]

Marsalis's traditionalist position led to a number of critiques of fusion jazz, crossover jazz, and free jazz. He presented a consistent and coherent, if for some misguided, critique of jazz musicians who in the late 1960s and '70s "went astray. Everybody was trying to be pop stars, and imitated people who were supposed to be imitating them. Then there's the school of music that sounds like European music people were writing in the '30s."[100] The first theme was how pop jazz musicians prostituted themselves to the commercial dictates of the popular music market. Another theme was how free jazz and Black Music were based on European classical music. The last thing Black Music artists were playing in Marsalis's eyes was race music. Another theme was that musicians who had yet to prove themselves proficient in the jazz tradition—musicians who only played fusion, crossover, or free jazz—were probably unable to play real jazz because it takes dedication and tremendous effort to become a true jazz musician. As Marsalis told *Down Beat* in 1984, "What the jazz musician has done is such a phenomenal feat of intellectual accomplishment that people don't believe it is what it is . . . these people are not sincere, and they don't want to pay the dues that it takes to learn how to play this music."[101] Another theme was how these musicians in their dashikis, African robes, leather pants, fringed vests, purple bell-bottom pants, or some other pop-minstrel style of presentation were destroying the image of jazz as a serious and sophisticated art form. And finally, these musicians were lowering the high standards of musicianship demanded in jazz and were leading younger musicians down a path of mediocrity. All these themes highlighted how jazz was on life support and fusion, crossover, and free jazz were pulling the plug.

His arrival, and what it signals, is especially important because there has been—as there always is—talk about the decline of jazz, and more than a few have sworn they've seen the art gurgling on its deathbed. The talk usually continues that all of the younger musicians are being lost to one pop fad or another, that the old hallmarks of discipline and adventure have been replaced by the slick and the predictable, and finally, that most younger players have neither a sense of history nor a respect for the accomplishments of their predecessors. But Wynton Marsalis is a perfect retort to those misconceptions because he has everything—virtuoso technique, passion, intellect, curiosity, a sense of history.

—STANLEY CROUCH, WYNTON MARSALIS (1982)[102]

Wynton Marsalis's biggest mentor and advocate was the black jazz musician and cultural critic Stanley Crouch. Crouch, once a black nationalist poet and free jazz drummer, went neoconservative in the late 1970s.[103] He immediately lambasted Black Music artists who were once his allies and friends as at best failing to play true race music—playing for white jazz audiences since the early 1960s ripped them from their black roots and led them down the path of European classical music—or incompetent hucksters fooling gullible white audiences with pseudo and minstrel-like black music.[104] He did not like the pop pablum of fusion jazz and crossover jazz either. But what is important is that Crouch remained a race man committed to race music just like Marsalis. They were simply neoconservative race men for a neoconservative time in America.[105] For these race men, their counterrevolution was against the undermining of the one true African American *art* jazz. And Marsalis and the new Young Lions were going to take the leadership in bringing America back to jazz, its greatest indigenous art. As Crouch wrote in the liner notes for Marsalis's 1987 album *Standard Time, Volume One*, "Marsalis and his men are placing themselves in a situation where their work has to be judged against the best of the entire tradition . . . the responsibility passed on to the more ambitious artists of each generation is to learn how to redefine the fundamentals while maintaining the essences that give the art its scope and its grandeur."[106]

Jazz is an art form and it expresses a Negroid point of view about life in the 20th century. It is the most modern and profound expression of the way Black people look at the world. . . . I have nothing against pop music, but I do resent the pretention attached to the entertainment of today. . . . I am shocked by how many Black people at the top of their professions are so gullible and worried about being accused of not identifying with the man in the street that they refuse to discern with the interest in quality that makes for a true elite.

—WYNTON MARSALIS, EBONY (1986)[107]

As Wynton Marsalis made clear in his 1986 essay in *Ebony,* the Young Lion was a strong advocate for jazz as race music. He disparaged both forms of populism found among jazz musicians in the 1960s and '70s, either the Black Music populist commitment to making music from and for the black urban "ghetto" or the fusion and crossover populism committed to performing jazz with more popular idioms from soul to funk. Marsalis was returning to a "politics of respectability" in his cultural politics of race.[108] In the view of Marsalis, Crouch, and other neoclassicists, jazz needed an "uplift" from the obtuse meanderings of Black Music and the shallow decadence of fusion jazz and crossover jazz. And true jazz could uplift the race, or at least middle- and upper-class blacks, from the even more shallow decadent popular black music. Their mission was to bring the world back to the sophisticated foundations of the jazz tradition, to move race music down a sure path of respectability and authentic development. As Marsalis argued in late 1984, "We are becoming a pop culture, with everything reduced to the lowest common denominator. . . . I don't mean to sound like a snob—I love pop music for what it is. . . . But we musicians should never forget that it is our job to educate people to stand up for excellence and quality. . . . When jazz musicians started playing pop music, they gave up their credibility."[109] Marsalis was a leader for a new vanguard for a neoclassical era. And he seemed to have succeeded in generating if not a movement a general trend of traditionalism in jazz.

> 1979 was the year of roots and everyone was digging them up. Musicians frustrated in the search for something new looked back and discovered a wealth of ideas in the neglected music of their own jazz heritage. Avant-gardists, fed up with small audiences and no respect, came in from the cold. . . . Young horsemen, armed to the teeth with schooled technique but lacking a sense of direction "rediscovered" bebop for the sheer joy of speed and complexity. Older musicians found their careers back on track and themselves regarded as elder statesmen, guardians of the tradition. Everyone was playing "in the tradition" or trying to learn as fast as they could. Critics hailed artists who returned to the fold and predicted a jazz renaissance; audiences breathed a collective sigh of relief and sat back to wait.
>
> —JOHN LAHEY, CODA (1984)[110]

By the mid-1980s, critics already were hailing a new renaissance in jazz that seemed to have incorporated not only a new generation of Young Lions and older mainstream jazz musicians, but also previous free, fusion, and crossover jazz musicians. Hailing the arrival of a period of "traditionalism," critics also hoped for a reinvigorated jazz market as well. Free jazz artists like David Murray and Henry Threadgill were heralded as experimenting *within* traditional jazz as part of this neoclassical turn.[111] By the end of the decade, for many in the jazz art world it seemed clear that a revolution had certainly occurred that led this art world into a new neoclassical era. As white critic John Ephland wrote in *Down Beat* in 1990, "When music historians look back, 1990 could become known as the year the "Marsalis revolution" came to fruition. . . . The surge of interest in these young artists suggest a trend not only toward fresh faces with chops to spare, but a renewed interest in the roots of jazz."[112]

The Final Encore: Davis and Race Music

> WM: . . . The thing is, if it'll sell records to call that stuff jazz, they'll call it jazz. They call Miles's stuff jazz. That stuff is not jazz, man. Just because somebody played jazz at one time, that doesn't mean they're still playing it.
>
> —WYNTON MARSALIS WITH A. JAMES LISKA, DOWN BEAT (1982)[113]

Miles Davis returned to the music scene in late 1981. Davis had no idea he was returning just when a revolution in jazz would shake the very foundations of aesthetic innovation and popularization that defined his career. Wynton Marsalis, in the *Down Beat* article in 1982 on the young trumpeter's rapid ascent in the jazz art world, quickly placed Davis at the center of his revolution. Although this time Davis was not in the vanguard of a jazz revolution. No, this time he was the problem demanding a solution. But Davis in 1982 had not actually fallen from grace in the jazz art world. While Marsalis in the 1982 *Down Beat* Readers' Poll had won top honors for musician of the year, album of the year, and trumpeter of the year, Davis won the second spot in all three categories.[114] And he had actually won top honors in the Readers' Poll the year before for best artist and album.[115] Davis also went on to win best album in the poll the next two consecutive years. And Davis continued to appear in the finalists for top album, trumpeter, and/or artist of the year in the *Down Beat* Readers' Poll until his death in 1991. More importantly, while Davis in his final years seemed less driven toward breaking musical conventions or playing along the avant-garde edge, his move toward the *popular* in his crossover jazz period still garnered positive reception among many critics and fans. And Davis remained one of the top commercially successful jazz musicians in the world. He just had to contend with a new traditionalist revolt that somehow viewed him as emblematic of the problems challenging an ailing jazz art world.

Davis returned to the jazz scene with great fanfare in 1981.[116] His return generated a huge buzz when it was announced he would be a headliner for the Kool Jazz Festival in New York City in July of that year. On his return, however, his new studio album and live performances faced mixed reviews. Even his old ally Leonard Feather was sadly disappointed in Davis's return tour. "This reporter has studied Davis' career and admired him unreservedly from his earliest bebop days, heard him launch one stylistic revolution after another, and observed with dismay his physical and artistic retrenchment. . . . Our Prince has come back; but the crown is perhaps irreparably tarnished."[117] While many critics continued to be disappointed in Davis, by the mid-1980s he seemed to have hit his stride with a strong group of young musicians and a well-received studio album, *Star People* (1983). Davis now returned to his mixed status of the early 1970s. Davis received mostly positive reviews after *Star People* (1983) by those who accepted his more crossover jazz style of rhythmic-bluesy-funk and mellow pop tunes, and mostly negative reviews by those who still felt he lost his moorings in 1969 as well as those who now felt he was even more hell-bent on commercializing his appeal. While his 1980s new material was more crossover pop jazz, the recorded output on his return was better received than his 1970s post–*Bitches Brew* studio albums. And Davis was actually gaining more popular acclaim in the music industry, receiving four Grammy Awards: three for his albums *We Want Miles* (1982), *Tutu* (1986), and *Aura* (1989), and a lifetime achievement award in 1990.

Davis, however, remained a recognized target of the young iconoclastic traditionalist Wynton Marsalis until Davis's death in 1991. For Marsalis, Davis epitomized all that ailed the jazz tradition from avant-garde excess, electronic gimmickry, crass commercialism, and decadent posturing. His view of Davis was so omnipresent that Canadian journalist Stephen Brunt in the *Globe and Mail* in 1985 called it the "Wynton Marsalis Theory."[118] Typical of Marsalis's comments throughout the decade on Davis was what he told the *Jazz Times* in 1983, "He [Davis] was never my idol. I resent what he's doing because it gives the whole scene such a letdown, because he's such a great figure in the music. He's contributed so much for him to totally turn his back on his responsibility as a great artist. It hurts the music more than it hurts me. It hurts the way people perceive the music. And I think Bird would roll over in his grave if he knew what was going on."[119] While Davis spoke little of Marsalis, when he did he made clear that the Young Lion had little *new* to offer the world. As Davis told the *Los Angeles Times* in 1984, "Wynton hasn't found his sound yet. He's got a lot of technique, but that's about it."[120]

> As usual, where Davis led, many followed. His pernicious effect on the music scene since he went rapaciously commercial reveals a great deal about the perdurability of Zip Coon and Jasper Jack in the worlds of jazz and rock, in the worlds of jazz and rock criticism, in Afro-American culture itself. The cult of ethnic authenticity often mistakes the lowest common denominator for an ideal. It begets a self-image that has succumbed to a nostalgia for the mud. What we get is the bugaboo blues of the noble savage, the surly and dangerous Negro who will have nothing to do with bourgeois conventions. . . .
>
> In this climate, obnoxious, vulgar, and anti-social behavior has been confused with black authenticity. This has led to blaxploitation in politics, in higher education, and in art—to Eldridge Cleaver, Huey Newton, and the Black Panthers . . . to the least inventive and most offensive work of Richard Pryor and Eddie Murphy; to the angry cartoon coons of Spike Lee and the flat, misogynist, gutter verse of Ice-T and racist rap groups like Public Enemy.
>
> —STANLEY CROUCH, NEW REPUBLIC (1990)[121]

At the end of the decade, Stanley Crouch sent a shock wave through the American cultural firmament with a no-holds-barred condemnation of post-1969 Miles Davis. No longer satisfied in making Davis responsible simply for undermining the jazz tradition, Crouch doubled-down and accused Davis of leading black activists and artists into a black hole of minstrel-like buffoonery and savagery in politics and culture. While Davis's controversial 1989 autobiography certainly inspired Crouch's critical pen, Crouch expressed what was a general neoconservative view of Davis and African American culture held by jazz traditionalists. It was such a view that laid the foundation for the traditionalist revolt as articulated by Marsalis and his allies like Crouch. This neoconservative movement sought to distance itself from both radical black nationalism and the black popular aesthetic. Crouch was expressing a black nationalist ideology, but one that distinguished itself as a cultural politics of respectability against what it considered a cultural politics of debasement in the African American community. Davis was a ripe target for Crouch and Marsalis for obvious reasons. For over thirty years, Davis was not only the icon of modern jazz but also an undisputed icon in the African American community as the quintessential cool, unrepentant, brilliant race man. The counterrevolution was in full force with Davis seemingly flaunting its efforts to legitimize jazz as a truly elite, bourgeois art form. Because for Marsalis and other neoconservative traditionalists, in the end, only by embracing the time-honored connection between social group status and high art would the race music jazz finally attained its rightful place as America's great art music.

Marsalis and the other Young Lions of the neotraditionalist movement certainly seemed contemporary to the moment of the Reagan Era of neo-conservatism in the United States. White jazz critic Gary Giddins in the *Village Voice* in 1984 sarcastically suggested that the Young Lions in their charcoal gray suits and neatly cropped hair seemed more like black yup-pies looking for establishment blessing than dashiki-clad race men rebel-ling against the system.[122] Davis in his post-1969 chameleon state of self-presentation, from all-black-leather-outlaw pose, to multicolor onstage outfits, to his broad-rimmed sunglasses, to even his green and red trumpets, seemed to hail from another more outlandish and antiestablishment time. Black cultural critic Greg Tate made a similar prescient argument about Marsalis versus Davis in the *Village Voice* only a month earlier than Giddens. Tate viewed Marsalis as the perfect black rebel for the times, more rebel in pose than substance. And in terms of "Wynton and Miles—well, not to backhand the brother, but that comparison ain't even a conversation, let alone a quip."[123] For Tate, Miles was the real thing, while Marsalis was a fac-simile of a hip rebel perfect for white consumption during a conservative era.

As we will see in another chapter, Miles Davis for over four decades did represent for the African American community the iconic postwar rebel race man as provocateur and outsider, a black musician who refused to accom-modate to the expectations of the white establishment. Wynton Marsalis represented a new race man in modern jazz, more similar to the premodern jazz race man sophistication and elegance of Duke Ellington. Marsalis was seeking entrance into the cultural establishment as a race man promot-ing the race music of jazz as the Great American Music. In the process, he changed the ethos of music making in jazz as well as the image of the jazz musician. And in truth, such a well-attired, well-spoken, well-educated, and well-trained jazz musician was the perfect candidate to found and lead Jazz at Lincoln Center in 1991. And as Herman Gray argues, in the "canonical project" of his neoclassical mission, Marsalis was an unquestionable success, making jazz respectable and establishing a jazz foothold in the American cultural establishment.[124]

Conclusion

> What excites me most about *Doo-Bop*, the joyous teaming up of Miles
> and young rapper and instrumentalist Easy Mo Bee, is the way Miles
> was playing in his last days. . . . I just wish he was still around to jam
> with folks like Ice T, Whodini, Queen Latifah, Public Enemy and Geto
> Boys. Miles's embrace and encouragement of the new has made an
> impact on musicians of all ages. It's a hell of an exit Chief.
> —ROBIN TOLLESON, DOWN BEAT (1992)[125]

It is telling that in his final years, Miles Davis reasserted his race music credentials in ways that spoke directly against the traditionalist turn in jazz. Similar to the hard bop rebel days of the late 1950s and early 1960s, Davis in his final years made strong connections to Africa and the anti-apartheid struggle in the albums *Sun City* (1985), *Tutu* (1986), and *Amandla* (1989). Wynton Marsalis preferred references to the *past* history, culture, and music of African Americans, not to their contemporary politics, culture, and music. And as white musician and music writer Robin Tolleson in *Down Beat* celebrated in 1992, Davis embraced the new *popular* in black culture, hip-hop and rap music, in his final studio project *Doo-Bop* (1992). Davis himself had come full circle, returning to the political and musical rebellion of his first love, bebop. His final creative burst made a direct link between the political culture of *bop* and the new political culture of *hip-hop*. While Davis was no longer leading a revolution in music making, he had the intuition to see where that next revolution was going to emerge.

Over the entire career of Miles Davis, we see how modern jazz and Afro-modernism grappled with various distinctions and contradictions during the avant-garde and neoclassical eras. One of the most fundamental questions was about the "power of black music" in the twentieth century. As Samuel A. Floyd Jr. argues, this question constantly brushed against the relationship between the vernacular and the cultivated, the popular and the high, the popular classes and the black bourgeoisie.[126] It was compounded by a modern jazz ethos with pretensions to high art status and legitimacy. And it was further compounded by a music industry little concerned with the agenda of race-conscious musicians or the uplift of the African American community. During the avant-garde era of modern jazz, the popular remained part of the mix of the "cultural moves" of black musicians from hard-boppers to Black Music to fusion jazz to crossover jazz. And what makes Miles Davis stand out as the iconic genius of modern jazz is how he made all these moves!

But Davis's final years marked a distinct disruption in this relationship, as neoconservative traditionalists like Marsalis rejected any relationship with *contemporary* popular music. Jazz was now a conservatory music. Ironically, a conservatory music more conservative than classical music in its obsession in preserving a jazz tradition—there is no postmodern jazz in the Marsalis universe. And while a marginal "jazz left" attempted to retain a bridge to the popular, as well as the avant-garde, since the traditionalist revolt, it has been the "Wynton Marsalis theory" of jazz that has found an institutional and commercial anchor for the jazz art world over the last fifteen years.[127] But overarching all these "cultural moves," regardless of their contradictory impulses, is the inescapable truth that Afro-modernism in all its guises fundamentally shaped the jazz tradition throughout the twentieth century. And it was this drive in the quest for race music in this century that gave America its true *classical art*: the one point all these race men and race women of black music could probably agree on.

But it would not be neoclassical jazz musicians and their race music that challenged the dire state of the African American community during the New Jim Crow. And while the jazz left since the 1990s continued the radical calls for music making and politics found in hard bop and Black Music,[128] another more powerful race music community would emerge in the performance venues and recordings of rap artists. The Afro-modernism that had informed jazz since the 1920s up into the neoclassical era was now captured by a new community of popular black artists. And these popular artists would revolutionize American music as black musicians had consistently done since the beginning of the twentieth century. Neoconservative cultural elites in the 1980s, however, were unable to see the rich potential of hip-hop culture as the new race music. Marsalis and his allies openly ridiculed and condemned hip-hop culture and rap music. Miles Davis, and other crossover jazz artists like Quincy Jones, fully embraced this culture. Race music, however, has a power of its own, and cultural elites ultimately cannot prevent it from capturing the imagination of their own community and beyond. And Davis, with his consistent genius at tapping the pulse of the popular, recognized the power of this new tradition in popular music making. Whether he tapped into this music simply for commercial gain and a desperate need to remain hip, or embraced it because it was the innovative and radical race music of the next generation, is irrelevant. Because as Davis proved over and over again in his four-and-a-half-decade career, having commercial savvy, a rebel attitude, insatiable creative drives, and an intuitive sense of the popular are not mutually exclusive. Well, at least they were not so for Miles Dewey Davis III.

Martin Scorsese

RIVAL NARRATIVES OF AUTONOMY IN AMERICAN FILM

> Why did a generation of movie lovers, born between the late Sixties and early Seventies, naturally gravitate towards Martin Scorsese? ... for many of us born during this period—arguably the Renaissance of American film—Scorsese was The Man, the artist to whom we would stake our first cultural claim. And more: For some of us, Scorsese *was* film, the director in whom we witnessed the great traditions collide—Fellini's expressionism, Italian neorealism, the French New Wave's iconoclasm, Hollywood classicism. . . . Thank you, Mr. Scorsese; your pictures mean everything to us.
> —ANDREW LEWIS CONN, FILM COMMENT (1998)[1]

Andrew Lewis Conn was not alone in his admiration for the American filmmaker Martin Scorsese. Many film critics, film directors, and moviegoers have viewed Scorsese as the most iconic filmmaker of the generation who defined New Hollywood in the 1960s and '70s. French minister of culture Jack Lang, for example, proclaimed Scorsese "the most important film director of his generation" when awarding him the Commander of Arts and Literature medal in 1991.[2] And no New Hollywood director, except for the more commercially successful Steven Spielberg, has been as consistent in their filmmaking over the last five decades. In a variety of ways, Scorsese has come to exemplify the New Hollywood auteur filmmaker celebrated fifty-years ago by film critic Andrew Sarris.[3] He has proven to be the most successful American filmmaker to have navigated the difficult balance between a position as an independent filmmaker and the power of the big budget Hollywood director. He certainly seems to be the genius who works both outside and inside the Hollywood system. At the same time, Scorsese's career directs us to the often-contradictory, and hard to exactly define, position of *independent filmmaker* in American film. As cultural critic D. K. Holm asks, "Can filmmakers ever be truly independent within the context of commercial cinema?"[4] Scorsese would certainly consider this one of the defining questions of his career—a question he constantly argued was answered in the various films he has made over the years.

In the last half of the twentieth century, the public stories about American film narrated a contested terrain over questions of independence, auteurship, commercialism, and aesthetics as artists and others positioned themselves in this art field. One set of distinctions in American film in this public story has been between avant-garde *experimental film*, commercial *independent film*, and mass-appeal *Hollywood film*. No absolute boundaries existed between these three genre communities, with techniques, aesthetics, artists, and producers not necessarily restricted to one or another community. But they certainly provided benchmarks of real distinctions and locations in the art field that motivated and shaped artistic and other practices and meanings in American film, and at times, generated considerable debate and hand-wringing. These artistic communities presented public stories about the nature of autonomy in filmmaking, the medium of film as art, the tastes and expectations of audiences, and the power of commercial and industrial forces in filmmaking. And hovering over these public stories was the seemingly death-defying power of shape-shifting Hollywood studios, from the collapse of the Golden Age studio system to the rise of the Blockbuster Age conglomerate system. Even in the midst of the Digital Age, Hollywood studios remain the dominant power in American film.

This chapter not only focuses on the questions of independence and autonomy in American film, but also on three aesthetics in American film during Scorsese's career: an avant-garde *pure aesthetic*, an independent *aesthetic of the real*, and a Hollywood *commercial aesthetic*. The sociologist Pierre Bourdieu argues that the *pure aesthetic* is an aesthetic of distance—emphasizing art, form, and expression distant from everyday life. He also argues that an *aesthetic of the real* is an aesthetic of the ordinary—emphasizing art, content, and experience close to everyday life.[5] The pure aesthetic common in avant-garde art also speaks to an art form as an impersonal medium, a blank canvas, in which artists explore their personal artistic muses as well as the aesthetic potential inherent in the medium. The aesthetic of the real common in political and popular art, on the other hand, speaks to an art form as a craft, representational, affective, and personal in a more biographic and societal sense. But as film historian Richard Maltby argues, Hollywood has been dominated by a *commercial aesthetic* that includes questions of form and content but also speaks to the importance of production values and a "regulated difference" that repackages the same ingredients into a new product with supposedly guaranteed mass appeal.[6] The contemporary universe of Hollywood comic book film franchises with star-name actors and actresses is the perfect example of this commercial aesthetic.

The various distinctions between a pure aesthetic, aesthetic of the real, and commercial aesthetic expressed themselves in the public stories about avant-garde experimental film, independent commercial film, and Hollywood mass-appeal film. Such distinctions expressed themselves also in how public stories spoke to the relationship between a filmmaker's life, art, and passions. This chapter looks at how the personal, the biographical, and the affective dimensions of a popular aesthetic of the real were evident in the public story of Martin Scorsese as a member of the independent film community. I will look at the evolution of independent film since the first rumblings of revolt against Hollywood in the late 1950s. I also will look at how the abstract, the formal, the personal, and the intellectual dimensions of a pure aesthetic emerged in the public story of an experimental film genre community that forged a path separate from Hollywood and independent commercial feature film. But I will also show how the public story of Scorsese as an independent filmmaker elided how the Hollywood commercial aesthetic significantly shaped his conception of himself as an independent filmmaker as well as the nature of his personal auteur films. The public stories of Martin Scorsese, Hollywood film, independent film, and experimental film have revealed in the second half of the twentieth century, and into the twenty-first century, the various ideas about autonomy and filmmaking that have structured the meaningful activity of artists, critics, producers, and others in the field of American film.

Martin Scorsese: Auteur of New Hollywood

The whole façade, the whole image of what mainstream filmmaking was, made me feel like an outsider. . . . The only thing I can do is to make movies as honestly as possible and take the risks—whatever it means—to do what you think is right. I'm just trying to make movies that if I'm alive 20 years from now, I can look at them and say, "You know, that's exactly the picture I wanted to make."

—MARTIN SCORSESE WITH BERNARD WEINRAUB,
NEW YORK TIMES (1995)[7]

Martin Scorsese is one of the few New Hollywood directors who have consistently made auteur commercial feature films up to the present. Many critics claim he is the most accomplished artistically of these directors, who include the equally successful but more mainstream Steven Spielberg. After New Hollywood's fall in the late 1970s, Scorsese remained connected to the world of independent film as well as the Hollywood film industry. Since his earliest days as a director, he has negotiated between artistic autonomy and commercial demand. As Scorsese reminded Bernard Weintraub in 1995, his calling as a filmmaker included a dedication to making personal, honest, and creative films. This is what has made Scorsese an icon of American independent film up to the present. This status has been buttressed by an extensive public story that since its beginnings in the late 1960s has remained remarkably consistent in its overarching themes and tropes.

A misunderstood moviemaking genius stuck in a Sisyphean struggle against all the puny producers and myopic studio suits of his time who will never fully understand or appreciate his cinematic sensibilities. . . . Scorsese is foremost a pragmatist who has achieved no small degree of satisfaction because he's learned to be successful within a grinding, ball-breaking system.

—TIMOTHY RHYS, MOVIEMAKER (2002)[8]

Scorsese's public story is about a filmmaker who has made personally relevant and artistically powerful movies but also has sought the big budgets and mass audiences only Hollywood could provide. His public story is the embodiment of *la politique des auteurs* that informed the independent film community.[9] This theory in the 1950s and 1960s celebrated film directors who incorporated personal vision within commercial feature film, whether the classic films of Jean Renoir and Howard Hawks or the postwar art cinema of Akira Kurosawa and Jean-Luc Godard. This theory informed the New Hollywood renaissance.[10] Scorsese is an archetype of the auteur filmmaker—a position of commercial independent film set between avant-garde experimental film and mainstream Hollywood film. That Timothy Rhys would provide in 2002 such a vivid description of the autonomy of Scorsese in *MovieMaker*, an independent film magazine, is testament to the enduring iconic status of this director in American independent film.

The *politique des auteurs* narrative includes tropes of personal vision, artistry, technique, risk taking, rule breaking, independence, and being-the-outsider, but also tropes of being pragmatic, a player, a negotiator, and a filmmaker who wants to make films demanding large Hollywood budgets. *Village Voice* film critic Amy Taubin in 1990 pointed to Scorsese's outsider-insider status: "Scorsese is an anomaly among contemporary film directors. For 20 years, he has managed to make utterly personal, deeply autobiographical movies that are bankrolled by the film industry. He's both an art-film director—the American equivalent of a Buñuel or Truffaut—and a 'player' in Hollywood."[11] In his 1996 documentary on American cinema, Scorsese again commented on his outsider-insider status: "Even today I still wonder what it takes to be a professional or even an artist in Hollywood. How do you survive the constant tug of war between personal expression and commercial imperatives?"[12]

Scorsese's public story has also emphasized his encyclopedic knowledge of classic American and European films. Scorsese in interviews constantly refers to the classic films that inform his specific works. Those who have worked with him also point to the large number of classic films he previews with his collaborators before each production. As Scorsese said in receiving the American Film Institute Life Achievement Award in 1997, "This award is meant to honor the masters of the golden age of the studio system. . . . They're the pioneers who created the grammar of film language. What we do now, they did before."[13] Scorsese's documentaries on American and Italian film, *A Personal Journey with Martin Scorsese through American Movies* (1996) and *My Voyage to Italy* (1999), attest to his commitment to classic American and European film. As the British Film Institute's *Sight and Sound* proclaimed, "Scorsese is famously . . . a hands-on historian of cinema, with his own vast print collection and encyclopedic knowledge."[14] An auteur like Scorsese does not reject the tradition of commercial narrative cinema but embraces it as essential to his personal vision. He works with this tradition as a "genius within the system."

The son of a clothes presser, the director grew up in Little Italy, where asthma and a frail physique prevented him from taking part in the macho, street-smart life around him. He spent most of his free time going to the movies, and those movies made him want, more than anything, "to be part of that incredible world of the creation of films."

Martin Scorsese's public story began when the *New York Times* in 1969 introduced to the world a young director from New York City's Little Italy. By the release of his acclaimed *Mean Streets* (1973), the details of his youth in Little Italy were being added to his public story.[16] Over time more details would be added about how his life experiences as a youth formed his passion for film as well as the themes in his films. In this story, Scorsese was born to be a filmmaker with memories as far back as a four-year-old kid mesmerized by watching the Hollywood classic *Duel in the Sun*. Making films was his driving passion and his ultimate salvation. As Hal Hinson commented in the *Washington Post* in 1991, "People make movies for a lot of reasons, but Scorsese makes them because he's hooked. His blood runs pure celluloid."[17]

Scorsese's public story is presented as a product of a history of human experience as lived in the social and cultural context of his life in Little Italy and as imagined in the world of film. What has been personal in Scorsese's art is not simply an aesthetic vision but an *affective* connection between his lived experience, his passion for film, and the stories in his movies. As Scorsese in 1986 told Peter Biskind and Susan Linfield in *American Film*, "It always comes down to whether I see myself in the film."[18] His films are portrayed as honest not only in how critics see them as starkly realistic. They are real in how Scorsese speaks to their "anthropological" sense—placing characters in historical settings to reveal the connection between individuals and the social. And he constantly speaks to personal connections to his film characters from Charlie in *Means Streets* (1973) to Jake in *Raging Bull* (1980) to Howard Hughes in *The Aviator* (2002). As Scorsese told *Rolling Stone*'s Anthony DeCurtis in 1990, "So the only criterion on the films I'm willing to take risks on is that it be truthful, that it be honest about your own feelings and truthful to what you know to be the reality around you or the reality of the human condition of the characters."[19]

Were it not for Scorsese's insatiable appetite for movies, however, it is conceivable that he would be dwelling today down on Elizabeth Street, where his parents were born and still live and where he himself grew up—a frail, asthmatic boy doing his best to keep pace with one of Little Italy's more rambunctious gangs.

In Martin Scorsese's public story, film was his only salvation from the two stereotypical paths available to a young Italian male in Little Italy in the 1960s: the priesthood or the mafia. This was a theme perpetuated by Scorsese himself, as film becomes the rare path out of Little Italy. "Coming from this little Sicilian village on Elizabeth Street, you might as well have said to me, 'You'll be living on the moon,' as saying, 'You'll make movies.'"[21] Scorsese also points to how there were no books in his home, how he was a terrible student who only made it to college because NYU would take anyone. "And, I've said it many times in interviews. I come from a home where the only things that were read were the *Daily News* and the *Daily Mirror*. . . . I mean, I'm not a fast reader, although I'm forcing myself to read as much as possible now. I'm sort of catching up on books that I should have read twenty years ago, forcing myself to read a lot."[22] His public story does not portray him as innately artistic, or innately intellectual. As Timothy Rhys points out in 2002, "To hear him tell it, one thing Martin Scorsese doesn't need is to be called an 'artist.' God forbid. No red-blooded American director ever claimed to be an artist anyway. 'Auteur?' Give him a break. 'Auteurs' don't come from Elizabeth Street."[23] Scorsese had an *affective* connection to a single, personally resonant art form—a popular affective appreciation more than an avant-garde aesthetic appreciation.

Scorsese's affective appreciation of the popular reveals itself in his film-making. Scorsese is celebrated for his respect and mastery of conventional film language and technique. It is the realism, honesty, and personal engagement not supposedly found in mainstream Hollywood film that are the foundations of Scorsese's independence. Although Scorsese has integrated nonconventional techniques found in early New Wave cinema and avant-garde cinema into his unique vision as an auteur, it is not a rejection of the tradition of commercial filmmaking or an emphasis on formal experimentation over story that defines him as a filmmaker. The popular aesthetic rejects art for art's sake—art focused on formal experiment—for the art of the real. As Scorsese says, "I come out of the narrative tradition . . . those are the films that I first saw and those are the films that made the most, the biggest impression on me. . . . I was raised on American films, which means story and narrative."[24]

The public story of Scorsese also has presented him as an outsider. Scorsese is portrayed as an outsider to mainstream Hollywood. As he told *Fast Company* in 2011 in talking about the end of the New Hollywood renaissance, "They saw me as outside Hollywood. You're gone; you're in independent cinema now, on the outside from now on."[25] But Scorsese is also portrayed as outside mainstream America. Since his beginnings as a film director, both Scorsese and others have emphasized his roots in the working-class ethnic enclave of Little Italy as setting him apart from mainstream America. Scorsese's uniqueness as an artist is more often associated with his life experience in Little Italy than with some abstract muse or intellectual agenda. Scorsese in this public story even positions himself as an outsider to Art. "To me, Bohemians are people in black-and-white movies, wearing black turtle-necks, reciting poetry I don't understand, talking in coffee houses that have a lot of brick. . . . I wasn't that hip that way."[26] But what is even more compelling is how a commercially successful and highly celebrated American filmmaker has been portrayed throughout his career as an artistic and social outsider. It speaks volumes about twentieth-century American art and society in how Scorsese's public story paints him as much an outsider, rebel, and autonomous artist as any avant-garde filmmaker in America.

Experimental Film: Avant-Garde Pure Aesthetic

> *Scorsese, Coppola* and *Malick* are relatively young, unmistakably talented, and much more independent of industry pressures than their Hollywood predecessors. They may stray a bit farther from conventional story-telling techniques than would an old-guard master like Howard Hawks; but their films remain fictional narratives. . . . The Whitney, on the other hand, is interested in filmmakers whose work involves no such artifices—filmmakers whose efforts are more closely related to the modern paintings hanging on the walls. . . . Ken Jacobs, one of the most innovative and influential avant-garde filmmakers, is constantly reminding us that no matter how life-like a cinematic image may look, it is ultimately the result of a beam of light projected onto a flat surface.
>
> —ROGER COPLAND, NEW YORK TIMES (1976)[27]

Roger Copland's comparison of auteurs like Martin Scorsese to avant-garde filmmaker Ken Jacobs underscored several distinctions between independent film and experimental film. One difference was auteurs' commitment to storytelling traditions found in Hollywood film versus avant-gardists' commitment to aesthetics similar to the visual arts. And while Scorsese was heading to independent or major studios, Jacobs was heading to the Whitney Museum of American Art. Like postwar art critic Clement Greenberg's claim that modern painting was the struggle with the pure form of a two-dimensional canvas, Copland also highlighted how experimental film held a similar pursuit of a *pure cinema*. Avant-garde visual art and film were not concerned with representation—an aesthetic of the real—but concerned with form—a pure aesthetic. Theorist Rudolf Arnheim predicted in 1965 that film was following "what modern art has done. By renouncing portrayal, the work of art establishes itself clearly as an object possessing an independent existence of its own."[28]

> If cinema is to take its place beside the others as a full-fledged art form . . . [i]t must relinquish the narrative disciplines it has borrowed from literature . . . it must develop the vocabulary of filmic images, and evolve the syntax of filmic techniques . . . [i]t must determine the disciplines inherent in the medium, discover its own structural modes, explore the new realms and dimensions accessible to it.
>
> —MAYA DEREN, DAEDALUS (1960)[29]

The experimental film community emerged as an informal network of filmmakers in Los Angeles, New York City, and San Francisco in the 1940s and '50s. By the 1960s, an art world of experimental film existed with cooperatives, societies, journals, distributors, theaters, exhibitions, and festivals.[30] Maya Deren was one of the founders of postwar American experimental film. In *Daedalus*, Deren reiterated an argument found in her earliest writings and talks that became a core theme in this genre community's public story. She lamented how film was trapped in the literary and theatrical traditions of Hollywood and promoted finding the medium's unique language. Deren represented a strand of filmmaking that defined experimental film and its public story by the end of the 1960s. This strand emphasized a *formalist* approach to film as a *visual art*, where images and sounds existed in a context outside the narrative-realism that formed the language of commercial film in America. As the film critic P. Adams Sitney declared in 1969, "The dominant evolution of the American . . . avant-garde cinema has been the pursuit of progressively complex forms."[31]

> Whatever it may have been in the past, the idea of content is today mainly a hindrance, a nuisance, a subtle or not so subtle philistinism. . . . This is why cinema is the most alive, the most exciting, the most important of all art forms right now.
>
> —SUSAN SONTAG, AGAINST INTERPRETATION (1966)[32]

In her highly regarded book *Against Interpretation*, Susan Sontag linked experimental film to the direction of avant-garde art away from the philistine

obsession with interpreting content. Experimental film mirrored the history
of avant-garde visual art toward greater abstraction. Such a trajectory was
not surprising, since many European avant-garde artists who experimented
in film before World War II migrated to the United States during or after the
war. Avant-garde film's link to modern visual art was clear to émigré Hans
Richter who had a major impact on postwar experimental film in America.
"These artists discovered that film as a visual medium fitted into the tradition
of art without violation of its fundamentals. . . . The connection to theater
and literature was, completely, severed. Cubism, expressionism, dadaism,
abstract art, surrealism found not only their expression in films but also a
new fulfilment on a new level."[33] European filmmakers brought the *cinéma
pur* of early European art film to American experimental filmmakers. Many
of these filmmakers were part of a larger avant-garde community of artists
centered in the bohemian Greenwich Village celebrated in Sontag's book.
So, it is not surprising that the public story of this film community would follow the general trajectory of the American avant-garde toward abstraction
in painting, sculpture, dance, and music.[34] As filmmaker Stan Vanderbeek
said at a New York Film Festival symposium in 1965, "artists and painters . . .
are going to be the new film-makers . . . they are our only hope."[35]

Pioneer Maya Deren's own work fell in what many called poetic film—
film that avoided the linear realism of commercial film and instead emphasized surrealist storytelling.[36] Experimental film began with artists supporting this poetic approach, others supporting a more formalist approach of
abstract image and sound, and finally others supporting the Direct Cinema
approach of unfiltered, nontheatrical realism found in documentaries and
low-budget narrative films. Into the early 1960s, all three approaches were
celebrated in experimental film's public story for rebelling against the big-
budget, stylized, polished, theatrical realism of Hollywood film.[37] During the
1960s, however, the core of the experimental film community abandoned
any connection to narrative film.[38] Experimental film's public story in the
1960s veered toward a more abstract approach to filmmaking.

Experimental film's public story also emphasized this medium's fall from
grace with the advent of Hollywood and sound film.[39] The story tells how
sound introduced the literary and theatrical traditions that corrupted the
true potential of film as a visual art. By the mid-1960s, the complete rejection
of the tradition of commercial feature film in this public story led avant-
garde critics to separate experimental film, called New American Cinema,
from not only Hollywood film but also American independent film and international art cinema.[40] The avant-garde community's public story now
was about distancing itself from not only Hollywood but also the emerging

auteur independent film community and its genre ideal. As major spokesperson Jonas Mekas, editor of the experimental film magazine *Film Culture* and film critic for the *Village Voice* from 1958 to 1972, argued in 1965, "Cinema has reached its maturity and can no longer be dismissed or reviewed or treated— neither by the audiences nor the critics—as a medium for telling stories. Now cinema, like any other art, has two ends, and they are far apart."[41]

By the 1970s, experimental film's public story separated avant-garde film from the Direct Cinema tradition it once celebrated, along with the *politique des auteurs* of international art cinema and American independent film. This story now hailed experimental film as a formalist, abstract, nonnarrative practice of filmmaking. Avant-garde experimental filmmakers, however, were avid writers espousing the philosophies behind their more conceptual work and commenting on other filmmakers and the state of cinema. Ironically, experimental filmmakers who lamented the written word's dominance of commercial film needed extensive prose to explain their purely visual and aural films. From Pierre Bourdieu's viewpoint, the appreciation of experimental film demanded a far greater level of cultural capital—the disposition to understand modern art—than the world of independent film and Hollywood film inhabited by Scorsese and others.[42]

> To rescue its proper place she reaches for conceptual elements from other arts: the metaphorically charged image of lyric poetry, the impersonal presentation of form unfolding in time found in dance, and the rhythmic and thematic structures which happen in music . . . this complex of ideas was gathered from many sources, including Deren's studies of the enlightenment, political philosophy, modernist poetics (Imagism, Pound), and psychology (Bergson, Jung)—all her academic studies brought into relation with one another.
>
> —BRUCE R. MCPHERSON ON MAYA DEREN (2005)[43]

In experimental film's public story, film is a medium of expression that the avant-garde artist uses to create art. As Bruce McPherson points out, Maya Deren was a poet, a dancer, an intellectual, and a filmmaker. The relationship between the artist and film is not portrayed in the public story of experimental film as *affective* or *personal*. Deren's *art*—like all experimental filmmakers' art—was a personal, affective expression, film was one medium in which to express it. Many experimental filmmakers were first *artists* and *intellectuals* before they were filmmakers. This explains why their public story rejected the craft-profession techniques of commercial filmmaking.

There was no affective connection to popular film in this narrative. Experimentalists approached film as a blank canvas in which to reinvent a pure art. As filmmaker Stan Vanderbeek said at the New York Film Festival in 1965, "There is a whole aura of professionalism that surrounds the film like a metaphysic, the mechanical metaphysic. . . . Anybody can basically learn all that you have to learn about motion pictures in say a month and you can even do that on a part-time basis. After that it only becomes a problem of artistic level and artistic ambition."[44]

> The New American film maker seeks to free himself from the over-professionalism and over-technicality that usually handicaps the inspiration and spontaneity of contemporary cinema, guiding himself more by intuition and improvisation than by discipline: he aims desperately, as his colleague action painter, or poet and dancer, at art in its very flight, at a free, a spontaneous inspiration.
>
> —JONAS MEKAS, FILM CULTURE (1960)[45]

Experimental film's public story also advocated for a "personal cinema." This was not the personal vision celebrated in Scorsese's public story, but an unencumbered personal vision of an avant-garde artist alone or with a small group of collaborators. Experimental film's public story rejected the large collaborative organization of commercial feature film.[46] It also rejected the professionalism of such films and promoted unskilled, amateur movies as authentic, experimental, and free. Personal cinema became more of a clarion call in the mid-1960s because of the constant rejection of experimental film by most filmmakers, critics, and audiences. As Jonas Mekas exclaimed in 1965, "The only aesthetically interesting work, however, is being done in the personal, private cinema . . . cinema that can be viewed and appreciated more in privacy than in public."[47] For the avant-garde, "public" became a derogatory term similar to how mass culture was used to describe Hollywood film. As the experimental filmmaker Stan Brakhage argued in his 1982 book, *Brakhage Scrapbook*, "A public Artist, with capitol 'a,' is as much admired by many, and of as little value to an individual life, as any professional . . . the true amateur, even when in consort with other amateurs, is always working alone, gauging his success according to his care for the work rather than according to the accomplishments or recognitions of others."[48]

Experimental film's public story espoused a highbrow *pure aesthetic* while simultaneously claiming an allegiance to amateur moviemaking. Avant-gardist Vanderbeek, at the New York Film Festival in 1965, predicted, "55%

of film-makers . . . women in home movies. If they ever got together they'd put everybody out of business."[49] This public story was contradictory in demanding a pureness based on a lack of film conventions yet was predicated on a sophisticated appreciation of symbolic and formal elements found in visual and sound art. As Direct Cinema director Karel Reisz complained in *Sight and Sound* in 1958, "Many of these films are incomprehensible without reference text-books."[50] Stan Brakhage in 1963 strongly advocated for a purity in vision, "Imagine an eye unruled by man-made laws of perspective, an eye unprejudiced by compositional logic, an eye which does not respond to the name of everything but which must know each object encountered in life through an adventure of perception."[51] Yet over thirty years later, experimental film advocate James Peterson argued that the position of early avant-garde artists like Brakhage was contradicted by the esoteric conventions of experimental film that continued to leave viewers frustrated and avant-garde advocates lamenting the narrow-mindedness of these viewers.[52]

> I accuse all our movie critics, and I accuse here *Time*, *Newsweek*, and *Variety*, and *The New York Times* and the *Post*, and absolutely all our newspapers and magazines (including most of the underground press) of committing an unforgivable cultural crime by reviewing only commercial films, only long-run films, for ignoring one-time film events.
>
> —JONAS MEKAS, VILLAGE VOICE (1969)[53]

Unlike Scorsese's public story, the public story of experimental film involved two opposing storytelling communities—the small community of avid supporters of experimental film and virtually everyone else involved in the public story of American film. Jonas Mekas and other avant-garde filmmakers and critics complained about experimental film having little support among critics and audiences. As early as 1960, Mekas complained that the "works of the New American cinema are criticized by audience and reviewers for their roughness and for their technical imperfections. Do we read books only because they are perfect?"[54] Even major film journals like *Sight and Sound* (British) and *Film Quarterly* (American) were often unfavorable to American experimental film. With the experimental film community centered in New York City in the 1960s, avant-garde filmmakers and critics were especially infuriated with their marginalization at such elite institutions as the Lincoln Center's New York Film Festival and MoMA.[55]

By the mid-1970s, experimental film's public story became less contentious, and less prominent in the public story of American film, as experimental film found a home at universities, art museums, art galleries, academic publications, and avant-garde film festivals.[56] As a *visual art*, experimental film gained institutional recognition from art museums and academia.[57] Even major mainstream festival and critics' awards would recognize experimental film—usually within the special genre of the short film—but separate from major screenings, panels, and awards. What emerged from the late 1960s and early 1970s was a more clearly bounded genre community of avant-garde experimental filmmakers ranging from subcultural "artisan avant-garde" filmmakers located in urban artistic communities to more established "institutional avant-garde" filmmakers at universities or other art institutions.[58] By the 1980s, "independent film" became almost exclusively a reference to the narrative-based independent film community in the public story of American film.[59] Major works on post-1970s American independent film, Emanuel Levy's *Cinema of Outsiders* (1999), Greg Merritt's *Celluloid Mavericks* (2000), Peter Biskind's *Down and Dirty Pictures* (2004), Geoff King's *American Independent Cinema* (2005), and Yannis Tzioumakis's *American Independent Cinema: An Introduction* (2006), all show experimental film's absence, outside of its early connections and aesthetic influences, in the public story of contemporary American independent film.[60] Experimental film, however, has remained a vibrant and noncommercial art world located in its own network of small distributors, microcinemas, collectives, galleries, museums, festivals, and colleges.

New Hollywood versus Experimental Film: Competing Forms of Autonomy and Aesthetics

> When movies, the only art which everyone felt free to enjoy and have opinions about, lose their connection to song and dance, drama, and the novel, when they become cinema, which people fear to criticize just as they fear to say what they think of a new piece of music or a new poem or painting, they will become another object of academic study and "appreciation," and will soon be an object of excitement only to practitioners of the "art."
>
> **—PAULINE KAEL IN ATLANTIC MONTHLY (1964)[61]**

The response to American experimental film in the 1960s and early 1970s on the part of many film critics and audiences was incomprehension, frustration, boredom, or ridicule. No group was more dismissive of experimental film than mainstream film critics like Pauline Kael. Kael, in her famous

Atlantic tirade, rejected the pure aesthetic in experimental film that demanded high levels of cultural capital to be appreciated. Kael and other mainstream critics emphasized a populist critique of experimental film. Kael, however, along with Andrew Sarris, spearheaded a new film criticism that made New Hollywood and the independent film community a success. As Shyon Baumann argues, this new film criticism was essential in the success of New Hollywood as well as the rise of the American auteur director.[62] Scorsese also has specifically acknowledged Kael's criticism as essential to his early success.[63] So, the public storytellers that supported New Hollywood film mostly rejected avant-garde experimental film. By the end of the 1960s, in the public stories about film, the auteur-independent and the avant-garde-experimentalist were in conflict over what constituted serious, autonomous film in America.

Pauline Kael, in her *Atlantic Monthly* piece, celebrated the populist foundation of commercial feature films. "The movies are still where it happens, not for much longer perhaps, but the movies are still the art form that uses the material of our lives and the art form that we use. . . . People go to the movies for the various ways they express the experiences of our lives."[64] Kael promoted what Pierre Bourdieu calls a popular aesthetic—an aesthetic of the real that is affective and ordinary, emphasizing content and experience close to everyday life.[65] Popular criticism also emphasized simple judgment—good or bad—with little exposition on the aesthetics of an artwork. As film critic Judith Crist argued, "I consider myself a journalistic critic. In other words, I am not confusing myself with the critic who is writing for *Film Quarterly* or for the little magazine with an equally small circulation. I am a mass medium person. . . . I think that you must inform, basically, letting people know whether this is something they should or shouldn't see."[66] But, even more middlebrow critics like Sarris merely emphasized a specific movie's relation to film history and a director's overall work.[67] Critics like Sarris simply provided a bit more expertise to their reviews than more popular critics like Crist. The criticism of Sarris, Kael, Crist, and other supporters of New Hollywood film also was based on the classical tradition of Hollywood. The experimental film community in their public story clearly rejected this history and tradition.

Scorsese's public story resonates with the popular *aesthetic of the real* espoused by mainstream film critics who supported New Hollywood. His approach was committed to the narrative and representational functions of film commended by mainstream film critics like Kael. Such a commitment, however, did not prevent Scorsese from being viewed by himself and others as a maverick, independent, innovative, experimental, and personal filmmaker. In following the aesthetic of the real, Scorsese's films were portrayed in his public story as affective, anthropological, character and narrative driven, about-lived-experience, respectful-of-tradition, well-crafted, larger-than-life, commercial, realistic, and popular. Scorsese, as a Hollywood outsider-insider, was an auteur playing *off the grain* of the Hollywood aesthetic of the real.

Experimental filmmakers, as complete outsiders, played *against the grain* of the Hollywood aesthetic of the real. They were committed to abolishing the narrative and representational functions of film. Avant-garde filmmakers, like Scorsese, viewed themselves as maverick, independent, innovative, experimental, and personal artists. But their public story also revealed that their pure aesthetic led their films to be abstract, nonnarrative, intellectual, rejection-of-tradition, underground, nonprofessional, radical, esoteric, and a marginal film genre. Both public stories celebrated independence, autonomy, and outsider status. But these public stories promoted opposing distinctions between auteur independent and avant-garde experimental film. Independent filmmakers sought viable audiences in search of meaning in film. Experimental filmmakers, however, practiced what Bourdieu calls "reverse economics," where failure of financial, institutional, critical, and audience recognition acts as proof of the pure value of their autonomous vision, experimental sophistication, and radical ideas.[68]

Independent Film: From The New York School to Indiewood

> These artists have come to realize that to compromise an idea is to soften it, to make an excuse for it, to betray it . . . the artist is an irreplaceable figure in our society. . . . The answer cannot be left in the hands of the money men, for their desire to accumulate material success is probably the reason they entered into film-making in the first place. The answer must come from the artist himself.
> —JOHN CASSAVETES, FILM CULTURE (1959)[69]

For many, John Cassavetes was the father of contemporary independent feature film.[70] In his 1959 manifesto, Cassavetes articulated one of the founding tropes of this genre community: independent spirited directors who enter Hollywood, enter at their own risk. Cassavetes was part of the small group who formed the New American Cinema in New York City in 1961. He was associated with the New York School faction of this movement.[71] Unlike their pure cinema avant-garde fellow travelers in New American Cinema, the New York School directors were committed to a Direct Cinema, or cinema verité, in making independent fictional or documentary feature films. Direct Cinema was based on an aesthetics of the real whether in Bert Stern's documentary *Jazz on a Summer's Day* (1959), Lionel Rogosin's docufiction film *Come Back, Africa* (1959), or Shirley Clarke's fictional film *The Connection* (1961). Overall, the New York School in the early 1960s encapsulated the basic features of what would become contemporary American independent film. These basic features included a distance from the power of the Hollywood studios. The New York School and independent film also followed an aesthetics of image, form, and technique influenced by New Wave cinema of the 1950s and set against the conventions of Hollywood film. And finally, both film movements were positioned left of the mainstream social and cultural politics of Hollywood.[72] If the centripetal force for the experimental film genre community was an abstract, nonnarrative pure aesthetic, the centripetal force for the genre community of independent film was a representational, narrative aesthetic of the real. The other major difference between these two genre communities was independent film's relation to the commercial market of feature films and its always fraught relationship with Hollywood. Experimental film, as we have seen, abandoned any connection with the feature film market and Hollywood.

The film career of Cassavetes incorporated all these dimensions of contemporary independent film. His first feature film, *Shadows* (1961), was independently produced, had a Direct Cinema gritty realism, and its story centered on three African American siblings and interracial relations in contemporary New York City. The 1961 version of this film, however, was a remake of a less polished 1959 version. Cassavetes wanted a more viable film for the commercial market of feature films. And the second version received mostly positive reviews, although experimental film advocate Jonas Mekas in the *Village Voice* lambasted Cassavetes's capitulation to commercial pressures.[73] Like the celebrated credit-card-financed, low-budget indie films of the 1980s and 1990s, Cassavetes was even celebrated for his DIY independent spirit working with a shoestring budget of $40,000.[74] Cassavetes also flirted with Hollywood. While he stridently argued against working in Hollywood, he made the mistake after the success of *Shadows* to try it anyway. After making two films, *Too Late Blues* (1961) and *A Child Is Waiting* (1963), he left Hollywood in disgust, never to return. Instead, he embarked on a fully independent career as a gritty realist, critically acclaimed filmmaker from *Faces* in 1968 to his last independent film *Love Streams* in 1984. Cassavetes became the icon for the "true" independent filmmaker of independently financed, produced, and distributed films. He was particularly iconic because his films gained national and international recognition even though he refused to submit to the whims of Hollywood money men.

> In the wake of *Bonnie and Clyde*, there is an almost euphoric sense in Hollywood that more such movies can and will be made. The reason is that since mid-1966, the studios have opened doors and checkbooks to innovation-minded producers and directors with a largess unseen since Biograph moved from Manhattan to Los Angeles in 1910. . . . Still, occasionally, one victory can change the world—or at least the part of it that produces films. *Bonnie and Clyde* is a conspicuous victory. It has proved to the industry that the "new movie" and "popular success" are not antithetical terms. Hollywood has sometimes acted as if money and art were incompatible. At worst, they can come together in a marriage of convenience. At best, they may even get to like each other.
> —"HOLLYWOOD: THE SHOCK OF FREEDOM IN FILMS," TIME (1967)[75]

Cassavetes's independent spirit certainly infused many of the New Holly-wood directors who made a deal with the devil in the late 1960s and '70s. Hollywood faced such mounting problems in the late 1960s it took a chance to stop the hemorrhaging by looking at the niche market of mostly college-aged youth demanding more than just shallow entertainment in their films.[76] As *Time* magazine noted in 1967, this opening up of Hollywood to more independent-minded directors and their more artful films seemed to allow commerce and art to coexist in ways not seen since the prestudio era. New Hollywood directors inspired by French New Wave, Italian Neorealism, and the New American Cinema suddenly saw opportunities not afforded John Cassavetes or Shirley Clarke in the early 1960s. Scorsese's first feature film, *Who's That Knocking at My Door* (1969), was inspired by French, Italian, and New American Cinema filmmakers.[77] In fact, Cassavetes was a mentor to a young Scorsese. Scorsese credits Cassavetes with inspiring him to leave Hollywood in the early 1970s in order to follow his own muse and quit making other people's films—at the time Scorsese had just finished directing Roger Corman's exploitation film *Boxcar Bertha* (1972). Scorsese made *Mean Streets* in 1973, which he credits as the film that launched his long career as an independent filmmaker.[78]

"Alice" is a distinct disappointment. Following the example of many of his contemporaries, Scorsese has capitulated to Hollywood; this time he has revived all the conventions of pop romance that he seemed to have repudiated in "Mean Streets." . . . Scorsese has reached an important turning-point in his career. He has done one shattering, uncompromisingly personal film that lost money, and he has done an enjoyable but hokey Hollywood comedy that is a box office hit. Now he has to decide which kind of success he wants.

—STEPHEN FARBER, NEW YORK TIMES (1975)[79]

Like Cassavetes, Scorsese's first widely acclaimed film, *Mean Streets*, would lead him back to Hollywood to make *Alice Doesn't Live Here Anymore* (1974). While his next film was a commercial success and many mainstream film critics celebrated its supposed feminist take on female independence, others were not so happy with Scorsese's return to Hollywood.[80] Stephen Farber, echoing the earlier advice of Cassavetes, wondered in the pages of the *New York Times* if America had lost one of its most promising independent spirits. Scorsese heeded Farber's warning and briefly left Hollywood to make the independent film *Taxi Driver* (1976). But the purse of Hollywood was irresistible to a director with hopes of making high-production-value films similar to those made during the Golden Age of Hollywood. So, Scorsese returned to make to two big-budget films in Hollywood, *New York, New York* (1977) and *Raging Bull* (1980). But the trope of selling out to the commercial aesthetics of Hollywood continued to haunt Scorsese. Even the critically acclaimed *Raging Bull* did not protect Scorsese from this criticism. *Cineaste*'s Don Georgakas was convinced that the production value of technical wizardry found in Scorsese's brilliantly filmed movie was far more important to the director than any compelling story. "From start to finish, *Raging Bull* exhibits a dichotomy between technical sophistication and thematic poverty. . . . Ultimately, one becomes aware of viewing a film that is anxious to make the viewer aware that, while it is supposed to look like a film made in the late Forties or Fifties, it could only have been made decades later. This kind of conceit and the devices used to elaborate it will either annoy or engage viewers, depending on their esthetic inclinations. In either case, they have little to do with boxing, human psychology, or even a good story."[81]

Of course, when it came to commerce versus art not all film critics held the views expressed in alternative film magazines like *Cineaste* that the Hollywood commercial aesthetic was too powerful a force to allow truly independent and critically engaging films. In 1984, Vincent Canby, echoing the earlier defense of New Hollywood by Pauline Kael and Andrew Sarris, celebrated the New Hollywood directors as the geniuses of the system. "Our best filmmakers are those who make the necessary adjustments to the system. Like Steven Spielberg, Martin Scorsese, Francis Coppola, and Lawrence Kasdan, among others, they must always express their idiosyncratic talents within more or less conventional films designed to meet the demands of the great mass market."[82] Unfortunately, Canby's celebration was more a faint memory, as the New Hollywood auteur had been abandoned by Hollywood years earlier. As film critic Stephen Farber noted in 1985, "The experience of these maverick filmmakers reveals a good deal about how radical the industry has changed in less than 20 years. They entered a business that, if it did not exactly encourage innovation, allowed opportunities to sneak a few subversive, oddball movies through the cracks. Just ten years ago the industry seemed far less monolithic than it does today. . . . In the days before *Jaws* and *Star Wars*, studio executives were only beginning to dream about the $100 million blockbuster at the end of the rainbow."[83] By the time Scorsese's film *Raging Bull* (1980) was released, the New Hollywood era was over. The question of independent directors like Scorsese balancing art and commerce in Hollywood seemed no longer a question worth asking, since the answer seemed to be a resounding NO. Scorsese, however, remained somewhat hopeful, as he told Farber that he hoped "to alternate low-budget independent efforts with more expensive studio films."[84] Of course, Scorsese did eventually follow this strategy, setting up an alternative model to the Cassavetes's strategy of no compromise. But as New Hollywood directors like Scorsese opted to continue to play with the money men of Hollywood, even if for a short while, other independent filmmakers held to the Cassavetes model of pure independence outside the Hollywood commercial juggernaut.

> Over the last 15 years radical Third World filmmakers, the women's movement, gays and lesbians, and the independent left in North America have produced four strong alternatives to the mainstream cinema. In fact, these four movements of film activity stand for more than an alternative. Because all four embody political movements that challenge the dominant society, and because many of the key films consciously challenge conventions of style and approach in dominant cinema, they are often referred to as counter-cinema.
>
> —PETER STEVEN, JUMP CUT (1985)[85]

While New Hollywood siphoned off some of the more creative young talent in independent feature film, another path of independent film was forged out of the New American Cinema movement. *Jump Cut* magazine in 1974 joined the older magazine *Cineaste* to become major publications for a genre film community dedicated to what *Jump Cut* called "counter-cinema," a political cinema influenced by various strands in leftist politics: new left, feminist, black power, and third world liberation. Or as *Cineaste* exclaimed in 1969, it had "become a magazine of cinema engage—a cinema engaged in the movement for social change."[86] This new genre community was dedicated to an aesthetics of the real that was informed by the Direct Cinema of New American Cinema. It also was influenced by New American Cinema avant-garde film, but rejected what it viewed as this genre community's abstract formalism and eventual distancing from the movement for social change.[87] As Peter Steven argued, in "the mid-1970s it has been possible to talk of a left counter-cinema: a cinema practice that looks to and identifies with political movements in society."[88] While countercinema had some popular successes in the 1970s, like Barbara Kopple's Academy Award–winning documentary *Harlan County U.S.A.* (1976), distribution and exhibition remained a constant problem for this genre community.

When Hollywood abandoned New Hollywood and independent films outside its commercial aesthetic in the late 1970s, independent feature film actually entered a period of growth. New Hollywood relied on what Susan Sontag called a new cinephile community of filmmakers, producers, and audiences whose demand for auteur films fell outside the narrow parameters of the Hollywood commercial aesthetic.[89] And truly independent film, completely outside Hollywood, was rising along with New Hollywood with films like Joan Micklin Silver's *Hester Street* (1975), Charles Burnett's *Killer of Sheep* (1977), and Rob Nilsson and John Hanson's *Northern Lights* (1979). As Karen Cooper, director of the major venue for independent film in New York City, the Film Forum, told the *New York Times* in 1982, the late 1970s witnessed the rise of independent films that distinguished themselves with "oblique narrative, something that has become stronger in the past seven years—a film that tells a story and in that sense, is traditional filmmaking but diverges from the commercial story films, usually in terms of editing or casting or any number or combination of production details which are altered or reshuffled to try to give a new angle to how we understand a chronological sequence of events."[90] Or as Geoff King, in his overview of American independent film, argued, beginning in the 1970s you had various strands of *playing off the grain* of traditional Hollywood film in terms of narrative, form, and genre.[91]

The institutionalization of independent film was consolidated in the early 1980s in a network of independent distributors, art houses, festivals, and nonprofit organizations all focused on supporting a film genre community committed to making independent film in the directions coming out of 1960s New American Cinema.[92] The Sundance Institute (1981) along with other nonprofits like the Independent Feature Project (1979) provided funding, workshops, and conferences to help independent filmmakers network, learn, and produce independent films. The 1980s also saw a large number of new distributors like Cinecom (1982) and Vestron (1981), who were joining older independent distributors like New Line Cinema (1967) in financing films and distributing them to art houses and even mainstream theaters. The most successful independent distributor, Miramax, was formed in 1979. The festivals that became the foundation of American independent film in the 1980s were Los Angeles Filmex (1971), Telluride (1973), Toronto (1975), Seattle (1975), Montreal (1977), and the US Film Festival (1978), which became the Sundance Film Festival in 1991.[93] Other factors also sparked the boom in truly independent film in the 1980s. Part of the boom was a new videocassette market demanding more content than Hollywood could supply.[94] Vestron was one of several home video companies that invested directly in independent film. And in the late 1970s, the Public Broadcasting System (PBS) and the National Endowment for the Humanities (NEH) also began providing grants for independent film production.

> The day of the American independent movie is at hand . . . of more than 500 films produced in Hollywood last year, some 300 were produced by the so-called independents. . . . From Cinecom in New York and Vestron in Connecticut to Island and Skouras in Los Angeles and FilmDallas in Texas, maverick distribution companies are popping up to handle the new flood of independent productions, often producing the films themselves. In the Utah mountains, Robert Redford's Sundance serves as a creative cocoon—and economic angel—to get alternative visions onto the screen. . . . The moment is at hand for the indies. . . . The American cinema hasn't had its batteries seriously recharged since the explosion of talent in the early '70s. The resources are there as never before. The new companies are in place, the support groups aiding and abetting, the audience waiting. Lights, camera, action.
>
> —"HOLLYWOOD GOES INDEPENDENT," NEWSWEEK (1987)[95]

The 1980s and early 1990s certainly seemed to point to an era of true independent cinema incorporating a wide breadth of critical and commercially successful films.[96] *Newsweek* in 1987 already noticed the impact of the institutionalization of film production, distribution, and exhibition outside the control of big Hollywood studios. It noted the stars of new independent film, including Spike Lee, Oliver Stone, Joel and Ethan Coen, Lizzie Borden, John Sayles, Robert Townsend, and Jonathan Demme. Not surprisingly, *Newsweek* compared the rise of independent film in the mid-1980s as a moment as important as the rise of New Hollywood in the early 1970s. And in 1992, *New York Times* film critic Janet Maslin noted that the next new wave of independent films were "made uncompromisingly, and on a shoestring, they were as well acted and entertaining as anything the studios had to offer.... The change of direction appears to be part of a broader shift.... Whatever else these new film makers will accomplish, they are helping to forge a path others can follow."[97] Her list of new directors included Carl Franklin, Julie Dash, Quentin Tarantino, Allison Anders, Nick Gomez, and Gregg Araki.[98] The impact of a decade of institutional support for independent film showed not only a remarkable commercial boom but also a striking diversity of directors and films. The independent film magazine *Cineaste* certainly saw a new era in independent film. "The turn of the decade has brought with it the reemergence of a normally marginalized force in American cinema: the independent filmmaker. Dubbed the "Rise of the Indies" by film festivals across the country, this new wave of auteurs has ushered in a rejuvenated spirit of hope."[99]

> As the century comes to a close, Hollywood has finally caught up with the explosion of creative energy that had been operating outside the studio mainstream. Faced with a fast-emerging demographic wave of restless young moviegoers, the major studios have wooed, embraced and perhaps co-opted a fresh generation of film talent.... As a group, the New New Wave directors are cocky and assertive, but without the hubris, pretense and drug-fueled mania of the '70s-era directors.... They're also pragmatic—they don't have the instinctive hostility toward studio "suits" that marked much of the indie film movement of the early 1990s.
> —PATRICK GOLDSTEIN, LOS ANGELES TIMES (1999)[100]

The commercial instincts of Hollywood in the early 1990s began to sense something profitable was ripe for incorporation. And major players in the field of independent film, especially Miramax and Sundance, saw an opportunity to transform the commercial feature film market dominated by Hollywood fare since the rise of the blockbuster era in the late 1970s. For many, Quentin Tarantino's *Pulp Fiction* (1994) was the trigger that set in motion the full integration of independent filmmakers into Hollywood, with Miramax leading the way.[101] The film already had a hefty budget of $8 million and had star power with Bruce Willis, John Travolta, and Uma Thurman. Miramax decided to follow the saturation booking strategy used by Hollywood for blockbuster films. The wide release of *Pulp Fiction* brought a first weekend gross of $9 million and brought in over $100 million in domestic box office. Suddenly, independent films from quirky and visionary independent directors were viewed as potentially profitable as blockbusters. Once again, the question of balancing commerce and art, and negotiating with the money men of Hollywood, returned to independent film. By the end of the decade, as Patrick Goldstein of the *Los Angeles Times* suggests, there were hints that a new generation of independent filmmakers, less embedded in the independent film community of the last two decades, was entering Hollywood. Hollywood also began to incorporate the "independent spirit" into its blockbuster machine, hoping to bring some quality and substance to its commercial aesthetic. Bryan Singer gained acclaim with his independent films *Public Access* (1993) and *Usual Suspects* (1995). By the end of the decade, Singer went blockbuster with the seventy-five-million-dollar *X-Men* (2000). Another acclaimed independent filmmaker Christopher Nolan, after making *Memento* in 2000, went Hollywood with the $45 million *Insomnia* (2002) and then the $150 million *Batman Begins* (2005). Maybe Cassavetes was right. Commerce always wins over art with the money men of Hollywood.

> Studio involvement meant small budgets were boosted; more marketing was required to recoup; stars were required to guarantee box office. "Indiewood" was born. . . . It's a story in which the only moral seems to be that more always means less. There is no end to it. Like a dinosaur, Miramax lumbers on while, down in the basement, indie films are still being made by the visionary, warped minds. . . . For my part, I can never get over why you need $100 million to tell a half-baked story. What's wrong with a pencil?
>
> **—WILL COHU, THE TELEGRAPH (2004)**[102]

I don't think they've been totally mainstreamed. One of the legacies of [the '90s] is these films that have been dubbed "Indiewood" films that exist in this middle ground between the big Hollywood movies and the traditional independent film. One hates to be forced back to a sort of vague fuzzy concept like "independent spirit," but they are movies that are suffused with a kind of independent aesthetic. And I think these movies are, for the most part, quite good.

—PETER BISKIND WITH TIM ROBEY, THE TELEGRAPH (2004)[103]

Will Cohu and Tim Robey of the London *Telegraph* were covering the 2004 release of Peter Biskind's bestseller *Down and Dirty Pictures: Miramax, Sundance, and the Rise of Independent Film.* The book lambasted the once-independent film studio Miramax and the supposedly independent film festival Sundance for aiding and abetting Hollywood's integration of independent film into its industrial system of filmmaking in the 1990s. In other words, Biskind's book lamented how Miramax and Sundance killed the independence of independent film. For Cohu, like many filmmakers and critics, the return of independent film as a commercially attractive property for Hollywood was the death knell for independent film. But Biskind seemed to suggest to Robey that the question of whether Indiewood killed the "spirit" of independent film was not a simple question to answer. As if defining independent film, let alone its spirit, was ever easy. But in some ways "Indiewood" was the perfect term for the inescapable contradiction in commercial feature film in America. On the one hand, independent film had been defined since the days of the Hollywood studio system by its distance from the Hollywood studios. On the other hand, most independent film that had reached a mass audience had some relationship to the Hollywood studios. Hollywood studios also had the power of the purse for those independent filmmakers who, against Cohu's better judgment, wanted to make one-hundred-million-dollar films. And Martin Scorsese was such a director who was happy to spend that amount on his films. He returned to Hollywood with the critically acclaimed *Goodfellas* in 1990, which was released in 1,070 theaters and reached number one in weekend box office.[104] And his star-studded epic film *Gangs of New York*, released by Disney-Miramax in 2002, cost just over $100 million. I have a suspicion that Cohu had this film in mind when he derided Miramax as a lumbering giant and ridiculed big-budget "independent" film.

As much as Biskind's book was received as an indictment of the incorporation of independent film back into the Hollywood logic of pure commerce, it was far more the ruminations of a cinephile over the complicated relation between the outsider-insider auteur filmmaker and the pressures of the commercial aesthetic of Hollywood. The old question of the balance between art and commerce refused to go away. Earlier in 2000, Biskind did an extensive interview with five of the "new new wave" generation of directors for *The Nation*. He interviewed successful Indiewood directors Allison Anders (*Sugar Town*, 1999), Alexander Payne (*Election*, 1999), Kimberly Peirce (*Boys Don't Cry*, 1999), David O. Russell (*Three Kings*, 1999), and Kevin Smith (*Dogma*, 1999). The discussion reveals the practical approach of this generation of independent filmmakers. While maybe not as full of hubris as the first New Hollywood auteurs, they demonstrated the same willingness to work within the system, but aware of the pitfalls and limitations of balancing commerce and art in Hollywood. Both Kevin Smith and David O. Russell argued that Miramax and Sundance actually transformed Hollywood and popular audiences rather than the other way around. Indiewood did not prevent low-budget independent films from being made and distributed, but it did get Hollywood to support higher quality, challenging, director-driven commercial feature films. And it made audiences more sophisticated in their tastes and expectations. And to bring the whole story of auteur independent film full circle, Alexander Payne noted that "Scorsese talks correctly about the film director as smuggler."[105]

Maybe Janet Maslin was correct. Independent film goes in cycles, and "the studios have a lot to do with setting the conditions in which those cycles can occur. A corporate penchant for risk taking, in the years after the unexpected box-office success of 'Easy Rider' in 1969, helped bring forth or encourage an astonishing array of new names. Martin Scorsese, Robert Altman, Woody Allen, Francis Ford Coppola, Paul Mazursky, Steven Spielberg, and George Lucas all established their reputations in the late 60s and early 70s, when marginal-seeming young film makers captured and revitalized Hollywood's mainstream."[106] And twenty years later, another generation of Indiewood directors captured and revitalized Hollywood's mainstream, even as blockbusters filled the multiplexes across the country and Hollywood studios followed their global strategy of synergy and franchise building. Even Biskind in 2004 noted that regardless of independent film losing the type of clout among the money men of Hollywood it held in the late 1990s, it had established its own independent field of film that would keep this genre community healthy regardless of the cycles of boom and bust of independent filmmaking in Hollywood.[107] Which was a wonderful insight given that the Great Recession of 2008 actually initiated the decline of Indiewood and a bust for independent film in Hollywood. As Michael Cieply noted in the *New York Times* in 2009, "The glory days of independent film, when hot young directors like Steven Soderbergh and Mr. Tarantino had studio executives tangled in fierce bidding wars at Sundance and other celebrity-studded festivals, are now barely a speck in the rearview mirror."[108]

Martin Scorsese: A Reconsideration of the Iconic Auteur

Silence is the cheapest film (from a budget stand point) that Martin Scorsese has made since *Kundun* back in 1997, which cost him $28 million. The likes of *Gangs of New York*, *The Aviator*, *The Departed*, *Shutter Island*, *Hugo*, and *The Wolf of Wall Street* all cost between $80 million—$150 million to make, while *Silence*'s budget was, at most, $50 million—and maybe even as low as $40 million, depending on reports.
—"THE MAJOR SACRIFICES MARTIN SCORSESE HAD TO MAKE
   TO COMPLETE SILENCE," CINEMABLEND (2017)

Scorsese's return to the gangster genre after two decades is one of the most highly anticipated films currently under development. . . . *Silence* may have been his 28-year-old passion project, but it was mostly ignored by audiences, grossing only $7 million in the U.S. opposite a $40 million budget. Something tells us the same fate won't meet the director's next project, which carries an even bigger budget and bigger stars.
—"9 THINGS YOU MUST KNOW ABOUT MARTIN SCORSESE'S
   $100 MILLION 'GOODFELLAS' REUNION," INDIEWIRE (2017)

Given the struggles of independent film, and its boom and bust relationship with Hollywood, we return to assess how truly "independent" Scorsese has been as the consummate outsider-insider and whether his strategy of film-making has provided a viable model for independent film. Since Scorsese told Steve Farber in 1985 of his trade-off strategy of one big-budget film for Hollywood, one low-budget personal film for him, this trope has remained a part of Scorsese's public story. Just as in 2017 Scorsese's personal-passion film *Kundun* (1997) is mentioned in relation to an equally personal film *Silence* (2017), so *Last Temptation of Christ* (1988) we are told in his public story was a personal-passion film before *Kundun*.[109] As Scorsese told Gavin Smith of *Film Comment* in 1998, "usually I have my own projects lined up. I like to do film I want to do, but then again, the way this business has been going, I have to slip in a *Cape Fear* or even a *Casino* to a certain extent—because that wasn't on my agenda, it was on Hollywood's agenda for me."[110]

But what does it mean when a personal-passion film costs $28 million or $40 million? What does it mean if *Gangs of New York* (2002), which in Scorsese's public story was a passion for nearly thirty years, cost $100 million or his personal homage to early film, *Hugo* (2011), cost $150 million.

What does it mean when *Cinemablend* claims a forty-million-dollar-budget film involves major "sacrifices" on the part of Scorsese? What does it mean when virtually every headline announcing Scorsese's next film, *The Irishman*, includes its $100 million price tag? If indie producer John Pierson told Peter Biskind in 2000 that "I think that you can still use budget levels as a fair criterion. Anybody who is making a film for less than $100,000 is an independent filmmaker . . . by the time you get to *Good Will Hunting*, it's just not worth the breath. It's like, Oh, come on now. It's the oh-come-on-now factor."[111] Then what does *Good Will Hunting* (1997) costing $10 million say about Martin Scorsese as an "independent" filmmaker? What does it mean when comic book blockbusters like *Captain America: The First Avenger* (2011) and *Thor* (2011) cost the same as Scorsese's personal-passion film *Hugo* (2011)? Scorsese's answer to these questions was presented to the world of independent film in his keynote address for the 1990 Independent Spirit Awards, the top award ceremony for independent film. He said, "being independent doesn't mean making low-budget films without studio backing . . . it is a way for being innovative out of inspiration as well as necessity."[112]

Certainly, anyone who has seen Scorsese's *Silence* will agree it is not a Hollywood film. And anyone familiar with Scorsese's public story and oeuvre of religious-themed films knows that the testing of faith, the main theme in *Silence*, has always been a personal obsession with a director who when only an adolescent contemplated the priesthood. And even a film on Hollywood's agenda for Scorsese, *The Wolf of Wall Street* (2013), which cost $100 million and earned $392 million, was a uniquely Scorsese film. As indie director Alexander Payne argued, Scorsese takes his "smuggling" seriously as the premier auteur of Hollywood. And maybe that's the crux of the matter. If the original meaning of "auteur" was a director who could pursue his personal vision *within* the studio system, Scorsese is the premier auteur of contemporary Hollywood. No other director can command such a high price for their personal-passion films, nor place their imprint so deftly in their supposedly Hollywood films. But to claim oneself as an outsider-insider is a bit of a far stretch. In certain ways, this returns us to the original query Steven Farber made in 1975 about a young promising New Hollywood director. "At his best he is an intransigent artist committed to unvarnished truth on the screen . . . he is also a film buff with a taste for Hollywood showmanship and an abiding affection for kitsch. Scorsese is going to have to come to terms with those conflicting impulses before he makes too many more movies."[113] Forty years later, Scorsese has certainly come to terms with his two conflicting impulses: his passion for the Hollywood tradition of filmmaking and his passion for playing off the grain of this tradition and imprinting a personal vision in all his films.

What personal-passionate films like *Kundun, Gangs of New York, Hugo,* and *Silence* tell us about Scorsese's commitment to an aesthetics of the real is that his artistic vision has become firmly wedded to the commercial aesthetic of Hollywood film. Scorsese's anchor in the commercial aesthetic of Hollywood is in his addiction to the production value that has always permeated Hollywood film. As Maltby argues, Hollywood film is as much about the *feel* and *emotion* of a film as about its form or content.[114] Often production value in Hollywood film, however, resolves down to examples of spectacular effects whether the burning of Atlanta in *Gone with the Wind* (1939), Munchkinland in *Wizard of Oz* (1939), the kaleidoscopic transformations of buildings and landscapes in *Inception* (2010), or the 3-D wizardry of Scorsese's *Hugo* (2011). But production value is far more than spectacular effects. Production value permeates every aspect of a Hollywood film from star power, costume, makeup, staging, filming, sound, to final editing. Production value works at both obvious and more subtle levels. What one imagines as the gorgeously meditative images in *Kundun* or *Silence* are as much a reflection of high-production value as the elaborate staging and computer manipulation of 1860s Five Point Ghetto in New York City in *Gangs of New York.* When Scorsese celebrates "the pioneers who created the grammar of film language. What we do now, they did before," he speaks of a grammar built on the production values of the "golden age of the studio system."[115] And part of the mass appeal of Hollywood film is this subtle and not so subtle production value found in a film like Clint Eastwood's thirty-million-dollar-budget *Million Dollar Baby* (2004) to Christopher Nolan's one-hundred-million-dollar-budget *Dunkirk* (2017). It's also what leads to *Million Dollar Baby*'s $217 million box office and *Dunkirk*'s $525 million box office. It's what led to Scorsese's one-hundred-million-dollar-budget *The Wolf of Wall Street*'s $392 million box office. And it's this box-office power of Scorsese that has allowed him to be the "outsider-insider" of Hollywood.

But the production value of the commercial aesthetic of Hollywood film was what the pioneers of New American Cinema rebelled against. It was the distance from this production value in Scorsese's earlier films *Who's That Knocking at My Door* (1967), *Mean Streets* (1973), and *Taxi Driver* (1976) that Steven Farber in 1975 saw in conflict with the commercial aesthetic of Hollywood. So, John Cassavetes would not be wrong to point to the artistic "sacrifices" Scorsese made in the compromises involved in his success as an "outsider-insider": how these compromises affected his personal-passionate films or how they prevented Scorsese from always following his personal muse. This tension, of course, has defined contemporary independent film since the rise of New Hollywood and has persisted in the rise of Indiewood. And it is a compromise Scorsese has consistently pointed to in his public story on working within the Hollywood studio system. He would argue, and he would be correct, that he only was able to make *Silence* because of the $392 million box office of *The Wolf of Wall Street* and the anticipated box office of the 125- to 150-million-dollar budgeted *The Irishman*.[116] But the question remains whether we can take as a veritable truth that as Scorsese said, "I am the movies I make. And I know they're not to everyone's taste. My old parish priest once told me that my work has too much Good Friday and not enough Easter Sunday."[117] One could easily argue that Scorsese's films also have too much Hollywood magic-glitter as well. Nor is his model seen as particularly viable or attractive to younger independent filmmakers. Even successful big-budget independent filmmakers like Quentin Tarantino, with his forty-four-million-dollar-budget *Hateful Eight* (2015), and Paul Thomas Anderson, with his thirty-two-million-dollar-budget *The Master* (2012), have remained outside the Hollywood studio system to make their films.

Conclusion

Cinema is a specificity of vision, it's an approach in which everything matters. It's the polar opposite of generic or arbitrary and the result is as unique as a signature or a fingerprint. It isn't made by a committee, and it isn't made by a company, and it isn't made by the audience. . . . But the problem is that cinema as I define it, and as something that inspired me, is under assault by the studios and, from what I can tell, with the full support of the audience . . . when you add an ample amount of fear and a lack of vision, and a lack of leadership, you've got a trajectory that I think is pretty difficult to reverse. . . . There are fewer and fewer executives who are in the business because they love movies. . . . You've got people who don't know movies, don't watch movies for pleasure, deciding what movie you're going to be allowed to make. That's one reason studio movies aren't better than they are, and that's one reason that cinema, as I'm defining it, is shrinking.

—STEVEN SODERBERGH, SAN FRANCISCO INTERNATIONAL
FILM FESTIVAL (2013)[118]

In 2013, Indiewood wunderkind Steven Soderbergh let the world know he was not happy with the state of Indiewood and the general crass-cluelessness of Hollywood suits. Before his keynote address at the San Francisco International Film Festival, he had announced his retirement from commercial feature films. His keynote was partially his public explanation of why he was retiring from Indiewood. Of course, like Scorsese's brief sabbatical from Hollywood in the 1980s, Soderbergh returned in 2017 with his feature film *Lucky Logan*. And while it had a hefty $29 million budget, it was independently produced and distributed outside the Hollywood juggernaut. It certainly seemed that Hollywood remained the center of gravity in commercial feature film where the state of independent film shifted with the currents of change in Hollywood. On the other hand, Soderbergh's ability to make a truly independent film for $29 million shows that independent film has established a subfield of filmmaking able to support such high-budget gems like *Lucky Logan* outside Hollywood. Of course, the question remains of what future awaits both independent film and Hollywood as the Digital Age marches on with streaming video being the next new threat to theatrical release feature films and the power of Hollywood studios. Scorsese's new film, *The Irishman*, is being financed by the digital streaming service Netflix![119]

Soderbergh in 2013 was haunted by the same questions of autonomy, art, and commerce that defined the New American Cinema in the late 1950s and 1960s and the world of independent film from the 1970s to the present. They are also the same questions that Martin Scorsese and others have asked in his public story as an icon of New Hollywood and independent film. The point of this chapter, however, is not whether the public stories of New American Cinema, New Hollywood, Martin Scorsese, experimental film, independent film, and Indiewood have been true accounts of autonomy, art, and commerce in American film. They represent different strands of storytelling in American film about autonomy or independence that have been honestly felt by artists, critics, producers, and audiences. They are strands of storytelling that provide the contours of many of the contradictions and conundrums faced in creating cinema or movies—movies are what Hollywood committees make—when faced with unavoidable questions of long-term support for those who make them as well as reaching and affecting large audiences. These public stories also have articulated general distinctions between a pure aesthetic, an aesthetic of the real, and a Hollywood commercial aesthetic in film in America over the last half of the twentieth century and into this century. A repertoire of terms emerged that distinguish the autonomous and nonautonomous, art and commerce, actualized and alienated, unique and industrial, pulp and substance in the ongoing public stories told about

American film. Yet the repertoire of distinctions active in American film involved not only shared terms but also very contentious oppositional terms of distinction between competing film communities and Hollywood.

This chapter shows how the distinctions that informed American film were revealed in the public stories that have been told about it. These distinctions informed the tropes of collective storytelling, which in turn, shaped how individuals—artists, critics, producers, exhibitors, curators, audiences, and so forth—approached film. In other words, public stories in the field of film represented what sociologist Ron Eyerman argues are collective structured meanings that inform, in part, the actions, interpretations, appreciations, and emotions of those active in an art field.[120] Furthermore, the storytellers in the public stories of American film were embedded in a cultural politics that no single actor had control over. A filmmaker's words and art influence their public story, but they do not control other storytellers in this tale, whether critics, artists, curators, journalists, or others. A public story tells us something about particular artists like Martin Scorsese, but also something about how individuals collectively understand an art field, such as American film, at a particular historical moment. So, "indie," "amateur," "experimental," "mainstream," "blockbuster," "suits," "Indiewood," and many other terms commonly used in the public stories of postwar American film were the building blocks in which storytellers contributed to this public story, artists made films, critics reviewed films, and audiences appreciated films.

This chapter also is not about whether Martin Scorsese remained true to the auteur ideals of his first years as a filmmaker or whether the commercial aesthetic of Hollywood has affected his filmmaking in too negative a way. It is unquestionable, however, that Scorsese has been a major artistic vision and public intellectual in American film since he began his career. And it seems equally clear how his public story and art speak directly to the persistent questions posed in American film since the fall of the Hollywood studio system and the early revolt of New American Cinema. This chapter highlighted how such a seminal figure negotiated his personal visions and practical concerns through the competing forces and interests in American film. And the career of Martin Scorsese, and his public story, is also truly remarkable in its consistency and resilience. As *The Wolf of Wall Street* (2013) and *Silence* (2013) show, Scorsese has kept to his promise to satisfy Hollywood's agenda for Marty in order to fulfill Marty's own agenda in filmmaking. And we'll see how well his 125- to 150-million-dollar budgeted Hollywood reunion of *Goodfellas* does in the box office and what auteur delights Martin Scorsese might have smuggled into the package to boot.

PART II

The Biographical Legends of Rebels

Interlude

"The Biographical Legends of Rebels" is concerned with the intersection of biography, social identity, and selfhood in the public stories of Miles Davis and Martin Scorsese. While the term *biographical legend* originally referred to how personal biography shaped the reputation and reception of an artist,[1] my work expands on the scope and power of biographical legends. Such legends in the public stories of Davis and Scorsese spoke not only to their art but also to the American experience writ large. Race, ethnicity, and gender would significantly shape these two public stories. Both artists embraced their roles as active voices for their respective communities. Both artists openly connected their artistic visions with their racial and ethnic identity. And both artists expressed deeply troubling interconnections between their gender identities and their racial and ethnic identities. But crucial to understanding the power of biographical legends is to recognize how they are products of a collective telling of these biographies and their significance. Not only artists, but also critics, journalists, and others construct public stories. So, to understand the biographical legends of Davis and Scorsese, we must understand how the collective nature of the storytelling made their public stories special expressive spaces for transcoding the broader ideological conversations and imaginative interpretations that have defined the racial and gender formations in the United States from the 1950s to the present. As I mentioned in the introduction, the Heroic Age of American Art opened up an invitation for a robust new cultural politics. Public stories about American art became collective cultural politics on a large scale.

Miles Davis would become an iconic African American musician challenging the jazz art world and the broader racial formations of Jim Crow and

New Jim Crow America. Martin Scorsese would become an iconic Italian American filmmaker and chronicler of the American experience. But how their respective embracing of racial and ethnic identity played out in their public stories and careers was starkly different. The unbridgeable racial divide in the American racial formation would shape far different forms of rebellion and far different responses to these art rebels. Two starkly different biographical legends emerged: one of an "unreconstructed" black man who lambasted the relentless and indestructible power of Jim Crow America, and another, of an "unmeltable" Italian American who became, over time, a quintessential white ethnic American. As Scorsese came to celebrate how white ethnic Americans were the foundation of the modern American experience, and how the American Dream eventually opens to all immigrants and social groups, Davis remained focused on how this dream was continually deferred and denied for African Americans. In other words, Davis and Scorsese gave witness in their public stories to two very distinct, if not diametrically opposed, encounters with the American experience.

The social distance and micropolitics of race relations also informed the telling and interpretation of Miles Davis's and Martin Scorsese's public stories. The modern jazz art world was fundamentally shaped by the social distance between white and black musicians, critics, entrepreneurs, and fans. Such a social distance existed from the microlevel of everyday interaction, to the practice of music making, to the telling of public stories. Unlike Scorsese, Davis confronted a very contentious collective telling of his public story that reflected not only his challenging of the race relations of the jazz art world and Jim Crow America but also the multimirrored interpretations of his actions, demeanors, and words. Being an "unreconstructed" black man in America was a far more perilous, and far more often misinterpreted, role than being an "unmeltable" Italian American. The public story of Miles Davis reveals the racial minefield that all African American artists navigated in a world dominated by a white racial imagination. Scorsese's biographical legend meshed easily with the dominant narratives and self-serving delusions of post–civil rights America, while Davis's biographical legend rubbed against such narratives and delusions. As we will see, it was the contrasting receptions of these two artists' public stories, generated by the racial divide in America, that led to the so-called enigma of Miles Davis as the "evil genius" of jazz.

The public stories of Davis and Scorsese also showed how their gender identities were inseparable from their racial and ethnic identities. The intersectionality of race, ethnicity, and gender expressed itself powerfully in both these public stories. An intersectional feminist perspective highlights two distinct expressions of gender identity in these public stories.[2] First, black and white masculinity in the racial imagination negotiated distinct contours of rebellion and masculinity. So black and white hypermasculinity would be experienced and interpreted differently, even while simultaneously reaffirming hegemonic masculinity and the gender formation in America. Second, the normative power of hegemonic masculinity also seemed to resolve both black and white hypermasculinity within a male gendered imagination, so that such expressions, except for a few rare moments, were rendered as taken-for-granted in music and film.

The following two chapters will show how the racial, ethnic, and gendered tropes of these iconic artists' biographical legends speak volumes to the continuing power of the racial and gender formations in the United States during the Heroic Age of American Art. Such tropes speak not only to how such social identities shaped the actual art and lives of Davis and Scorsese but also to how these social identities acted as ciphers for interpreting these artists' art, actions, demeanors, words, biographies, and even selfhoods. The public stories of Miles Davis and Martin Scorsese show in surprisingly, and often disturbing, ways how the racial and gender imaginations work in tandem in the collective storytelling of American art, the American experience, and the personal biographies of our most iconic artists. And as we will see, these imaginations often act to make invisible the true nature of race and gender relations as such truths are *lost in translation* through the power of the white and male imaginations in America.

Miles Davis

THE UNRECONSTRUCTED BLACK MAN IN MODERN JAZZ

> That fear—the knowledge that a single false step while wandering inside the maze of the white man's reality could blast you back home with the speed of a circus artist being shot out of a cannon—is the kryptonite that has lain under the bed of every great black artist from 1920s radio star Bert Williams to Miles Davis to Jay Z.
> —JAMES MCBRIDE, KILL 'EM AND LEAVE (2016)[1]

> Certain African-American cultural figures—in music, in movies, in sports—rose above what was manifestly a divided, unjust society and in the process managed to seem singularly unruffled. They kept themselves together by holding themselves slightly apart, maintaining an air of inscrutability, of not quite being known. They were cool.
>   Who did this idea adhere to? People are welcome to make lists of their own, but there are some examples that we can all agree upon. Miles Davis was cool.
> —QUESTLOVE, NEW YORK MAGAZINE (2014)[2]

A fine line has always existed for African Americans between being cool and being unruly. And African Americans have always faced the fear of violating the "racial etiquette" that defines everyday life in America and the dangers such disruption poses. This existential state of being black in America, what James McBride calls racial kryptonite, was the case for cool, zoot-suited African Americans—along with their cool, zoot-suited Mexican American brethren—who were beaten and stripped of their clothing in the streets of wartime Los Angeles during the Zoot Suit Riots of 1943. It was the case for a young African American named Trayvon Martin shot for wearing a hip-hop-identified hoodie on the way back from a convenience store in Sanford, Florida, in 2012. And it was the case for Miles Davis one night in August 1959 at the age of thirty-three. While taking a break from a gig outside a New York City jazz club, dressed in one of his famous tailor-made suits, he received a life-threatening clubbing by an undercover policeman for standing his ground against an unreasonable order to move down the street. Miles survived, but never forgot.[3]

As Questlove suggests, Miles Davis would top the list of anyone's coolest American icons of the twentieth century. Davis is so emblematic of American cool that Joel Dinerstein begins his 2017 book on the origins of post–World War II cool with a prelude on Davis.[4] And on that night in August 1959, Davis was already recognized as an icon of cool by such publications as *Time* and *Esquire*.[5] But being an icon of cool, and one of the most acclaimed jazz musicians at the time, had no purchase that night in New York City. But this undercover cop was not the only person who found Davis unruly. In fact, what strikes me in the public story of Davis up until his death in September 1991 was how critics, journalists, and others would just as likely refer to him as ill-tempered, angry, arrogant, or even racist than as cool or a genius. While Davis would be recognized as the most creative artist in modern jazz and an iconic symbol of coolness in America, he was also, readers were constantly reminded, an enfant terrible of American art. Even in his death, obituaries continued on the theme of Davis as the "evil genius" of modern jazz.

Questlove argues that coolness is a form of negotiation and resistance in a white dominated world. Coolness for others is viewed more as a survival strategy.[6] It has been for African American men a form of negotiation or resistance or survival in what Michael Omi and Howard Winant call the racial etiquette of the United States.[7] Coolness was both a resistance to and a defense against the constraints of deference, subordination, and discrimination imposed on African Americans. It was a dance around the kryptonite of race relations in America. It seemed obvious to me that what made Miles Davis problematic in the eyes of so many telling his public story was more than simply a reflection of contradictions in his behavior, demeanor, and opinions—such contradictions existed and were often acknowledged by those who knew him best—but also reflected a response to his dance of *resistance* and *refusal* to defer to the racial etiquette of the white world around him. He was, as the black writer Quincy Troupe, who cowrote Davis's autobiography, once called him, an "unreconstructed Black man."[8] This dance of resistance points to how his artistic rebellion was intimately linked to his struggle as an African American male in both a Jim Crow and New Jim Crow America. This dance was also linked to a jazz art world that regardless of its liberal color-blind ideology continued to perpetuate the subordination of black musicians in some fashion for most of Davis's career.

This chapter is about how Miles Davis articulated in actions, demeanors, and words his racial identity and rebellious politics as an African American male artist. But for black jazz musicians, coolness, rebellion, and blackness were complex dynamics of selfhood, self-presentation, and reception. The social distance between blacks and whites, for example, overdetermined a multitude of reinterpretations of black musicians' coolness, blackness, and rebelliousness. So, what came to be called the "enigma" of Miles Davis was not only his *supposed* contradictory nature but also the equally contradictory and multiple reinterpretations of his rebellion against racial etiquette and Jim Crow America. That is why Davis as an icon to the African American community was interpreted differently than he was for white Americans. Another complex dynamic in the coolness, rebellion, and blackness of black jazz men was the intersection of race, gender, and sexuality. Black masculinity was central to the selfhood and self-presentation of black jazz musicians as well as their interpretation by white critics and fans. And while black masculinity in jazz was certainly empowering in its challenging of whiteness, it was also complicit in its own self-destructiveness and willful sexism.[9] The public story of Davis certainly will show that his life as an unreconstructed black man was an act of cultural resistance that black critic Greg Tate argues was a "a paradigm for how Black people wanted to position themselves in relation to the American experience."[10] But it will also show how this politics was *lost in translation* as whites interpreted him with their own racial imaginations, and Davis constructed an image of a violent misogynist that Sherrie Tucker argues circulated "amid the ideological contours of a marketplace in which such constructions are commonplace and expected, not to mention profitable."[11] Davis's inscrutable and irreconcilable persona speaks volumes to the contours of race and gender in American art and society during his life and up to the present.

Prelude: Crow Jim in a Color-Blind Art World

The first overt rumblings of Negro racism in jazz were the white musicians' cries of "Crow Jim." It had always been generally accepted that whereas whites might be prejudiced against Negroes, Negroes were always openminded and free of prejudice about whites. This, of course, was never the actual case. The Negroes' survival had depended on making whites see and believe what they wanted to see and believe. Among the "angry young men" of jazz in the middle and late 50s (Miles Davis, Max Roach, Charlie Mingus), Negro musicians noted for their racial views also happened to be popular and were heralded as musical innovators.

—BROOKS JOHNSON, "RACISM IN JAZZ," DOWN BEAT (1966)[12]

African American Brooks Johnson was writing at a time when the jazz art world seemed to be in the midst of a serious racial conflict over the practice, meaning, and ownership of jazz. Even though black musician Archie Shepp reminded *Down Beat* readers a year earlier of the racial conflict being waged on the streets of America, "I am, for the moment, a helpless witness to the bloody massacre of my people on the streets that run from Hayneville through Harlem,"[13] the power of a liberal color-blind ideology in jazz led to the irony that the racism Johnson was referring to, and the racism most preoccupying jazz criticism at the time, was the supposed racism of black musicians toward white musicians, white critics, white audiences, or in the case of Miles Davis, simply white people in general. For many white critics and white musicians, jazz's color-blind ideology had been under siege by race-conscious, angry black musicians since the mid-1950s. The Crow Jim controversy over black racism was covered in a variety of periodicals ranging from *Harpers, Down Beat,* and *Playboy* to the *New York Times.*[14]

Accusations of Crow Jim reached their peak during the 1960s, but went as far back as the 1930s in the jazz art world. In the late 1930s and the '40s, these accusations referred to white critics and fans, especially in Europe, who preferred black jazz musicians, occasionally to the exclusion of white jazz musicians. Genuine jazz for some white critics and fans in the United States, and most white European critics and fans, could only be played by black musicians.[15] By the mid-1950s, however, Crow Jim started to refer to the idea that many black musicians and their allies believed black musicians played a distinctly different, better, and more authentic *modern* jazz than white musicians. Miles Davis created a ruckus in 1955, for example, by claiming that the famous white jazz musicians Dave Brubeck and Paul Desmond could not swing.[16] Crow Jim accusations also stemmed from the threat posed by the race-conscious music agenda of black musicians and the supposed pressure in their community not to hire white musicians. Crow Jim was clearly a response by white critics and musicians to the Afro-modernist agenda, outlined in chapter one, of black musicians laying claim to a black music tradition and practice that had been culturally appropriated by white musicians, critics, and audiences. Black musicians were simply taking back a race music that was rightfully theirs. Such Crow Jim laments, however, ultimately failed. By the mid-1960s, black musicians had wrested significant dominance in performance, recordings, and critical attention in a jazz art world previously dominated by white musicians.

> Streaming blood from wounds on the head, Miles was taken to jail and his temporary cabaret card . . . was lifted. The first hint that police officials thought that Miles (admittedly known throughout the music business for arrogance, general cantankerousness and a well-developed Crow Jim attitude) might not be entirely in the wrong came the next day: He was told he could have his card restored "on demand."
>
> —"THE SLUGGING OF MILES," DOWN BEAT (1959)[17]

Down Beat's first news report on the beating of Miles Davis in front of the jazz club Birdland in New York City in 1959 speaks succinctly to how deep the racial rift in jazz was by the end of the 1950s. At a moment when one of the most acclaimed jazz musicians was beaten nearly to death, the editors of a top magazine for jazz musicians found it irresistible to point to Davis's supposed arrogance and Crow Jim attitude. This news report clearly demonstrated how Davis for many white critics was at the center of the Crow Jim problem in the jazz art world. Such a positioning of Davis seems incongruous since he was famous for working with white jazz musicians since the late 1940s. White arranger Gil Evans was one of his most important collaborators and closest friends. But Davis's early association with Crow Jim sets the context for understanding the multimirrored interpretations of his public persona in his public story. It speaks to how this accusation articulated something beyond the mere claim that black musicians were superior jazz musicians or preferred to work only with black musicians. And while Davis was committed to an Afro-modernist agenda of race music, the accusation of Crow Jim hurled at him reflected more the social distance between white and black members of the jazz art world and the threat posed by Davis in challenging racial etiquette and Jim Crow America. As a committed "race man"—a black man who was unyielding in his calling out of racism and challenging of Jim Crow America—Davis elicited a public story that spoke volumes to the dynamics of race in the jazz art world and his refusal to perform blackness to the expectations of white critics, journalists, and audiences. It also speaks to why Davis became a major celebrity in the black press and remained an icon of coolness and resistance to many black artists like Questlove up to the present.

The Enigma of Miles Davis

> The incredible thing is that Miles Davis goes out of his way to achieve the worst public relations to be found in the entertainment business. His rudeness and ill-manners in his utterances and actions have turned his international following into a mass schizoid phenomenon. They clamor after the wonderful sound of the horn while they are forced to dislike the man who plays it. . . . When critics rebuke his manners, he broadcasts his acidulous opinions of critics. He states his conditions to night club entrepreneurs . . . and unless they are willing to meet his conditions they are graphically told what they can do with their contracts.
>
> —ALEX HALEY, CLIMAX (1961) AND NEGRO DIGEST (1961)[18]

Alex Haley first published the quote above in "The Swinging Life of Miles Davis" for the pulp men's magazine *Climax*. Three months later it was reprinted in the *Reader's Digest* for African Americans, *Negro Digest*, as "The Two Faces of Miles Davis." The two titles alone tell you of the multimirrored fun house in which the world viewed Davis: swinging hipster with attitude or Janus-faced race man with attitude. Or as jazz critic Joe Goldberg wrote in 1965, "Psychoanalyzing Miles Davis has, in certain circles, assumed the status of a party game."[19] It was Barbara Gardner, in 1960, who consolidated Davis's reputation as Public Enigma No. 1 in her *Down Beat* article, "The Enigma of Miles Davis." "There is no room for the middle stance. You choose sides, and you play on your team. He is either the greatest living musician or he is just a cool bopper. He is handsome and a wonderful individual or he is ugly and a drag."[20] As an avid boxer, Davis clearly translated the use of fancy footwork to outmaneuver your opponent to his elaborate performance, on- and offstage, in the jazz art world. But his performances were not merely strategic ruses, or negotiations of the racial minefield that pervaded

American music, but also honest expressions of selfhood and social identity. If anything stands out in his public story, it is the *consistency* in his unpredictable persona, ill-temperate viewpoints, and creative impulses as a public figure and jazz musician over forty-five years. It is this overall consistency that is the key to understanding the significance of Davis's reputation as a supposedly enigmatic "evil genius."

Haley, Goldberg, and Gardner pointed to the contradiction Miles Davis posed to many, but not all, critics and journalists writing his public story. It was a contradiction that remained part of his public story over his entire career. Outside of the general consensus that Davis was the most innovative jazz musician in the second half of the twentieth century, another defining trope of his public story was the arrogant or angry artist who turned his back on audiences, intimidated club owners, promoters, and booking agents, kept most fans at a cold distance, and was a leader of few words with his sidemen. What strikes me was why such an obsession occurred in his public story. Why was Davis's onstage persona harped on by so many jazz critics? Why did the harping continue after Davis, his sidemen, and sympathetic critics provided sensible reasons for his on- and offstage behavior contradicting the view of him as an arrogant musician with a general nasty temperament? Why did it continue despite Davis's huge fan base with sold-out clubs and concerts? Why did some critics imply Davis mistreated fellow musicians when virtually all his sideman, while noting Davis as a man-of-few-words, lauded his leadership and musical mentorship? Davis certainly could be ill-tempered, impolite, and provocative offstage, especially toward white club owners, concert promoters, booking agents, and record executives. But there were plenty of intemperate and impolite men in jazz. However, Davis was the only "Prince of Darkness" or "evil genius." Critics and journalists over Davis's career seemed constantly searching for why such an arrogant and nasty artist was the most popular jazz musician in the world and the respected mentor and friend of many of the most accomplished and innovative musicians in modern jazz.

> Once musicians stopped thinking of jazz as something that was fun to play while entertaining people, a dreadful reaction against the audience began to really set-in. For many, the members of the audience had always been square; now they became virtual enemies, or so it would seem from watching their attitude on the stand. The realization that they were *artists* seemed too much for some musicians.
>
> **—BILL COSS, METRONOME JAZZ 1958 (1958)**[21]

Critic Bill Coss was lamenting the ethos that defined the onstage performance of not only Miles Davis but also his generation and later generations of modern jazz musicians. Other critics like Nat Hentoff supported
jazz musicians demanding performance spaces not burdened by inattentive
audiences, the loud ambient noise of night clubs, and "cigarette girls who sell
teddy bears."[22] Davis's basic performance style was to enter onstage, begin
playing a tune, not announce any of the next tunes, not introduce his sidemen, ignore the applause of his audience, and go offstage when not playing.
And even as critics like Coss and others complained about the blasé and
arrogant attitude that pervaded all modern jazz, Davis still could not escape
blame. An article in the *Los Angeles Times* in 1965, for example, pointed to
the "Miles Davis Syndrome" as responsible for the arrogant and alienating
behavior of all modern jazz musicians.[23] Davis himself summed up his reputation to Alex Haley in a 1962 *Playboy* interview. "Some critic that didn't have
nothing else to do started this crap about I don't announce numbers, I don't
look at the audience, I don't bow or talk to people, I walk off the stage, and
all that. Look, man, all I am is a trumpet player. . . . I ain't no entertainer, and
ain't trying to be one. I am one thing, a musician."[24] Davis, his sidemen, and
others provided ample reasons for why he behaved this way. They argued
that he was an artist and not an entertainer. That he left the stage so as not to
distract from his sidemen's solos. And that he did not engage with audience
members offstage because he was concentrating on his group's performance.
As his famous sideman Julian Cannonball Adderley explained to readers of
the black newspaper *New York Amsterdam News* in 1961:

> People are always talking about the bad side of Miles Davis. Now, this
> is a point of view I just don't agree with at all. Not that I think he's an
> angel, but he's like anybody else: He's a human being, and probably one
> of the most misunderstood cats in jazz. Miles thinks out everything he
> does before making decisions . . . he has a reason for everything he plays
> or does. Take this business about Miles leaving the bandstand. He's told
> me: "Cannon, if I don't have anything to do and I just stand there, I only
> draw attention away from you or anyone who's playing a solo, so I cut
> out." You see what I mean?
>
> —JULIAN "CANNONBALL" ADDERLEY,
> NEW YORK AMSTERDAM NEWS (1961)[25]

Up until Davis took a five-year hiatus from the music scene in 1976, his on-
and offstage reputation continued to persist. As John Rockwell wrote in the

New York Times in 1974: "Miles Davis is not an easy artist to understand. . . . Mr. Davis's coldness to his audiences—which, it must be reiterated, is part of a personal mystique that many in the audience Friday found attractive— showed itself in his wandering lackadaisically on and off the stage . . . and in an anticlimactically curtailed second half of the concert."[26] Even on his return to the music scene in 1981, critics speculated on whether he would bring back his old persona. Wayne Svoboda in the *Wall Street Journal* warned readers what to expect from Davis just before one of his comeback concerts, "The legendary trumpet player is noted for his erratic behavior at performances. He has been known to play briefly with nary a glance at the audience and then walk off-stage leaving others in his group to carry on. Sometimes, he simply hasn't shown up for scheduled performances."[27] While Davis actually surprised critics and audiences with a friendlier onstage demeanor during his last decade performing, his old onstage reputation remained a core trope in his public story during this period up to his death.

> Miles Davis is a walking X-rated dictionary. He is not an easy person to put into words; not even his own. His expletives would cause a waterfront loan shark to wince. . . . To observe Miles Davis and appreciate his music is to look and listen through a kaleidoscopic medium. No constants exist. . . . The life of Miles Davis is a musical epic of which he is creator, hero, anti-hero, and deus ex machina. . . . Still to the majority, he is militant, rude, violent, egocentric. Perhaps he is a combination of all these and more to varying degrees, but to know him is to respect him . . . yet from his music and lifestyle has emerged a cult of hundreds of thousands of musicians and fans who emulate him in every respect— the course language, arrogant attitude, stage presence, and even the low dry voice.
>
> —FREDERICK MURPHY, "MILES DAVIS: THE MONSTER
> OF MODERN MUSIC," ENCORE (1975)[28]

Frederick Murphy in 1975 once again showed the overarching image of Davis as the "Prince of Darkness." Murphy also projected the confusion among certain critics and journalists that reached as far back as Gardner's 1960 original piece on Public Enigma No. 1, when she expressed confused surprise "that despite all the criticism of his stage manner, the readers also voted him jazz *personality* of the year."[29] While Murphy, Gardner, and other critics imagined a silent majority who found Davis arrogant, aloof, angry, violent, or whatever other negative attribute attributed to the trumpeter, they could not explain away his huge popularity, charismatic presence, and iconic status. So, part of the contradiction of Davis was how such a supposedly dark figure could be celebrated as the epitome of cool. It was clear that the aloof, silent Davis was viewed by many as the icon of hipness. This is evident in Sascha Burland and Robert Reisner's description of Miles Davis in the men's magazine *Nugget* in 1958.

> In their midst, cool and crisp in a white, tapered Italian suit, Miles Davis slumped against a flagpole rope with the casual air of a star aerialist in a traveling circus. Heavy dark sunglasses shut out the whole spectacle. His handsome baby face carried no expression other than an occasional suggestion of a brief grimace as he reacted to a particularly loud smile, too close for comfort. To remain isolated from crowds or people who don't interest him, Miles insulates himself within a portable vacuum, a very successful device particularly when it's accompanied by sharp tongued sarcasm. People at whom Miles slings his impish barbs usually scatter in hasty retreat. This practice has not given Miles an altogether loveable reputation. But this is okay with Miles.
>
> —SASCHA BURLAND AND ROBERT REISNER,
> "THE MIDNIGHT HORN," NUGGET (1958)[30]

Many in the jazz art world were unable to process the cipher of hipness that Mile Davis projected to thousands of fans. In frustration, as early as the 1950s, jazz critics complained about the "cult of personality" that infected this art world. This critique revealed the social distance between white jazz critics and jazz musicians and their audiences, since such "problematic" personalities were often the most celebrated and commercially successful jazz musicians. We return to the racial kryptonite of how the unclear distinction between coolness and unruliness infested the jazz art world. In other words, the social distance in the jazz art world clearly manifested itself in how the most problematic of jazz musicians in the cult of jazz were black musicians like Davis. Jon Panish and Ingrid Monson have emphasized how the racial social distance in the jazz art world led white critics, writers, and fans to exotify and objectify the bad behavior of black musicians as rebellious cool. Burland and Reisner's reference to sunglasses and a portable vacuum—signifiers of aloofness—were a manifestation of the white gaze glancing across the social distance of race in interpreting Davis. For Panish, this white gaze was incapable of seeing this social distance from the vantage point of the black musician who was negotiating the racial etiquette imposed in the racial minefield of Jim Crow America. I want to add, however, how this social distance also allowed negative stereotyped readings of "cool" black males as angry, irrational, disrespectful, and racist.

> Miles broods in his beautiful town house, teaching his son to box so that he won't fear white men, raging at every corner of a world that has made him wealthy, a world that is now . . . filled with proud little boys who call themselves Miles Davis. He is a man who needs to shout, but his anger is trapped in a hoarse whisper caused by an injury to his vocal cords. The frustration shows.
>
> Onstage, he storms inwardly, glaring at his audience, wincing at his trumpet, stabbing and tugging at his ear . . . he still creates a mood of terror suppressed—a lurking and highly exciting impression that he may someday blow his brains out playing . . .
>
> Racial woes are at the heart of much bad behavior in jazz, and the racial question is largely a confusion between life and art.
>
> **—"JAZZ: THE LONELIEST MONK," TIME (1964)[31]**

These comments in a *Time* feature on Thelonious Monk were a public meditation in the top national weekly in the United States on the angry race men of jazz. And once again, Miles Davis was the standout winner for "angry black man." And as if to sum up the social distance between black race men and liberal white critics and journalists, this journalist from *Time*, probably with white jazz critics as his main sources, made the final step in the overall charade of the color-blind ideology of the jazz art world. A charade that claimed American racism certainly fed into the bad behavior of black musicians, but any rational, calm individual would know that the racial question should be left out of music making in the color-blind world of jazz. Davis hated this article. As Leonard Feather told the readers of *Melody Maker*, "Miles's name was gratuitously invoked during a passage that implied he is raging at the world, that his music is a curse at white people, whom he hates, and that he is teaching his sons to box so that they will not fear whites. . . . The absurdity of hinting that Miles Davis is a bigot is obvious to anyone but a 'Time' editor."[32] For Davis and others, critics and journalists' critiques of his onstage and offstage persona had clear racial overtones. In 1962, Davis argued that "even in jazz—you look at the white bandleaders—if they don't want anybody messing with them when they are working, you don't hear anybody squawking. It's just if a Negro is involved that there's something wrong with him . . . I know damn well a lot of it is race. White people have certain things they expect from Negro musicians—just like they've got labels for the whole Negro race."[33]

But the enigma Miles Davis posed to critics and journalists was not simply his onstage persona. His behavior offstage was equally part of his public story as the supposed "Prince of Darkness." Davis, for example, was known for his dislike of and caustic behavior toward jazz critics since the 1950s. As Stanley Goldstein noted in a 1960 *Playboy* exposé, "If Davis is not anti-white, he is largely anti-jazz critic. . . . Among the critics, Miles has only a few personal friends. . . . To writers he doesn't know, Miles can be traumatically caustic or bewilderingly outrageous. . . . Davis himself, however, is sometimes hurt at the way he's occasionally treated in the press."[34] Of course, black jazz musicians in general were not big fans of white jazz critics.[35] And the vociferous debate among jazz critics over the supposed Crow Jim of black musicians in the 1950s and '60s only added fuel to the fire. Davis's own distain in actions and words for jazz critics was both an expression of a collectively felt antagonism black jazz musicians had toward white jazz critics and a response to the personal attacks Davis had endured since the early 1950s.

Given the social distance between whites and blacks in the jazz art world, all black musicians constantly negotiated the racial etiquette infused in their relationships with whites. What underlay the public story of Davis was how his relationship with white jazz critics revealed no attempt at deference to their power and privilege over defining modern jazz to white readers. In his interaction with jazz critics, Davis certainly had his career in mind. But in reading his overall public story, I suggest that these interactions were also political. For Davis, when it came to race, the personal was always political. Because in his view, the personal was always steeped in the world of Jim Crow. His public story shows how Davis inherited this attitude from his race man father. The lack of deference to jazz critics was in part a purposeful reminder of the racial social distance in the jazz art world. It expressed a selfhood and social identity Davis consistently displayed in action and words his whole career. As we will see, as a race man provocateur, Davis actively worked to remind the whites he interacted with that they were living in a Jim Crow world where whites were the real problem.

This is clear in how Miles Davis was not only caustic toward white jazz critics, but showed no deference as well to white club owners, concert promoters, or record executives. Gardner, in her *Down Beat* meditation on the supposedly enigmatic Davis, introduced what would be another running theme in his public story, "Ask any club-owner where he has worked. Most will say, 'He's a headache, but the customers flock to hear him.'"[36] Popular anecdotes of his occasionally caustic relationship with jazz entrepreneurs constantly appeared in his public story. The most popular story was how he permanently damaged his vocal chords from yelling at a white promoter after a throat operation. This is what led to his famous hoarse voice. Other anecdotes included punching a white concert promoter for docking Davis $100 for being late, or Davis refusing to perform a two-set concert unless the promoter paid him the amount he felt was fair. His caustic relation to white entrepreneurs remained part of the Davis public story. As Chris Albertson wrote in the *Saturday Review* in 1971, "Club owners and concert promoters have been known to go into a rage over Miles's seeming detachment, but conformity is not part of his vocabulary, and, despite the constant criticism, he has for twenty years remained the dark, brooding, wandering loner who doesn't care if he is regarded as an eccentric genius or a bellicose bastard."[37]

But Stanley Goldstein, like many other defenders of Davis, argued in 1960 that "Miles does present a cactus-like, unapproachable front (or back, as is often the case) to the jazz public; but he is an unusually warm, spontaneously generous and witty friend to those few he allows to know him after hours."[38] In other words, in the interracial *public space* of the jazz art world, Davis acted differently than in the more *private spaces* of his life. All the sympathetic descriptions of Davis's behavior suggest that he was performing or negotiating his relationship to others in the jazz art world, and part of his "blackness" was to refuse to show deference to white fans, club owners, concert promotors, or record executives. And Davis only expressed what most black jazz musicians felt about the jazz art world: that many white club owners, concert promoters, and record producers were exploiting them as artists.[39]

Every colored American, no matter where or how he studies his 3 R's, has been well educated in the all-important 4th R—race relations. At home, in school, at church, the fundamental lessons on how to get along with white folks have been pounded into the Negro. Living in a white society, he has been forced to study these lessons hard and well in order to survive. Failure too often has been disastrous—if not fatal. . . . While Negroes have had to study how to get along with whites, few whites have ever taken the pains to learn to get along with Negroes. . . . When the newly enlightened white liberal crosses the color line and cultivates Negro friends with all the best of intentions, too often he unwarily falls into many racial traps as a result of his ignorance of the 4th R . . . There are Negros though who are not as tolerant and are as wont as not to administer a tongue lashing to would-be "white friends."

—"ETIQUETTE OF RACE RELATIONS," EBONY (1949)⁴⁰

Miles Davis was known to be unpredictably caustic in general regardless of who he was interacting with, white or black. John Rockwell in the *New York Times* in 1974 described the reputation of Davis's general demeanor. "And then there is Mr. Davis's blackness, and his hostility to the white music business and to the white audiences he must attract in order to earn a living. But part of that hostility seems endemic to his character, and would appear to manifest itself as much to his collaborators and to the black part of the audience as it does specifically to whites."[41] But since the 1950s, Davis was known for often adding the signifier "white" to the mix of his outbursts in his interactions in the jazz art world and outside it. He had no qualms about reminding critics, entrepreneurs, or anyone else that they were white. The everyday *politics* of Davis's performance of "blackness" was to turn the tables in the usual dynamics of racial etiquette where, as the editorial above from *Ebony* pointed out, African Americans had no choice but to remember their race in every interaction, while white Americans could be oblivious to theirs. And as *Ebony* suggested, sometimes a race man has to remind white Americans of the unspoken 4th R in American racial etiquette. And as an unreconstructed black man, Davis's everyday politics was to remind white Americans as often as possible of their white privilege. As Don DeMichael told *Rolling Stone* readers in 1969, "He never denies his blackness. . . . In almost any conversation with him, he makes reference to the difference of being black and being white in this country. His frankness has caused him to be called racist. He most certainly is not."[42]

The salt in the wound of defying racial etiquette was Davis's refusal to appreciate his success under the "guiding hands" of white entrepreneurs. He certainly was one of the highest paid jazz musicians in the world beginning in the late 1950s. In 1960, where top jazz musicians like John Coltrane and Cannonball Adderley were making $350 to $400 a week at club dates, Miles Davis was making $3,500 to $4,000 a week at club dates and $3,500 for a two-set concert.[43] He told *Ebony* in 1961 that he was earning $150,000 a year as the most celebrated jazz musician in the world.[44] But something more was at work in Davis's relationship with the white entrepreneurs in jazz. The politics of Davis was not simply about his treatment as a black artist, although he had little trust in the white-controlled industry. But Davis used his success to agitate against the general racism in the music industry and American society.

Miles Davis was also notoriously caustic to executives, and everyone else, at Columbia Records. By the end of the 1960s, he would relentlessly criticize Columbia Records for its racism and lack of support even as he became the highest paid and longest contracted jazz musician at the company.[45] In the 1970s, he complained constantly of how the white executives and promoters as Columbia had no clue as to how to market his music to black people. As Davis told Stephen Davis for the *Real Paper* in 1973, "I mean, they don't even try to go into the black neighborhoods and sell records. They tell me, 'We want to introduce you to a new audience,' but that audience is always white! . . . All I tell 'em to do is sell the music black, not to put no white girls on the cover with no pants on and stuff like that. Sell it black. Like I like Sly, man, James Brown. . . . I like to look at black people . . . I don't listen to the Rolling Stones and any of that shit."[46] Davis ended his thirty-year association with Columbia in 1985. He joined Warner Brothers where he remained until his death in 1991.

And Negroes who try to act the way they think other people want them to act bug me worse than Uncle Toms.

—MILES DAVIS, EBONY (1961)[47]

Black people are acting out roles every day in this country just to keep on getting by. If white people really knew what was on most black people's minds it would scare them to death. Blacks don't have the power to say these things, so they put on masks and do great acting jobs just to get through the fucking day.

—MILES DAVIS, MILES: THE AUTOBIOGRAPHY (1989)[48]

What the public story of Miles Davis reveals is that the real enigma of Davis was his refusal to follow the racial etiquette expected in the jazz art world. It was not his onstage performance persona that was the problem. This persona is what made him the most financially successful jazz musician of all time, the greatest icon of modern jazz, and the persistent epitome of cool up to the present. Placing aside the most common trope of his public story—his onstage persona as the core of his enigma—what emerges is that the enigma of Davis was his offstage persona in the world of jazz and American music. What becomes clear is that Davis refused to reconstruct himself not only for jazz audiences but also in his everyday interactions and conversations with white critics, journalists, club owners, concert promoters, booking agents, record executives, police officers, or any other white he encountered in his life. He never stopped "tongue-lashing" at the white world behind Jim Crow America. Of course, on the other hand, as Marc Crawford pointed out to readers of *Ebony* in 1961, in responding to "an angry columnist who accused him of being nasty. Miles shot back: 'I've got news for you. I been nasty all my life.'"[49]

Robin D. G. Kelley, borrowing from the work of anthropologist James C. Scott, argues for the need to recognize the infra-political in the everyday lives of African Americans. The infra-political is the "daily, unorganized, evasive, seemingly spontaneous actions" that "form an important yet neglected part of African-American political history."[50] He points to how southern working-class African Americans would sabotage, steal, refuse to work, yell at bus drivers, and perform other acts of resistance that made up their infra-politics: a politics outside the recognized and legitimized forms of politic behavior. I would argue that Miles Davis was a master of infra-politics in his workplace, the jazz art world, and his life in Jim Crow America. His refusal to show deference, his constant berating of white entrepreneurs and critics, his refusal to perform because of some perceived mistreatment, his onstage behavior, and his constant use of the signifier "white," were all part of an infra-politics of resistance. For Davis, inspired by his father, perceived of himself as a noncompromising race man: an unreconstructed black man not willing to perform the racial etiquette of the jazz art world and Jim Crow America. And in his role as race man, Davis also was willing to spread the *hidden transcripts* of the African American community about just what they thought about Jim Crow America.[51]

The Unreconstructed Race Man as Provocateur

> **Mainspring:** White folks. White people are responsible for my success. They make it so hard for you that a long time ago I got mad and made up my mind to be two, three times as good at whatever I decided to do. If I was white I probably wouldn't have had the drive. **Most paradoxical quality:** People claim I'm a paradox, that I don't act like they think I ought to. They want me to entertain them. I'm a musician and that's all I do. I'm not an actor or dancer, either. I just can do one thing, play my music.
>
> —MILES DAVIS, "SELF PORTRAIT," ESQUIRE (1962)[52]

One of the most famous quotes by Miles Davis was from his self-portrait in *Esquire* in 1962. That Davis pointed to white people as his inspiration to become the most celebrated jazz musician in the world, and the final barb that had he been white, he never would have attained such a pinnacle of success, perfectly speaks to Davis's stance throughout his career as a race man provocateur. This was not only in everyday conversations and interactions as discussed in the previous section, but also in interviews for the jazz and general press. As Davis made clear in *Esquire*, if he was an enigma to others, it was because he did not comport himself in a way white people deemed appropriate. And while in this self-portrait he was referencing complaints about his onstage persona, he and others would defend at other times Davis's behavior and words offstage. Davis would not only refuse to accept the dictates of American racial etiquette but also openly remind the world of the strife between white and black America. What becomes clear in the public story of Miles Davis is that throughout his career his music, behaviors and words were as *infra-political* as they were *personal* and *artistic*.

As noted in the previous section, probably the biggest *infra-political* weapon in his arsenal of performing blackness was his use of the word "white" as ultimate signifier of Jim Crow America. While notorious for his use of the term "motherfucker," his use of the term "white," usually in a negative sense, appeared far more often in his interviews. Whether talking about musicians, club owners, promoters, record executives, or people in general, "white" was the signifier of choice. His constant use of "white" and "black" in his interviews obviously was a major factor in accusations of Davis as racist. Given the reality of the "white" and "black" world of Jim Crow, the irony was not lost on Davis. When a friend asked about the charges that he was racist, Stanley Goldstein reported in 1960 that Davis laughed and said, "I don't have time to Jim Crow. I've been busy since I was thirteen years old, and I've known enough Crow myself. I wouldn't want to take the next thirty-three years to learn to be prejudiced."[53] He would, however, spend the next thirty-one years refusing in interviews to show deference to a world that remained fundamentally a Jim Crow racial order.

I argue that the basic view of Davis as angry, enigmatic, and, for some, racist, was shaped significantly by a white interpretation of Davis as an out-spoken, unreconstructed black man whose modernist pose onstage was inseparable from his offstage persona expressed in interviews his entire career. It was his very refusal in interviews to show the racial etiquette of *deference* and *silence*—African Americans censoring their feelings and viewpoints in order not to offend white sensibilities or challenge white privilege—that confounded the expectations of many white jazz critics and other whites in the jazz art world and beyond. Davis was a race man who refused such transformation of selfhood for the pleasure of white society. And Davis's words were viewed differently on the occasions when a black voice spoke in his public story. As black newspaper columnist George Pitts wrote in 1962 in response to Davis's frank comments in his (in)famous 1961 *Playboy* interview, "A pat on the back to Mr. Davis comes from this corner because he tells it like it is not only in his profession, but as it is in all facets of American life."[54] And Miles never stopped *telling it like it is* for his entire public story.

> DAVIS: What makes me mad about these labels for Negroes is that very few white people really know what Negroes really feel like. . . . But I know that pretty nearly all Negroes hardly have any other choice about how they feel. They ain't blind. They got to see what's happening. It's a thousand big and little ways that you run into the prejudices of white people.
>
> PLAYBOY: Do you, in your position as a famous Negro, meet prejudice?
>
> DAVIS: I told you, someway or other, every Negro meets it, I don't care who he is! . . .
>
> DAVIS: It ain't that I'm mad at white people, I just see what I see and I know what's happening. I am going to speak my mind about anything that drags me about this Jim Crow scene. This whole prejudice mess is something you would feel so good if it could just be got rid of, like a big sore eating inside of your belly.
>
> —MILES DAVIS WITH ALEX HALEY, PLAYBOY (1962)[55]

The years 1959 to 1962 marked a crucial turning point in Miles Davis's public story. Besides the major 1962 *Playboy* interview, a year earlier, Davis and members of his family did extensive interviews for *Ebony* and Stanley Goldstein did a *Playboy* exposé based on interviews with Davis and others familiar with the trumpeter. It was clear Davis was using extensive interviews to intervene in the telling of his public story. As we have seen, by 1959 the public story of Miles Davis had become one of a modern jazz genius who had gained a reputation, whether earned or not, of being enigmatic, arrogant, angry, and Crow Jim racist. As Miles told Marc Crawford for *Ebony*, "You goddam right I'm angry. . . . I don't like to stress race because I have friends of all colors. But everything I see around me stresses it. . . . It makes me prejudiced. All I want for my kids is a simple thing. To be free. To not have to think about color or anything."[56] As the *Ebony* and *Playboy* interviews show, Davis was attempting to provocatively turn the tables on the white jazz critics and journalists who wrote about him by reminding everyone that they did not live in a Crow Jim America, but a Jim Crow America. In particular, he was highlighting the ignorance of white liberals about the lives of black Americans just as the *Ebony* editorial, "Etiquette of Race Relations," did thirteen years earlier. And he was clearly reframing his angry and caustic behaviors and words as responses to the racial prejudice of whites in his life. This theme of racism pervading his and other black's everyday lives would remain a major a part of his contribution to his public story along with the always reliable refrain of white musicians not having what it takes to compete with black musicians in the world of music.

> Despite his lineage and respectable bourgeois background, Miles was no more immune than any other American Negro to the traumatic blow of a Jim Crow childhood. "About the first thing I can remember," he once told a reporter, "was a white man running me down the street hollering 'Nigger! Nigger!' My father went hunting him with a shotgun. Being sensitive and having race pride has been in my family since slave days."
> —MILES DAVIS WITH LEONARD FEATHER, DOWN BEAT (1964)[57]

From the early 1960s until his final years, Miles Dewey Davis III wanted the world to know of the pervasive nature of Jim Crow and the strong legacy of the Davis family not to take it sitting down or silent. The story of the Davis family included the role of racial kryptonite in their long family history. Davis's grandfather was a successful accountant in Arkansas. But all the wealth and land he had acquired was stolen from him during the consolidation of the Jim Crow South. He was forced to flee to the state of Missouri. In the 1961 *Ebony* article on Davis, this is the backdrop to the story of his father hunting a racist white man who called a young Miles "Nigger!" The Davis family's vigilance against the racial kryptonite of Jim Crow America was clearly an often-told family tale that was also repeated in Davis's public story. It was first told by Dr. Miles Davis II, trumpeter Davis III's father, in the 1961 *Ebony* article. But as Quincy Troupe wrote two decades later in the music magazine *Spin* in 1985, "Miles comes from a politically conscious family . . . a long and distinguished line of Davises who were extremely proud of their heritage and didn't take shit from anyone. . . . Miles father was a 'race man' who favored Marcus Garvey's Back to Africa movement over the integrationist tendencies of the NAACP. These ideas were passed on to young Miles. Doc Miles once took a shot gun and went looking for a white man who had called young Miles a nigger (he couldn't find him)."[58] Miles Dewey Davis III would be a vocal unreconstructed race man for his entire career. While driving in New York City with jazz critic Don DeMichael in 1969, he let Don know the state of race relations in the present and foreseeable future and his refusal to buckle under to Jim Crow.

> "White people own all this shit," he said, hunching over the wheel and peering up at the buildings. "Own the whole country," I added. "They don't own me." "You got a white booker, haven't you? A white record company?" "They do what I tell them to do, man. They don't own me. I make my own records. We're just in business together. I mean it's all right to be in business with a white man, but for him to own everything and dictate to you is outdated, and it was outdated when I was born. I've never been that way in my whole life and I never will be. I'd die before I'd let that shit happen. . . . See all those colored here? It'll be just like this 20 years from now. That's what burns me up."
>
> —MILES DAVIS WITH DON DEMICHAEL, ROLLING STONE (1969)[59]

Up until his five-year hiatus from music in 1976, Davis remained as fierce a race man as his father. As he told Jimmy Saunders in a 1975 *Playboy* interview, "White folk fill you up with all that shit about Jesus, and then you get out there believing that holding hands we shall overcome."[60]

Miles Davis also continued to criticize the racism permeating the world of American music. By 1969, Davis adopted the 1960s nationalist black art movement's rejection of what they believed were white labels imposed on black music. He also continued to claim that white musicians and black musicians existed in distinct music cultures. He told DeMichael in the *Rolling Stone* interview in 1969, "I don't like the word rock and roll and all that shit. Jazz is an Uncle Tom word. It's a white folks word."[61] He told *Newsweek* in 1970 that "it's a white man's world. . . . The record companies make idols out of white artists. They don't sell black artists like that. . . . Man, you know whites are going to hold onto the power and the money. . . . That's what makes our music different. It comes from a people who have had to learn to make the white man move."[62] In an *Encore* interview in 1975, he told Frederick Murphy, "I don't play rock. Rock is a white word. And I don't like the word jazz because jazz is a nigger word that white folks dropped on us. We just play *Black*."[63]

> LF: Have you heard any rock groups that interested you?
> DAVIS: I haven't heard anything coming from the white kids with the long hair and shit. I like to hear the Motown Sound and James Brown, them funky singers.

LF: You put it on a racial basis, yet some of your most rewarding associations have been interracial.

DAVIS: You don't understand. What I want to hear doesn't come from a white musician. . . . What I want to hear, like rhythm and blues, it comes from black musicians all the time. . . . It's because I'm black, Leonard. I'm not white. . . . I'm just saying that white people cater to white people and black people cater to black people. It's just a normal thing.

LF: Your ideal world basically is still an integrated world, isn't it?

DAVIS: Right. But I think it won't work. . . . Most black people would like to see everybody integrated, you know? A lot of black people want to be like white people: they think white people have a level that they want to try to reach. That's even sad, you know? People can live together, but all that old shit hasn't stopped.

—MILES DAVIS WITH LEONARD FEATHER,
"THE DEFINITIVE DAVIS," PENTHOUSE (1972)[64]

In his interview with jazz critic Leonard Feather for *Penthouse* in 1972, the various threads of Miles Davis's ongoing commentary on Jim Crow America and American music came together as Feather pushed him on his continued insistence that black musicians played a different music from white musicians. Davis refused to back down as the provocative race man who remained committed to race music. And Davis continued to perform in interracial music groups. Once again, the old Crow Jim argument resurfaced where white jazz critics refused to see the general point, as expressed by Davis, that black musicians came from a distinctly different music culture than white musicians. He also refused to accept the delusion of the liberal color-blind ideology of the jazz art world that black race consciousness was a hindrance to an integrated American society. He also refused to acknowledge that anything had fundamentally changed in Jim Crow America. As he told Chris Albertson in 1971, "I am not a Black Panther or nothing like that. . . . I don't need to be, but I was raised to think like they do and people sometimes think I'm difficult because I always say what's on my mind, and they can't always see what I see."[65]

What is striking is how obvious Miles Davis's comments on American music and American society are not the rantings of some irrational, angry race man, but the clear-eyed analysis of the contemporary state of race relations. It would be difficult to imagine that things were going well in the United States in the late 1960s or early '70s. Those were heady, radical times.

And with the death of Jimi Hendrix in 1970, as Jack Hamilton argues, white musicians and critics had completed their cultural appropriation of rock and roll.[66] Davis's commentary on the white labeling of jazz, rock and roll, and rock were clear rejections of the cultural appropriation of black music that was happening once again in American music. And his commentary that the old shit had not stopped and twenty-years down the road the state of Jim Crow America would be basically the same was just as astute. The irony in one regard was that the once provocative race man of the 1950s and '60s was now spouting out words that were spouting out of the mouths of black radicals across the United States and in the pages of jazz journals and rock magazines like *Jazz Magazine* and *Rolling Stone*. Even young white Americans were adopting the radical chic of the black power movement.

And during the 1950s, '60s, and '70s, Davis was not the only provocateur race man or race woman in jazz. Ingrid Monson provides a detailed history of the parallel development of race-conscious politics within the jazz art world and its development within the wider African American community. The whole Crow Jim "problem" in the 1950s and '60s involved the radical politics of black jazz musicians like Max Roach, Abbey Lincoln, Charlie Mingus, Archie Shepp, Jeanne Lee, Cecil Taylor, and Marion Brown among others. As white jazz critic Nat Hentoff told readers of the *New York Times* in "The New Jazz: Black, Angry and Hard to Understand" in 1966: "As black jazzmen took themselves and their art more seriously, they increasingly utilized their music to tell what they felt about life in America and, in particular, about their experiences as Negroes in America. . . . Also on the ascendant was their pride in being black. . . . In the jazz of the nineteen sixties, black consciousness has reached new levels of concentration and intensity . . . an attempt to underline their sense of collective identity with black people."[67]

> Man, he was a star and the whole goddamned effing world was gonna know it! And more than that, he was gonna rub their noses in all that fame of his, and do it with all the black arrogance he could muster. So, all those whiteys bought his records, told him they were *mad* about him, went to his concerts in droves—well, he was just gonna turn his back and play that trumpet, look cold and mean and splendid in the spotlight, and let them come to him, because he was Miles and didn't even need a surname to be remembered by. Just Miles . . . So here he is, a black man in his forties who plays trumpet of all things, not even guitar, and he's a bonafide superstar, the ONLY jazz superstar so far as all those out there in the great global village of rock and roll and beyond are concerned.
>
> —MICHAEL WATTS, TODAY'S SOUNDS (1973)[68]

The difference between Miles Davis and the other black jazz provocateurs, however, was that he was not simply a jazz musician. He was a certified *popular music* icon. His status was clear to both the *Melody Maker* and Michael Watts. In the British music magazine's review of the contemporary state of popular music, *Today's Sounds*, artists were arranged under sections related to their power as pop icons, like Leonard Cohen and Cat Stevens as the "poets" of popular music. The chapter "Miles Davis," however, stood by itself, with no section head, as the very last chapter of the book. It was the only chapter featuring a jazz musician. Even among the younger icons of pop—David Bowie, Lou Reed, Stevie Wonder, Bob Marley, Bette Midler, and others—Miles Davis stood alone. The bona fide, ultimate cool black race man. The "cult of personality" jazz critics lamented in the 1950s remained as strong as ever for Davis. But he no longer wore tailor-made Italian suits or cardigan sweaters, but snakeskin pants, suede long-fringed vests, and leather boots, but still with those cool sunglasses. The enigma of Davis remained up to his leaving the music scene in 1976. The race man as provocateur was as admired and popular as ever. Even as jazz critics lambasted his lack of musical prowess in these waning years, Davis remained the "evil genius" of jazz.

The Hip-Hyper-Masculine Race Man

> Miles Davis has an image. Nasty and notorious, arrogant and whimsical, he does nothing he doesn't want to do, and he makes a point of it. When he feels like biting his producer's ear, he bites. *That's a nice WHITE ear . . .* Irascible and insolent, he's the Evil Genius, the Sorcerer, the Prince of Darkness . . . his ascent to the peak of Bad Motherfuckerdom ensures his currency even among people who don't make a steady diet of jazz. . . . It's his magnetism, his sexuality, his hubris. And his talent for trouble: cops arrest him for narcotics and brass knuckles and .25 caliber automatics, beat him over the head outside Birdland. Racketeers shoot through the door of his Ferrari and he breaks both legs smashing up his Lamborghini. A woman sues him for unlawful imprisonment and menacing in his apartment, a man for being thrown down the stairs. Miles Davis is a pop star.
> —DAVID BRESKIN, ROLLING STONE (1983)[69]

The ultimate enigma of Miles Davis as a celebrated pop icon is how the social distance of race in America guaranteed a *reinterpretation* of his behaviors and words by white Americans. Ingrid Monson, Jon Panish, and Nichole T. Rustin argue that the social distance between black and white America has acted to rob the *agency* of African American artists in terms of the interpretation of their attitudes, actions, and words by white Americans.[70] I have emphasized Davis's public story as in part a reflection of his *infra-politics* as a black jazz musician. But if anyone understood how useless your intentions and politics were as an African American artist it would be Davis. From the very beginning of his career, he confronted whites' reinterpretations of him. The quote above from *Rolling Stone*'s David Breskin suggests that for many white critics, journalists, and fans, the *infra-politics* of Davis was totally lost in translation. His racial rage and critique of Jim Crow America was for many subsumed within a white gaze of cool hypermasculine blackness. As Monson, Panish, Rustin, Gray, and Kelley point out, masculinity was inescapably interwoven with blackness in jazz and American music.[71] So, Davis's racial outrage was subsumed under a white male gaze of black masculinity that haunted jazz and popular music. And unfortunately, Davis's own performance of black masculinity in the racial minefield of American music led, over time, to his own complicity in creating the Bad Motherfucker mystique of hipness. And this complicity ultimately led to the controversial autobiography that would forever change his legacy as an American icon.

> And since masculinity or virility has always been so essential to art, and is now being touted to the jazz public as being most definitely a part of that which is funky, it should be stressed that obvious strength, which can be mere posturing, hardness, or viciousness and the vicarious salacious or obscene are not necessarily part of masculinity. Real strength, which is real virility, is frequently gentle, because it can afford to be, and it is less concerned with overt actions, of whatever kind, because it has security in its wholeness.
>
> —BILL COSS, METRONOME JAZZ 1958 (1958)[72]

The number of times white critics used the term "virile" in the 1950s and '60s to describe black musicians and their music making is quite astonishing, assuming, unlike white critic Bill Coss, that virility has nothing to do with music making or art. They used it almost as often as they used "angry," sometimes in the same sentence. Coss was finishing a long, convoluted diatribe on the difference between white cool jazz and black hard bop. This diatribe rambled from the funky virility of hard bop, to the effeminate gloss of cool jazz, to the crisis in masculinity in America, to finally his conclusion that "real" virility is often gentle—a reference to white cool jazz. Anyone questioning whether white male critics and fans were unconsciously negotiating their masculinity through jazz musicians need only read this article to see the light. And Coss again reveals the double-edged sword of male blackness in American culture—its constant shifting in the white male gaze from object of coolness to symbolic castration. At least, according to Coss, white cool jazz musicians were secure in their wholeness, unlike the lack of wholeness of black hard-boppers. This is what Monson, Panish, and Rustin mean by the robbing of agency and objectification of black musicians in the jazz art world.[73] Coss basically painted black musicians as one-dimensional, angry, virile men against white musicians as full-dimensional, gentle, introspective men.

> Thus, the singular thing about Miles Davis's celebrated trumpet playing, which is at last full-grown, is not its striking style but its genuine, though elusive, content. . . . The results are thrill feminine forays into the upper registers, cunningly heavy arpeggios, and a mutant melodic line . . . a view of things that is brooding, melancholy, somewhat self-pitying, and extremely close to the sentimental.
>
> **—WHITNEY BALLIETT, NEW YORKER (1961)[74]**

Whitney Balliett's review of a concert featuring Miles Davis is a perfect example of how white critics were constantly using metaphors of emotion, often gendered in reference, when reinterpreting jazz musicians' recordings, concerts, or club dates. Balliett's review shows that in the 1950s Davis posed a dilemma to many critics and fans as he defied in his singular music making the black masculinity they expected, consciously or unconsciously, in jazz. And even before his reputation solidified as the "Prince of Darkness," the contradiction between his music and his behavior befuddled critics and fans alike. As Leonard Feather wrote in 1960, Davis was "a musician whose melodic language on the bandstand is eloquent but whose speech off the stand consists largely of four-letter profanities."[75] Davis's distinct style of trumpet playing stood in stark contrast to the "virile" technical pyrotechnics of black trumpeters like Dizzy Gillespie and Fats Navarro. The most common term used in reviews, articles, and biographies of Davis was that his style was "lyrical." But like Balliett, many white critics fell into using terms that stood out as feminine in relation to the masculine terms found in reviews of other black jazz musicians. For example, Ralph Gleason commented in *Down Beat* in 1957, "Miles plays with a dainty, almost delicate manner." Contrast this to white critic Don Cerulli's comment on sideman Sonny Rollins's music making in a Davis club date that same year as "rough-edged and brimming with virility."[76] The most quoted, and infamous, comment on Davis's trumpet playing came from white critic Barry Ulanov. He claimed that Davis sounded like "a man walking on egg shells."[77] As white critic Martin Williams wrote in a memorial for Davis in 1991, "There was that old suspicion (also employed to undermine Stan Getz and Chet Baker) that somehow his playing was too 'feminine,' too refined, for jazz."[78] Needless to say, Getz and Baker were two of the most famous white cool jazz musicians of the 1950s.

Of course, a number of white critics awkwardly resisted or openly refuted the reinterpretation of Davis's music making as feminine. One sensed that these critics were clearly uncomfortable in Davis being feminized. Bill Coss writing in *Metronome Jazz 1958* assured its readers, "There is the almost fragile, though never effeminate, tracing of a story line which is somewhat above and beyond him."[79] Or in lambasting Ulanov's comment on egg shells, jazz critics offered a different reinterpretation of Davis's style. White critic Nat Hentoff assured the readers of *Esquire* magazine in 1959, "If Miles walked on an egg shell, he'd grind it to the ground."[80] Hentoff was even clearer in *International Musician* in 1961 on Davis's music making not indicating problems in the masculinity column. "In a period when much modern jazz is either batteringly 'soulful' or jaggedly experimental, Davis' work is deeply lyrical and sometimes can be exceptionally subtle and tender. It should be emphasized, however, that there is nothing fragile in Davis' introspective jazz."[81] Or as Martin Williams wrote in 1962, "But Davis the musician walks firmly . . . if he ever encounters an eggshell, his intensity will probably grind them to powder."[82]

By the early 1960s, however, white critics were no longer obsessed with the "feminine" nature of Davis's music making. As John S. Wilson wrote in the *New York Times* in 1961, "proving his all-around capabilities on the trumpet. He played with tremendous fire and spirit, soaring off into high note runs with confidence and precision, building lines bristling with searing emotion and yet retaining all the warmest, singing elements of his gentler side."[83] And now the moody, brooding, playing was part of the hip charisma of Davis as the new jazz icon of cool. As Ralph Gleason wrote in the *San Francisco Chronicle*, "Almost all of jazz's true leaders have been charismatic figures. . . . The latest, and in many ways the most potent influence of his order in jazz, is Miles Davis."[84] It seemed, in the early 1960s, white critics and fans had been able to resolve the confusion in their racial imagination over Davis's seemingly contradictory expressions of selfhood and masculinity. It turns out they got help from Davis himself as he quickly displayed his true masculine nature in his public story.

As mentioned previously, Miles Davis made a major intervention in his public story beginning in 1959 with extensive articles and interviews. Besides his self-presentation as an outspoken race man, he also presented himself as a race man steeped in hypermasculinity. His black masculinity was linked first to his family lineage with the story of his father, shotgun in hand, going after the white man who called young Davis III a "Nigger!" The Davis family's masculine resolve was evident in another story of how Davis III kicked his heroin addiction in 1954 by going "cold turkey" by himself over twelve days. Another theme in Davis's public story was his love of boxing. In the 1961 *Ebony* article on Davis, four photos were featured on his boxing obsession. As one caption suggested, "Miles heroes appear to be fighters more than musicians."[85] In his public story, Davis always sought out local gyms when touring, sometimes with a personal trainer. He also enjoyed feigning boxing during interviews, like when John Palcewski interviewed him for the men's magazine *Cavalier* in 1969. "Miles starts walking back toward the kitchen, stops suddenly and goes into a boxer's stance. He punches the air swiftly and rapidly and dances lightly around, grunting softly with the effort."[86] All of these tropes of masculinity in the Davis biographical legend would be repeated over and over when critics or journalists shifted to his life offstage.

By the late 1960s, Davis was transitioning from jazz icon to pop icon with his best-selling 1969 *Bitches Brew* captivating a new generation of young white rock audiences with his fusion jazz and hip "Prince of Darkness" persona. In his public story, Davis clearly ramped up his masculine pose. An interview in *Melody Maker* shows how Davis had fully embraced his mystique as the "Prince of Darkness."

ENNIS: I asked him if he'd describe himself as a militant and he
    exploded.
DAVIS: Militant? That ain't nothing. That's light stuff. If a man says
    something to me I don't like, I might kill him. That's beyond being
    militant. I've been through maybe a hundred killings in my head.
    Black militant—that's nothing but a load of White rubbish. You
    can't call me that.
ENNIS: He once knocked out three guys single-handed for annoying
    him. Basically, he's very strong.
        —JANE ENNIS, "MILES SMILES," MELODY MAKER (1973)[87]

In a 1973 *Melody Maker* interview, Davis announcing his constant fantasy of killing people shows how he began in the late 1960s to be far more angry, aggressive, and threatening. He was more than this. But as the race man provocateur was still espousing on Jim Crow America, he was also engaging interviewers and readers with a new hypermasculine aggression. It was a synergistic theme in his public story told through press coverage, music reviews, and Davis's comments on his run-ins with the law, gangsters, neighbors, and road posts. Of course, the late 1960s and '70s were a more radical time than the 1950s and early '60s, with angry black militants marching across the country. As bell hooks argues, "radical militant resistance to white supremacy, typified by the sixties and seventies black power movements, called out of the shadow of repression the black male body, claiming it as a sight of hyper-masculine power, agency, and sexual potency."[88] Huey Newton's 1967 photograph as a militant Black Panther made him as iconic as Miles Davis or Jimi Hendrix. And white rock critics and fans in particular seemed drawn and inspired by Davis's "Prince of Darkness" persona along with his stylish snakeskin pants, suede long-fringed vests, and leather boots. But while Davis was continuing to rant about racism in America and the music industry, these critics and journalists seemed more interested in his "Bad Motherfuckerdom" than in pursuing his thoughts on racism. Such attraction to Davis's troubled life, anger, and, at times, violent demeanor meshed well with their attraction to other aspects of Davis's hypermasculinity.

One striking aspect of the revitalized "Prince of Darkness" was how his troubled life seemed to speak to white critics and journalists about his rebel, cool hipness, rather than about the racist world in which he lived. References to his run-ins with the law as the "bad boy" of jazz and pop particularly speak to how critics and journalists lost in translation Davis's constant critique of racism in America. Virtually every time Davis talked about his interactions with police, he emphasized that he was stopped because he was black, and on certain occasions, because he was a black man with a white woman. Davis was not too subtle about this. He was never subtle about anything, except, of course, for his lyrical phrasing and intonation on the horn. In reference to his 1970 arrest in New York City for driving a car without registration and illegally possessing brass knuckles, Davis said, "It wouldn't have happened if I hadn't been a black man driving a red car."[89] Or as he told Quincy Troupe for *Spin* magazine in 1985, "The police make me mad, and I never say the things they want to hear. . . . I don't be saying 'Yessuh, boss,' or 'I'm taking the car to be washed and cleaned.' Shit like that. Man, 'cause the shit I be wearin' should tell any fool that I belong in the car!"[90] When Davis's 1986 album, *You're Under Arrest*, was released, Ken Franckling wrote in the *Sun Times*, "Davis is bitter about the problems he faced growing up black in white America. He has tangled with police over the years, with arrests and incidents he views as pure harassment. That festering bitterness prompted him to name his final Columbia album 'You're Under Arrest' . . . He says he did so 'because the police always f . . . with me . . . I feel like I'm ready to die in a war.'"[91]

Besides Davis's selected image as a hypermasculine, badass black man, his public story also projected the image of a black man living the *Playboy* fantasy in real life. Men's magazines made jazz music part of the "playboy" lifestyle. And by the 1960s, Davis's public story featured repeated references to his playboy lifestyle of money, fancy cars, fine clothes, beautifully laid out homes, and gorgeous women. As Nat Hentoff wrote in 1961, "Off the stand, Miles enjoys sports cars—he owns a Ferrari—and is considered the best dressed of all jazzmen."[92] In 1969, John Palcewski interviewed Davis in his home for the men's magazine *Cavalier*, "I look around the room. It resembles something out of Hugh Hefner's *Playboy* mansion."[93] And in 1970, the *New York Times* dedicated an article to the elaborately designed home of Davis in New York City.[94] As Harriet Choice told readers of the *Chicago Tribune* in 1974:

> And then there was the Miles Mystique. Accidents in fast sports cars, gorgeous pace-setting clothes, fights with agents and promoters, and above all, a seeming contempt for his audience. . . .
>
> When I arrive at Miles' apartment, in an old brownstone on the West Side, there is the "Prince of Darkness" himself, wearing a black patch over one eye and playing drums to a James Brown record wailing from above. Miles tells the girl who lets me in to take me upstairs. . . . The girl (who I later learn is named Loretta) goes over to the bar. . . . By now a tall, friendly young woman named Ruby has come in.
>
> **—HARRIET CHOICE, CHICAGO TRIBUNE (1974)[95]**

Besides cars, clothes, and gorgeously appointed homes, playboy Davis also surrounded himself with women. As female journalist Harriet Choice shows, journalists often described the women Davis seemed to always have around him along with his other possessions. While Choice was more matter-of-fact about describing these women, male journalists tended to be more impressed with this aspect of Davis's hypermasculine lifestyle. As early as 1961, Davis's relation to women impressed Stanley Goldstein as he told *Playboy* readers, "In addition, a sizable percentage of the women in a Davis audience find his apparent unapproachability challengingly attractive, and I expect some vivid daydreaming goes on among many female listeners when Miles appears on the stand."[96] John Palcewski's 1969 *Cavalier* interview sums up another aspect of playboy Davis's relation to women in his public story. "A pretty Negro girl comes into the room and leans over and whispers something in Miles' ear . . . 'Bitches are all the same,' he says . . . 'Yeah, they're all the same,' he continues. 'Nothin' different about any of them.'"[97]

Miles Davis was known to use the B word in his everyday conversations in the 1950s and '60s. And the normalization of misogyny in the world of American music was evident with misogyny itself never being part of the Ill-Tempered Miles trope. This was even the case as Davis began to use the B word obsessively in interviews as he ramped up his self-presentation of hypermasculinity. He used the word as often as he used the word "white." The only criticism in his public story, until his infamous 1989 autobiography, of his use of the B word was more about his racism than his misogyny. While Leonard Feather in his 1972 *Penthouse* piece on Miles Davis noted the trumpeter's use of the term "white bitches," its ill-tempered nature is resolved into his supposed racism, not his clear misogyny. And overall, Feather once again revealed the standard reinterpretation of Davis that suggested more the badass, hypermasculine, hip race man than the race man as a politically astute observer of Jim Crow. "Miles Dewey Davis has learned as well as any musician alive how to make music, women, money, and headlines, not necessarily in that order of importance but probably in that chronological sequence. The various sobriquets he has acquired along the way—Prince of Darkness, Public Enigma No. 1—attest to his ability to build around himself an aura of cultism and mysticism."[98]

It is clear that for most white critics, journalists, and fans of Miles Davis, besides revering him for his amazing history of music making, they mostly lost, in their own translation of his attitudes, actions, and words, the importance of the *infra-politics* of this provocative race man during the reformation of a New Jim Crow America. What is important to note is how in the eyes of many African American men and women, Davis, *Ebony*'s "Evil Genius of Jazz," was viewed in a far different light. In a thoughtful reflection in the *New York Times* on the importance of Davis, the black poet Amiri Baraka wrote, with the help of a few black musicians, on the importance of Davis as an iconic race man for the African American community:

For many years of my life, Miles Davis was my ultimate culture hero: artist, cool man, bad dude, hipster, clear as daylight and funky as revelation. . . .

Few artists of my generation, whether writers, painters or dancers, do not know the trumpeter's work . . .

. . . Davis was not only the cool hipster of my be-bop youth, but also the embodiment of a black attitude that had grown steadily more ubiquitous in the 1950s—defiance. . . . "When I think of Davis's influence, I think he's had a positive influence on black people in general," says Steve McCall, drummer and elder statesmen of the new music. "He transcended the slave mentality." . . .

Davis, both in print and in person, seems a man not only anxious to be appreciated and celebrated by blacks, but sensitive to the tragedy of race in this country, particularly as it relates to his musical and social life.

—AMIRI BARAKA, NEW YORK TIMES (1985)[99]

Of course, Baraka, like most male critics and journalists, white or black, failed to note Davis's ill-tempered attitudes and behaviors toward women and the overt misogyny expressed in his hypermasculine race man pose. The normalization of misogyny in American music, arts, and entertainment ran across the race line in America. And the posing of hypermasculinity was not exclusively the gift of Bad Motherfucker Miles Davis. Hypermasculinity ran rampant in American jazz and popular music. But as Nichole T. Rustin argues in the case of Charles Mingus, black artists had the additional pressure to perform a far more constrained and fraught masculinity in American culture.[100] And Davis seemed to have succumbed to the power of this hypermasculinity, and its concomitant misogyny, more and more during his career and life. And it seemed to serve both his selfhood and iconic status well. This was until he fell into the black hole of hypermasculinity in his 1989 autobiography: the final encore in his public story and biographical legend.

The Dark Prince Returns: The Still Angry Race Man's Fall from Grace

Even the plethora of decidedly chilling rumors regarding his imprisonment of women for days on end during the dark endless nights of the seventies. Maybe they know him because of his single-handed elevation of the fifties black hipster to a realm of treacherous grace which, through his sartorial elegance, his fat, bright sports cars and beautiful statuesque ebony-skinned women friends, his feisty hyperactive persona, spelt out to all and sundry, *I'm not as good as you*

are. I'm better . . . Again, that overwhelming adamancy, that patented
I'm Miles Davis and you're not vehemence.
—NICK KENT, THE FACE (1986)[101]

British rock critic Nick Kent showed the continued power of Miles Davis's
dark persona and hypermasculinity in the final years of his career and life.
Davis remained a popular icon as well as demanding huge fees for his live
performances and winning Grammys for his record albums. While controversial autobiographies were nothing new in American culture, it would
be hard to find one that generated as much controversy as Davis's 1989 autobiography. The autobiography was mostly about his music making, and
he demonstrated a generous attitude toward the musicians he worked with
over his entire career. At certain points, he was critical of a few musicians or
recalled classic stories of his bouts with famous jazz musicians, but overall
a remarkable telling of his music making. But Davis remained the race man
provocateur. So, he peppered his autobiography with a litany of incendiary
rants about his drug addictions, his scrapes in the music industry, his run-
ins with the law, his view of white people, his anger about Jim Crow racism,
and his playboy lifestyle.

But the most striking aspect of his autobiography was the unapologetic
telling of his misogynistic views and behavior toward women, including
domestic violence. Davis seemed to have entered a black hole of hypermasculine rage, becoming almost a caricature of himself as the "Prince of
Darkness." As one outraged reviewer joked, "as self-inflicted wounds go, his
autobiography is a masterpiece. My only suggestion is that, given the relentless use of a certain 12-letter word, the title should have been Miles: The
Mfr . . ."[102] And many were outraged and disappointed in the once celebrated
race man whose voice they heard in this autobiography. Some reviewers and
critics simply ignored, or viewed as irrelevant, the motherfucker parts of
the autobiography and focused on the parts about his music making. But for
many reviewers and others, the motherfucker parts became the one encore
too many for the "evil genius" of jazz.

Miles Davis the race man provocateur and badass hipster presented in
the autobiography was not much different from the Davis revealed in his
interviews since the late 1960s when he vamped up his image as the "Prince
of Darkness." The lists of criticism on how racism pervaded his career and
life were certainly not new and were expressed as far back as his earliest
interviews in the late 1950s and early '60s. And many of the incidences in

his life involving racism, his onstage and offstage persona, his drug use, and his run-ins with the law had already been revealed in his public story. Even his long history of illness, his struggles with pain, and his addiction to pain-relieving alcohol and drugs emerged in his public story on his return to the music scene in 1981. New anecdotes and more details certainly appeared in the autobiography to add fuel to his fiery provocations. But for most reviewers, critics, and others familiar with Davis's public story, this part of his badass race man persona was not new.

> I mean, they're just fucking up everything because they're so fucking greedy. I'm talking about whites who are doing this, and they're doing it all over the world. . . .
>
> America is such a racist place, so racist it's pitiful. It's just like South Africa only more sanitized today; it's not as out in front in its racism. Other than that, it's the same thing. But I always have had a built-in thing for racism. I can smell it. I can feel it behind me, anywhere it is. And the way I am, a lot of whites really get mad with me, especially white men. They get even madder when I tell them off when they get out of line. They just think they can do any kind of shit to a black person here.
>
> —MILES DAVIS, MILES: THE AUTOBIOGRAPHY (1989)[103]

In his condensed package of badass-ness, Davis brought everything to the table in his autobiography, repeating the various claims and criticisms that brought accusations of Crow Jim racism since the 1950s. And once again Davis used the signifier "white" throughout the book. His general condemnation of white cultural appropriation, racism, and general mean-spiritedness irked some reviewers.[104] And he doubled down even more on how white rock musicians, like white jazz musicians before them, could not play the black music they stole as well as the true owners of race music. As Davis exclaimed, "I hate how white people always try to take credit for something after *they* discover it. Like it wasn't happening before they found out about it—which most times is always late, and they didn't have nothing to do with it happening. Then, they try to take *all* the credit, try to cut everybody black out."[105] What is clear in his criticisms was Davis was challenging the idea that anything had changed in American music. Or that the old Jim Crow ways had changed. But nothing had changed in Davis's view. The exploitation of black musicians and the cultural appropriation of black music by white musicians, critics, and fans remained a tried-and-true tradition in America.

And more importantly, Davis pointed to how the old Jim Crow racism and racial order had not disappeared in the New Jim Crow America. He refused to ignore the reality he saw every day of his life.

Miles Davis as the hip, hypermasculine race man also permeated his autobiography, from his history of drug and alcohol abuse, his parallel history of going cold turkey at crucial moments in his career, his uncontrollable anger, his bouts of violence, his obsession with boxing, his inability to drive a sports car safely, his run-ins with the law, to his high-spending playboy lifestyle. Davis reveled in his "Prince of Darkness" hipster mystique. But what truly stood out in the self-presentation of his hypermasculinity was the unapologetic, cold, heartless, and vicious treatment and views toward women. Davis certainly made references to women as "bitches" and paraded his women in front of journalists before this book. And on his 1981 return to the music scene, he talked about his pimping women during his heroin addiction in the early 1950s. But his autobiography was the first time he wove in detail the role of women in his biographical legend. And their role was clear, either they were the very few idealized women in his life, or they were obstacles to his art, objects of his desire, or targets of his misogyny.

What stood out most starkly was his unrepentant abuse of and violence against women closest to him, as well as supposedly women he hardly knew. Beginning with his own father slugging his mother through a locked glass door when Miles was a young boy to his own slapping of his wife Cicely Tyson in their Malibu home in the mid-1980s, his autobiography was unrepentant in his misogyny. He ended his autobiography with a final screed against black professional women he had encountered in his life, "then, you get mad and might hit them. I used to get in those situations a lot with pushy women and I used to hit a few."[106] Davis was clearly unashamed about the violence he inflicted on women throughout his life. As Davis biographer Jack Chambers wrote for the *Globe and Mail*, "His autobiography crowns this twilight of his career. . . . Davis always claimed to be brutally honest, with emphasis clearly on brutality. That brutality, no doubt abetted by the number of brain cells he has killed in the drug bouts he celebrates in the book, adds up to a pretty sleazy self-portrait. The style might be called self-inflicted tabloid journalism."[107]

> I almost didn't do the piece because I thought Miles Davis had put a hex on me. I thought somehow he had found out that I was writing a piece suggesting that *he is guilty of self-confessed violent crimes against women such that we should break his albums, burn his tapes, and scratch up his*

CDs until he acknowledges and apologizes and rethinks his position on The Woman Question.

—**PEARL CLEAGE, MAD AT MILES (1990)**[108]

The black female columnist and writer Pearl Cleage emerged as one of the most outspoken critics of Miles Davis. In her 1990 book on violence against black women, she passionately evoked Davis's autobiography as the ultimate in black male misogyny with his unrepentant tales of violence against women. As Cleage told the *Michigan Citizen*, "Miles Davis is a musical genius, but that doesn't excuse or explain his violence towards Black women. It's time to factor in the way our Black male heroes treat their sisters before we decide who deserves to be admired and who does not."[109] But while Davis's autobiography had an immediate negative impact on his reputation, it did little to hinder his career during the last two years of his life. Nor did it prevent his iconic stature of coolness from remaining a permanent fixture of American culture. This should not be surprising given the normalization of misogyny and male violence in American culture. Violence against women is not an uncommon trait among the male "heroes" in popular culture, from Frank Sinatra to John Lennon to Eminem, or from Charles Mingus to Ike Turner to Dr. Dre. Misogyny and male violence crosses all social groups, whether class, race, ethnicity, or religion. And it is this *normalization* of Davis and other famous males' misogyny, hypermasculinity, and violence toward women that remains as much a poison in America as the racism of the New Jim Crow.

Conclusion

For nearly half a century, critics have come up with all sorts of phrases to describe the darkness and light that is Miles Davis. Miles commanded attention from every generation since the early days of the cold war, fostering undying devotion and disgust along the way. Even in death he remains the most revered and reviled artist on the planet.

—**ROBIN D. G. KELLEY, NEW YORK TIMES (2001)**[110]

Black Historian Robin D. G. Kelley, in reflecting on Miles Davis, on what would have been the trumpeter's seventy-fifth birthday, made another foray into what historian Sherrie Tucker calls Miles Davis studies.[111] Miles Davis studies is the attempt to reconcile in jazz histories the positive rebelliousness of hip black masculinity with the negative consequences of its misogyny and homophobia. Kelley decides to unite the supposed warring sides of the cool and the dark Davis through what he calls the "pimp aesthetic" in black culture. My intention is not to delve into this argument, but only to highlight that Kelley is not the first to discuss the role of pimp in performances and self-conceptions of the hip and the hypermasculine. Besides, Davis himself claimed to pimp off women during his days of heroin addiction in the early 1950s. My intention is to use this analogy of the pimp to return to the argument that the infra-politics of blackness in jazz and popular culture cannot be easily separated from questions of gender and sexuality in a culture obsessed with the sexualization and objectification of people of color.[112] And in vacillating between playboy and pimp, already racially coded in white and black in the 1950s and '60s, Davis succumbed to his own complicity in performing these roles. As Clyde Taylor argues, "like other mythogenic people, Black men are, as if in self-defense, prolific generators of self-descriptive legends."[113]

Greg Tate, in his 1991 *Village Voice* memorial to Miles Davis, pointed to a more challenging and compelling conflict in understanding this icon: the irreconcilable conflict between the celebrated unreconstructed race man who refused to defer to the racial etiquette of Jim Crow America in his attitudes, behaviors, and proclamations and the ugly hypermasculine hipster who celebrated his deviant and misogynistic behavior. As Tate wrote, "As much as I love Miles, I despised him after reading about those incidents. . . . I'd loathe any muffukuh who violated women the way he did and relished having the opportunity to tell the world about it. Miles may have swung like a champion, but on that score, he went out like a roach."[114] Like Tate, my intention is not to reconcile these two Miles Davises. And like Tate, I certainly do not intend to excuse the misogynistic Miles Davis. Davis's misogyny is ultimately inexcusable as it is in any male in America.

The ultimate tragedy, however, is the normalization of misogyny in American popular culture and the dynamics of hypermasculinity, black or white, that reinforces or naturalizes this misogyny up to the present. I can say that it is mostly, although not exclusively, African Americans who have grappled with this tragic contradiction in the life and public story of Miles Davis, and in the cool pose more generally. Jazz studies more recently has grappled with questions of hypermasculinity and the white racial imagination. But in the public story of American music and popular culture, this is far less the case. In the popular white racial imagination, the dark side of black hipness and cool—the racialized and gendered construction of cool—still seems less important than the rebellious, nonconforming, virile reinterpretation of cool. Three recent works on cool, Lewis MacAdams's 2001 *Birth of the Cool*, John Leland's 2004 *Hip: The History*, and Joel Dinerstein's 2017 *The Origins of Cool in Postwar America*, all begin by eliciting Miles Davis and discuss him at length.[115] Yet they never mention the dark-side of Davis's ill temper or misogyny, or the problems of hypermasculinity, or the white racial imagination in American cool. In fact, unlike Kelley, Leland does not even see the problem of misogyny in his celebration of the pimp-player aesthetic in cool.

> To those who knew him, Miles was an enigma, a seemingly impenetrable self, a self that retreated the closer one got to him. Even with the distance of time, he resists interpretation as tenaciously as some cool-surfaced character from a novel by Alain Robbe-Grillet.... He offered whites and blacks alike entrée to what they took to be a certain kind of blackness.
> —JOHN SZWED, SO WHAT: THE LIFE AND TIMES
> OF MILES DAVIS (2002)[116]

So, a lot has been *lost in translation* in the reinterpretation of Miles Davis. The terrible irony is that the two contradictory Davises Greg Tate attempts to grapple with, the unreconstructed race man provocateur and the unapologetic hypermasculine misogynist, seem to have been lost in the white imaginary memory of the coolest icon in American history. If Davis remains an enigma and icon of blackness for whites and blacks alike, as jazz studies scholar John Szwed argues, it is through very different racial imaginations. Much as scholars and critics have grappled with the politics of hip-hop culture up to the present, which contains the same contradictions of race men provocateurs and cool black hypermasculinity, so we need to contend with this contradiction in jazz history and the life and career of Davis. But as much as Davis fell into a black hole of hypermasculinity, he also shaped a public story as a race man who refused to defer to the racial etiquette that permeated his life or be silent about the oppression of Jim Crow and New Jim Crow America. That his last recorded studio album, *Doo-Bop*, linked his own birth as an artist with the burgeoning hip-hop movement in title and music, is testament to Davis remaining connected to the heartbeat of African American cultural resistance—both the good and the bad. To grapple with Davis's public story is to grapple with the most crucial issues still facing America and the African American community today.

Martin Scorsese

A SOJOURN FROM ITALIAN AMERICAN TO WHITE ETHNIC AMERICAN[1]

> We are an odd couple, Marty and I, I grew up in a placid suburb of Milwaukee, Wisconsin, cosseted by my middle-class family—loving, indulgent, always avoiding openly expressed emotions. . . . Marty's young years were, of course, the opposite, spent mainly in Little Italy on New York's Lower East Side—working class, but also criminal class, with the Mafia providing much of the neighborhood's half-hidden social organization and control. There was an element of danger on—well, yes, all right—the Mean Streets of his boyhood. . . . In talking with him I've often felt we are like immigrants from two different countries meeting on neutral ground and discovering that we can communicate in a third language: the language of film.
>
> —RICHARD SCHICKEL, CONVERSATIONS WITH SCORSESE (2011)[2]

What first struck me reading film critic Richard Schickel's introduction to *Conversations with Scorsese* was the year it was published. In 2011, how were American-born Martin Scorsese and Richard Schickel like immigrants from different countries? Scorsese certainly had emphasized his Italian American roots since his early years as a filmmaker. And Schickel only mimicked Scorsese's own musings about his youth in a Little Italy full of wise guys.

But one significant change had occurred by 2011. This once fervently self-identified Italian American had become a self-identified white ethnic. Now the struggles of Irish immigrants in *Gangs of New York* (2002), Irish American wise guys and cops in *The Departed* (2006), or multiethnic criminals in *Boardwalk Empire* (2010–14) resonated as much with Scorsese as the young punks from Little Italy in his first critically acclaimed film *Mean Streets* (1973). And while German American Schickel viewed himself and Scorsese like immigrants from foreign lands, they had more than film in common. They both shared an identity as white ethnic Americans. The very recognition of their ethnic roots pointed to what Matthew Frye Jacobson calls a new "hyphen-nationalism" at the end of the twentieth century: an identification of European ethnics as sharing and defining the American experience.[3]

This chapter explores Martin Scorsese's evolution in his public story from a strongly identified Italian American to a more broadly identified white ethnic American. This public story—in films, books, television, radio, journals, and newspapers—has been told by various storytellers, including critics and journalists as well as Scorsese. No contemporary Hollywood director, however, has contributed as significantly to his own public story. Similar to how Alfred Hitchcock contributed to his rise as a celebrated auteur, Scorsese has shaped the reception of his films through an active and constant construction of his *biographical legend*.[4] Scorsese emerged as a director and public figure when auteur theory dominated film criticism. While Marc Raymond argues that Scorsese's artistic choices and public image purposefully constructed his artistic reputation as a director, I argue that his biographical legend as an Italian American was just as crucial to his reception as a celebrated Hollywood auteur.[5] The connection between biography, social history, cinematic tradition, and his films defined Scorsese's auteur brand as a filmmaker committed to creating not only aesthetically sophisticated films but also deeply personal, honest, and authentic films. The consistency of this connection for six decades—from the 1960s to the present decade—suggests how powerful this framing was for both Scorsese and others.

For most of his career, Scorsese was a self-created talisman of the Italian American experience. Scorsese's public story constantly shifted from authentic expressions, to exotic stereotypes, to Hollywood clichés of Italian America. Scorsese's public story and films fed into a popular fascination with Italian Americans.[6] Scorsese cast such a powerful spell as an Italian American that his narrative transformation into a white ethnic points to the power of hyphen-nationalism during this period. The White Ethnic myth acted to resolve certain ambiguities in Scorsese's public story. This story began with

Scorsese, as a working-class Italian American, revealing the false promises of the American Dream. Later, however, the story shifts to Scorsese, as an internationally acclaimed American filmmaker, celebrating white ethnics' struggle toward, and eventual realization of, the American Dream. Weaving through Scorsese's evolution into a white ethnic American was an obsession with a hypermasculinity intimately linked to the performance of ethnicity in his films. While Scorsese's biographical legend spoke little to *his* masculinity, except, as Laura Mulvey would argue, in his masculine command of the camera and male gaze,[7] as an auteur director he was constantly returning to portrayals of hypermasculine protagonists and other hypermasculine characters that often led to controversial receptions in his public story.

For many critics, Scorsese's films, more than any other contemporary filmmaker's, present a singular vision of America.[8] What is quite striking, however, is how Scorsese's vision evolved so closely along the path charted by Matthew Frye Jacobson and David R. Roediger in their analysis of how European immigrants in the twentieth century transformed into white ethnics.[9] Jacobson also points to a transformation from an American foundational myth based on Plymouth Rock to one based on Ellis Island.[10] As we will see, however, Scorsese's transformation was from the myth of Little Italy to the myth of Ellis Island. His public story charts the evolution of the 1960s ethnic revival into the hyphen-nationalism at the end of the twentieth century. It shows how the "unmeltable" European ethnic American of the revival became the white ethnic American of a new nationalism. It also shows how parallel to this evolution in American racial ideology was an equally powerful and problematic evolution in gender ideology and hegemonic masculinity tied to the racial imagination of male white ethnic Americans. The shadow of Scorsese's transformation is how the collective telling in the public story of such a critically acclaimed artist transcoded a mythology of white ethnicity and expressions of hegemonic masculinity. Such a shadow is testament to the power in the institutional and cultural regime of hyphen-nationalism and hegemonic masculinity in the United States that obscures in memory, creative imagination, critical appreciation, and art the power and legacy of white male privilege.

Being Ethnic and White in America

This chapter is based on work in race and ethnic studies, critical whiteness studies, and critical rhetoric studies. Scorsese's public story is first a case study of the transformation of white ethnic identity to white racial identity in the *racial formation* of the United States at the end of the twentieth century.[11] In race and ethnic studies, Richard D. Alba and Mary C. Waters were the first to recognize the beginnings of such a transition.[12] Leading into the final decade of the last century, Alba predicted that changes in educational, occupational, marriage, and community patterns that previously promoted singular European ethnic identities during the ethnic revival of the 1960s and 1970s were leading to a new multiethnic "European American" identity with its own myths of "its place in American history and the American identity."[13] White ethnics retained an identification with their ethnic backgrounds such as Italian American, but they were doing it within a broader European American white racial identity.[14] And this new identity as a white ethnic only gained strength into the twenty-first century.

This study shows how such a "possessive investment" in white racial identity and hyphen-nationalism has worked to mask white privilege in the United States under the rhetorical guise of multicultural and color-blind ideologies.[15] Scorsese's public story is a *liberal* version of multicultural and color-blind hyphen-nationalism.[16] It is an example of what Eduardo Bonilla-Silva calls "abstract liberal" color-blind ideology.[17] This liberal version recognizes that racism persists in America and must be combated, but ignores the deep-seated nature of institutional racism and the persistence of white privilege. Scorsese's public story also confirms how *whiteness* is not a clearly delineated, coherent, or stable form of social identity, cultural distinction, or political ideology. Instead, *whiteness* is a multifaceted, contradictory, intersectional, and constantly morphing identity and ideology.[18] This story also shows, however, how *whiteness*, even in its various shape-shifting forms, "reproduces white power and privilege, while simultaneously denying its existence."[19]

Scorsese's public story is compelling when investigating white ethnic and racial identity in a number of ways. Scorsese emerges as a *public intellectual* in the early 1970s when Hollywood film is first recognized by artists, critics, and audiences as not just pure entertainment but as an expression of the unique vision and/or biography of a director. And no other director of Scorsese's generation embraced the role of autobiographical director more than he. His public story, therefore, represents the intersection of film, criticism, history, and *biography* in a public intellectual's struggle to "recuperate, reconstitute and restore" his white identity.[20] This struggle crisscrosses multiple sites in multiple narrative forms in films, documentaries, reviews, interviews, award ceremonies, and so on. This public story reflects the personal and artistic journey of Scorsese as well as the *collective* rendition of this journey by Scorsese, critics, journalists, and others. My presentation of Scorsese's public story, therefore, is not intended to judge him, but to situate this artist within a broader collective renditioning of race and ethnicity across different discursive fields that was clearly transcoded by him and many other voices in his public story. It presents a compelling case study in critical rhetoric studies in showing how public intellectuals, with Scorsese as a main interlocutor, have constructed whiteness around a collective narrative about the films, biography, and passions of the most celebrated American filmmaker of the last fifty years.

Scorsese as Public Intellectual and New Hollywood Italian American Directors

No other Hollywood director has so actively attached autobiographical and sociohistorical narratives to their films, career, and life than Scorsese. Scorsese was not only an acclaimed filmmaker but also a major *public intellectual*. Scorsese's public story, unlike any other Italian American director of his generation, synergistically linked a fictional account of American history and the Italian American experience with a nonfictional public accounting of his autobiography and the American experience. This connection between autobiography, social history, and his filmmaking, as well as Scorsese's encyclopedic knowledge of film history and aesthetics, defined Scorsese's auteur brand. Scorsese's oeuvre has been more than his films. It has included the extensive narrative he has woven for six decades about his life, films, and the Italian American and American experience.

The Italian American directors who joined Scorsese during the 1960s and 1970s New Hollywood revolution were Francis Ford Coppola, Michael Cimino, Brian De Palma, and Abel Ferrara. None of these other directors present as compelling a case study in terms of the *explicit* importance of their ethnic identity and biographies in their public stories, the *explicit* importance of the sociohistorical contexts of their films in their public stories, or their *self-identification* as public intellectuals. No other director's public story significantly linked their Italian American identity and autobiography to their films and careers as consistently as Scorsese's public story from 1969 to the present. None of these directors have explicitly highlighted in their public story the sociohistorical significance of their films over this same period. And finally, no other director has maintained a presence as a public intellectual over the same period. In other words, Scorsese's films and public image as a filmmaker and public intellectual have stood out as quite unique for his, or for that matter any, generation of American filmmakers.

Francis Ford Coppola stands out with his fame as the director of the Godfather trilogy. But these were his only films about the Italian American experience. And Coppola's public story emphasized his distance from the world inhabited in these films as an Italian American who grew up in a middle-class family.[21] In fact, in his public story, he only accepted directing the first Godfather film because he needed the money.[22] In Coppola's public story, the intimate connection between autobiography, ethnic identity, and filmmaking has not been a major theme. His biographical legend has focused on the tragic tale of an auteur filmmaker's struggle against the ignorance of the Hollywood establishment.[23]

Brain De Palma and Michael Cimino did not self-identify in their public stories as Italian American filmmakers, nor did they incorporate the Italian American experience significantly in their films. De Palma waited over a decade, and over ten films, before making the Italian American gangster comedy *Wise Guys* in 1986. And his more acclaimed gangster films, *Scarface* (1983) and *Carlito's Way* (1993), were based on Latino characters, and *The Untouchables* (1987) was centered on FBI agent Eliot Ness. And while Abel Ferrara has made films centered on Italian Americans, including *China Girl* (1987), *Dangerous Game* (1993), and *The Funeral* (1996), his limited public story has emphasized his rebel stance as an exploitation film director, not his Italian American background.

What is striking in Scorsese's public story is the continued relevance of his Italian American identity, even as he shifted to a more shared white racial identity as a white ethnic. Robert Casillo points out how Coppola, De Palma, Ferrara, and Scorsese's interest in Italian America in their post-1990 films significantly diminished.[24] But Casillo is focused on their films and the Italian American experience. So, while Scorsese's films since *Casino* (1995) no longer showed a concern with presenting the Italian American experience, unlike his fellow Italian American directors, his public story, including his films, continued to elicit his Italian American identity, but now in relation to a shared European American experience. Scorsese is unique in the power of his ethnic identity, autobiography, and sociohistorical vision as filmmaker and public intellectual that makes his case study a perfect lens into the evolution of the White Ethnic myth in the American imagination from the 1960s up to the present.

Scorsese's Public Story I: The Kid from Little Italy

> Were it not for Scorsese's insatiable appetite for movies, however, it is conceivable that he would be dwelling today down on Elizabeth Street, where his parents were born and still live and where he himself grew up—a frail, asthmatic boy doing his best to keep pace with one of Little Italy's more rambunctious gangs.
> —GUY FLATLEY, NEW YORK TIMES (1973)[25]

Martin Scorsese's public story began in 1969 by introducing the world to a young Italian American director whose film, *Who's That Knocking at My Door* (1969), had an "Italian-American milieu" clearly based on "first-hand experience."[26] With Scorsese's *Mean Streets* (1973), the *New York Times* introduced readers to details of this young filmmaker's childhood in Little Italy. Over time, his public story expanded on his youthful life experiences and his early passion for film. In this story, Scorsese was born to be a filmmaker with memories reaching back to a four-year-old kid in a dark theater mesmerized by the Hollywood classic *Duel in the Sun* (1946). Making films, we were told, was his passion and salvation. A passion and salvation linked in Scorsese's public story ultimately to his life as the quintessential *Italian American* filmmaker.

> It wasn't until 1950, when he was 7, that his father had a fight with the landlord and the family moved in with his grandparents on Elizabeth Street, in Manhattan's Little Italy. That's where the asthmatic little boy sat by the third-story window and gazed down at the grocery stores and the bums stumbling over from the Bowery and at the local tough guys, of course. . . . And when the boy later was able to make films himself, he began with his own version of home movies, re-creating what he'd seen framed out that window.
> —PAUL LIEBERMAN, LOS ANGELES TIMES (2002)[27]

Scorsese's public story reads like a *made in Hollywood* biopic. In 2002, Paul Lieberman repeated the same story told over a quarter century earlier by Guy Flatley. Scorsese as an *Italian American* filmmaker remained a central trope for over thirty years. Scorsese contributed extensively to this biography. And as a kid from Little Italy, he had a strong Italian American identity. And while his public story emerged when the ethnic revival reimagined the European ethnic in America, all the scholarship points to how an individual with his background—urban working class, living in an ethnic enclave—would *feel* Italian American not by choice, but experience.[28] But what is equally clear, is being an urban, working-class Italian American was part of Scorsese's success as a filmmaker. It was an asset, not a liability.[29] Scorsese's self-identity as an Italian American led his public story, including his films, to resonate with the symbolic ethnicity that conservative Michael Novak in 1972 celebrated in *The Rise of the Unmeltable Ethnics*.[30] Scorsese was clearly an unmeltable Italian American for at least thirty years.

In his public story, virtually every aspect of Scorsese's career brings us back to his youth in Little Italy. As Les Keyser put it, "Scorsese's adult fixation with punishment and redemption, with suffering and acceptance, and with salvation through physical sacrifice, so manifest in *Raging Bull*, *Taxi Driver*, and *The Last Temptation of Christ*, has its roots in his own rites of passage in an urban jungle."[31] And if not his youth, aspects of his art are connected in some fashion to his personal life. All of Scorsese's films are *personal*. Scorsese has even pointed to his most commercial films, *Alice Doesn't Live Here Anymore* (1974), *Color of Money* (1986), and *Cape Fear* (1991), as still being personal. As Scorsese said in the *New York Times* in 1985, "People have said I make personal films. . . . How can I make a movie that isn't?"[32] It is the *personal* that also makes Scorsese an independent, creative filmmaker and not a Hollywood hack. So as Scorsese told *Playboy*'s David Rensin in 1991, "I've *always* tried to blend 'personal' movies with inside the industry."[33] The personal nature of his art, of course, was always inexorably conjoined to his identity as an Italian American.

> Scorsese owes much to cinema. It led him to discover a world other than that of his "crowd" and the Mafia; it helped him move out of their paralyzing clutches and beyond their hysterical taboos; finally, it provided him with a means for self-expression there where his friends remained caught in the codes and modes of behavior of the streets.
>
> —MICHAEL HENRY, POSITIF (1975)[34]

Film in Scorsese's public story was his salvation. This story constantly refers to two stereotypical paths—the priesthood or the mafia—as the only options for a young male from Little Italy. Richard Combs repeats this trope in his 1981 review of *Raging Bull* (1980), "Romantically, the options facing the young Scorsese have been summed up as: priest or Mafioso. Instead, he made movies, sublimating the other two."[35] Such claims were quite remarkable given the fact that Scorsese's immediate family, most of Little Italy, and a vast majority of working-class Italian Americans did not work for organized crime or the church. Yet Scorsese himself perpetuated this theme. As he told Michael Henry (Wilson) in 1974, "When you grow up in Little Italy, what are you going to be other than a gangster or a priest?"[36] For Scorsese, film became his route out of Little Italy.

Themes of the mafia and church were in the reviews of Scorsese's films. With his first two feature films based in Little Italy, reviewers saw these films as a window into a world unfamiliar to their readers. Jeremy Janes viewed 1968's *Who's That Knocking at My Door* as an honest effort "to examine thoroughly the specific spiritual hazards with the Italian American life style."[37] For many reviewers, *Mean Streets* (1973) acted as an authentic anecdote to Coppola's romanticized epic of the Italian American experience in *The Godfather* (1972). Paul Zimmerman wrote, "Scorsese has obviously reached deep into his own life and mind to paint the underside of the *Godfather* world, a dark, grimy, violent cul-de-sac which grinds its young men to powder between the rigid codes of the church and the street."[38] David Denby pointed out that "*Mean Streets* shows what *The Godfather* left out—the neighbourhood chiselers, loan sharks and screw-ups who prey on their own community and each other, sucking money out of ordinary people, hustling for ten-dollar bills."[39]

The authenticity critics celebrated, however, sometimes veered into exotic voyeurism, like critic Kevin Thomas's review of *Mean Streets*: "Scorsese plunges us into the dank, self-enclosed world of back alleys, red-neoned (and therefore inferno-like) taverns and dreary tenement apartments—an insidiously corrupt world in which frustration frequently erupts into violence."[40] Or as critic Tom Milne wrote, "we are taken on a tour of the no-exit hell of Little Italy, where every avenue of escape is blocked either by the meanness of the streets themselves or by the pressures of family obligations. . . . Held in precarious balance with the struggle for survival of the mean streets, and never for one moment acknowledging the sound of the death-rattle, Italian religion, honour and family display a serene façade of solidarity."[41] Clearly, Milne forgot that Scorsese actually made an exit from the "no-exit hell" known as Little Italy.

Scorsese worked hard to convey the authenticity of his films. In 1972, he told Jeremy Janes that his film *Who's That Knocking at My Door* (1969), was "about Italian Americans. . . . The church and sex, especially. . . . And the Adoration and Worship of the Mafia, without ever really getting it."[42] Scorsese rarely qualified the Little Italy tropes of mean streets and the church. For example, he did tell the *Los Angeles Times* in 1974 that he got "into the streets, even into a gang, 'but it wasn't heavy with us, like the *Mean Streets* characters, it was mostly social: We drank lots of wine, hung out on corners, picked up girls. . . . We never dealt drugs or hot goods or ran numbers like real hoods.'"[43] And he further admitted to the *New York Times*'s Guy Flatley in 1973 that "the majority of people in Little Italy are hardworking, decent people."[44]

In Scorsese's public story, it was exceedingly rare to read criticism of the portrayal of the Italian American experience found in his biography and films. There were a few early critical articles such as Foster Hirsch's review of *Mean Streets*. "Scorsese's characters, at any rate, are ethnic stereotypes; stage Italians as predictable and as overstated in their flamboyant gestures and earthy speech as stage Irish or stage Jews."[45] But most criticism appeared in the Italian American community[46] and barely made it into the public story outside this community. Most critics and journalists, like Andrew M. Greeley, viewed Scorsese's work as a rare exception of authentic portrayal. "No American artist since James T. Farrell has understood as well as Scorsese what neighborhood loyalties mean to ethnic groups. . . . 'Mean Streets' is not a pretty movie and some Italian American leaders were offended by it. They should not have been. It was a work of art that I believe could only have been what it was if it came out of the Italian immigrant experience."[47]

Crime and church have remained a trope in Scorsese's public story to the present. Mark Kermode noted in 2010, "Growing up among 'gangsters and priests,' Scorsese outdid even *Godfather* director Francis Ford Coppola as the definitive cinematic chronicler of the American underworld with his hard-hitting movies."[48] And while his acclaimed mob genre films—*Mean Streets* (1973), *Goodfellas* (1990), *Casino* (1995), and *Departed* (2006)—significantly shaped the ongoing reception of his work in his public story, virtually all his films somehow reflected his youth as an Italian American. While Scorsese left the church during his college years, the Catholic magazine *America* still commented in 2007, "Whatever his current religious beliefs may be, Scorsese is one of the most Catholic of artists, whose oeuvre paints a convincing portrait of the effects of sin, grace and redemption."[49] His early Catholicism and its lingering spiritual questions are even linked to aspects of Tibetan Buddhist Dali Lama's life in Scorsese's *Kundun* (1997).[50] Scorsese's Catholicism continues to define him in his films and public story. In an extensive interview with the filmmaker in the *New York Times* in anticipation of his film *Silence* (2016), a film about the persecution of Catholic Jesuits in Japan he passionately wanted to make for twenty-eight years, Paul Elie noted, "from the beginning, he has revealed himself to be an artist of intensely

Catholic preoccupations, and the poisoned arrow of religious conflict runs straight through his career."[51]

Scorsese's public story also speaks to his liminal position as an urban, working-class Italian American. Scorsese was born in 1942. At the time, his family lived in the neighborhood of Corona in Queens, New York. In his public story, Scorsese remembers the trauma when at seven he moved back to Elizabeth Street in Manhattan's Little Italy where his mother and father were born thirty years earlier. His father was forced, due to financial troubles, to return to his old neighborhood. Scorsese remembers the "suburban" Queens neighborhood of green backyards with trees and safe streets compared to the scarier streets of Little Italy. From the broken promises of Corona to the mean streets of Little Italy, Scorsese remained a strongly self-identified urban, working-class Italian American.

Most critics view Scorsese's films of American life as unromantic, dark views of American society. As Ellis Cashmore notes, "The American Dream and the way it motivates the quest not so much for money but for the type of 'success' money represents is obviously dominant in Scorsese's America. . . . In fact, everybody's endeavor ends up in tears. This is an America that, for all its democratic ideology and Christian doctrine, upholds a culture in which the vast majority of those who chase the Dream will be broken by it."[52] The dark side of the American Dream was prominent in his films about Italian American life from *Mean Streets* to *Raging Bull* to *Goodfellas* to *Casino*, although the dream is never an uplifting tale of self-made success for Scorsese's male protagonists all the way to a more recent film like *The Wolf of Wall Street* (2013). This warped American dream is always a path riddled by violence, corruption, obsession, amorality, betrayal, and often sociopathic drives. As critic Michiko Kakutani wrote in 1983, "One of the things that Mr. Scorsese has captured best in his films is a sense of American life—not so much life lived in the mainstream, but life lived on the margins, where the promises of the Dream seem both alluring and elusive."[53]

Scorsese's America, however, is a white-male-centered world of marginality, broken dreams, and violent masculinity. The lone exceptions were two early films, *Boxcar Bertha* (1972) and *Alice Doesn't Live Here Anymore* (1974), both of which were not personal projects, and the latter film he did to win favor with Hollywood.[54] Jonathan J. Cavallero points to how Scorsese does not present a sentimental view of the Italian American community, but a critical view of its insularity, limited horizons, violence, and bigotry.[55] But Larissa M. Ennis shows how such entrapment only highlights how in Scorsese's gangster films, and I would argue all his films about the Italian

American experience, the white ethnic male characters remain marginal to the mainstream. These "off-white ethnics are 'others,' victims rather than villains of racial/ethnic discrimination"[56] But in Scorsese's public story, we see how Scorsese is also constructing *himself* as an "off-white" protagonist in a much broader narrative. He is not simply like other filmmakers of his generation applying genre conventions to create the off-white gangster.[57] He has linked *personal biography* with *narrative conventions* to create a greater verisimilitude between his films and the Italian American experience. His films gain a greater "epistemic authority" through the larger rhetorical narrative in his public story of the *personal* and the *creative*.[58] The "off-white" director, who had only the mafia and the church as his limited horizons, was blessed by his passion for film to avoid the terrible fates his "off-white" real-life friends and fictional protagonists faced as "unmeltable ethnics" shutout from a WASP monopolized American Dream.

A number of scholars have pointed to how the authenticity of Scorsese's films has been questionable as well as problematic in terms of representing the Italian American experience.[59] And the social and historical accuracy of a film's narrative or characters, as opposed to its visual representation of a period or place, has never been a major goal in Hollywood.[60] This chapter, however, is not about the validity or authenticity of Scorsese's films, but about how Scorsese and others in his public story laid claim to such authenticity in his vision of the Italian American community and American society. This essay shows how Scorsese's public story was a major influence on "feeling" Italian in American popular culture during the ethnic revival. But the ethnic revival was more than just a popular culture phenomenon or individual foray into symbolic ethnicity. It also was part of a regime embedded in the culture industry, civic organizations, academia, and government.[61] For example, Scorsese's documentary *Italianamerican* (1974) was underwritten by the National Endowment for the Humanities for the 1976 Bicentennial. It was this regime that set the path for Scorsese's transformation at the turn of this century from an Italian American to a white ethnic who embraced a new hyphen-nationalism in the American imagination.

Scorsese's Public Story II: The New Immigrant and the American Experience

Like many of his films, "Gangs" has its roots, Scorsese says, in stories that "came out of the cobblestone." During his Elizabeth Street days, he sometimes found refuge in nearby St. Patrick's Cathedral, built

in 1809. It struck him that the name didn't sound Italian at all, and his schoolboy questions led to tales of "the people that came before us." One told how early Irish immigrants once massed in front of the cathedral to repel a mob of Know Nothings, the "nativists" who despised the riffraff fleeing Ireland's potato famine. Scorsese decided that his neighborhood showdown marked "the acceptance of what America's supposed to be . . . letting in the immigrants."
—PAUL LIEBERMAN, LOS ANGELES TIMES (2002)[62]

Scorsese's public story changed in the first years of this century. This change was not simply in the ideas he expressed but in a revision of his past to fit his new preoccupations. Scorsese makes clear to Paul Lieberman that *Gangs of New York* (2002)—a film about Irish immigrants in mid-nineteenth-century New York City—was a very *personal* story. It was a story that resonated not only with tales told in his youth but also with the stone masonry of his local church. It was a tale of the struggles and successes of European immigrants of the nineteenth and early twentieth centuries that in his story formed the foundation of the very buildings, streets, and people of New York City. It was the American experience writ large. As Scorsese reiterated eight years later in an interview about this neighborhood, "There's something about the cobblestones, the walls, and the nature of the buildings. . . . There was something about that area that was just reeking with story, not just the sanitized ones, this was really how the people lived and suffered and struggled— immigrants, coming to New York and settling there."[63]

Scorsese's public story had recurring anecdotes and themes that linked his personal life to his filmmaking. A good example is Saint Patrick's Cathedral mentioned in his interview with Paul Lieberman. Until 2002, this church in his public story represented Catholicism as a core part of his filmmaking. As late as 1998, Scorsese in a *Newsweek* essay dedicated two paragraphs to Saint Patrick's and how its Catholic iconology and theatricality influenced his sense of filmmaking.[64] There was no mention in over thirty years of his public story of Saint Patrick's cobblestones radiating stories of early Irish immigrants. This theme of stories *in his youth* about "the people that came before us" first appeared right before the premiere of *Gangs of New York*.

At around the age of seven or eight I became aware of an older history to the Manhattan neighborhood I grew up in. . . . Though my neighborhood was then an Italian American area, there were indications to a young person that it hadn't always been.

—MARTIN SCORSESE, INTERVIEW (2003)[65]

Even Scorsese's iconic Italian American Little Italy was transformed into a multiethnic tale. In the past, Scorsese mentioned how Little Italy was surrounded by neighborhoods populated by other ethnics and minorities. But like the Italian American communities in his earlier films, the Lower East Side was not portrayed as a melting-pot paradise in his public story. As he told the *New York Times* in 1973, "It's the ghetto that creates prejudice. . . . My brother took a look at him, and then turned to me and said, 'Oh, he's only a dirty Jew.' And that is one of my earliest memories. . . . We hated the Irish too."[66] But by 2003, Scorsese's memories changed. He told radio host Terry Gross that moving to Manhattan's Lower East Side as a child made "such a strong impression—so many cultures thrown together, so many religions, so fascinating. . . . So, this was the city for me, the center of a world that way."[67] In his public story, the theme of a multiethnic Lower East Side was replacing the theme of Italian American Little Italy.

Scorsese's revised public story also expressed identification with the experience of European ethnics. In his public story, Scorsese had discussed certain films in his youth and college years that had a deep impression on him. In 1995, he introduced a new film to his story. In *A Personal Journey with Martin Scorsese through American Movies* (1995), Scorsese introduced Elia Kazan's *America, America* (1963) as an influential film. "I'm often reminded of Kazan's film *America, America*, the story of his uncle's journey from Anatolia to America, the story of so many immigrants who came to this country from a very, very foreign land. I kind of identified with it. I was very moved by it."[68] This film was about the journey to America by persecuted Turkish Greeks at the turn of the nineteenth century. Scorsese's public story now pointed to his viewing this film in the 1960s as a college student. More important is how he claimed to identify with the Greek immigrant experience. The theme of identifying with other white ethnics also appeared in reference to another Elia Kazan film, *On the Waterfront* (1954). As Scorsese wrote in *Rolling Stone* in 2003, "In *On the Waterfront*, Marlon Brando's name may have been Terry Malloy, but for me he was an Italian American from the Lower East Side."[69] Scorsese now linked his Italian American experience with the history of the Irish and other white ethnics in America.

This transition in self-identity in his public story is telling in two ways. First, Irish American and other white ethnic main characters certainly appeared in Scorsese's earlier films, in particular *New York, New York* (1977), *Goodfellas* (1990), and *Casino* (1995). But these films were not set in Irish American or other white ethnic communities. In Scorsese's public story, *New York, New York* was an homage to the Hollywood musical. That the film's main character, Johnny Doyle, was Irish American was not critical to the story.[70] And the importance of Irish American Jimmy Conway in *Good-fellas* and Jewish American Sam Rothstein in *Casino* was their outsider status in the Italian American–dominated worlds portrayed in these films. The shift in self-identification with Irish Americans and other white ethnics in his films *and* public story only began with the 1995 reference to Elia Kazan's *America, America* and the premier of *Gangs of New York* in 2002. And second, while this transformation was later evident in Scorsese's crime films and television shows—*The Departed* (2006), *Boardwalk Empire* (2010–14), and *The Wolf of Wall Street* (2013)—now populated by an equal opportunity off-white ethnic criminal class,[71] the film *Gangs of New York* would signal a more significant rhetorical twist as the transformation from a white ethnic identity to a white racial identity was linked to an emerging color-blind hyphen-nationalism.

In Scorsese's revised public story, ever since he picked up Herbert Asbury's *Gangs of New York* while house-sitting in 1970, he dreamed of making a film about the nineteenth-century gang life depicted in this book. Like his other passionate project, *The Last Temptation of Christ* (1989), this film had been a *personal* mission delayed for a long time. *The Last Temptation*, however, was mentioned in his public story years before its release in 1989, while no mention was ever made in his public story about his quest to make *Gangs*. In 2002, a film about Irish immigrants suddenly became Scorsese's longest personal project. As Gavin Smith wrote, "For veteran Martin Scorsese, *Gangs of New York* has been a long, long road . . . and it took two decades of frustrated attempts before he was finally able to get his long-cherished project off the ground."[72] It is quite striking how such a passionate project—and Scorsese's identification with the Irish American experience—never surfaced in the public story of this Italian American until the year of the film's release in 2002.

> Having said all that, what fascinates me about the beginnings of large-scale immigration is how it tested the values America was supposed to embody. . . . But with the Irish coming into America, as I said, the values the country was supposed to represent were tested for the first time . . . blacks were attacked in the Streets of New York, so the racism in the film is pretty strong. The melting-pot idea began to emerge with the arrival of the Irish in the 1840s. . . . and this "nativism" becomes the film's political basis.
>
> **—MARTIN SCORSESE WITH IAN CHRISTIE, SIGHT AND SOUND (2003)[73]**

Scorsese in *Sight and Sound* presented the common political framing of *Gangs of New York* by the director: the struggle of the Irish against Nativist intolerance in the mid-nineteenth century. The film represented this struggle as a fundamental building block of the American experience in practical, political, and moral terms. As Scorsese told the *Hollywood Reporter*, the "film is about the struggle for freedom, the individual struggle cobblestone by cobblestone. But it is a film that ultimately examines what America is, what it's supposed to be and ultimately what it is to be an American."[74] In Scorsese's public story, Irish immigrants come to represent how the white ethnic experience, from old-world immigrants to subsequent generations, encapsulated the great American experiment—the fulfilling of the ideals of liberty, equality, and individual achievement. The statement that the Irish immigrants of the 1840s were the first to challenge these values is quite remarkable. Even more remarkable is how Scorsese also observed, "So there was a lot of suffering and many deaths, before assimilation began to happen. But it's important for people today to realize that the Irish suffered for everyone, even before the Italians."[75] Here Scorsese again views the core of the American experience as shaped by the European "new immigrants" who came to the United States in the last half of the nineteenth century and first two decades of the twentieth. In other words, the Irish suffered for all the subsequent waves of white ethnics who came to define the American experience. The suffering of African Americans, and other minorities, remains marginal to his story.

> Surely no filmmaker has issued such a brazen challenge to the verities of American history. . . . It is more than coincidence, surely, that Scorsese's immigrant troika—the priest, the cross-bearer, the man carrying his obscene gang standard—replaces here the old Yankee Doodle Dandy flag bearer and fife-and-drum icon that goes back to the Revolution. The "Gangs" advertising tagline is "America was born in the streets," and we are made immediately to understand that Scorsese means it, that by his lights the real America, the one we know today, did not really exist before immigrants fought their way in.
>
> **KEVIN BAKER, LOS ANGELES TIMES (2002)[76]**

Scorsese was not alone in seeing the American experience in his film. For critic Kevin Baker, the *Gangs of New York* became an ode to the true roots of the American experience: not the Founding Fathers and their Yankee brethren, but the European ethnics of the great wave of new immigrants. Ann Hornaday made a similar connection, "Scorsese captures the churn of an evolving democracy, celebrating the emergence of a vital new polyglot culture even as he acknowledges the European culture that had to be abandoned to create it."[77] Or as *New York Daily News'* Jami Bernard suggested, "the overall effect is of a larger truth, that today's melting pot is yesterday's witches' brew."[78] Baker, Hornaday, and Bernard provide examples of how Scorsese's public story resonated with the shift from Plymouth Rock myth to Ellis Island myth found in a new hyphen-nationalism.

Other journalists criticized *Gangs of New York* as a historical fantasy that lost sight of the racial politics of the time. J. Hoberman, for example, labeled the film a "hothouse historical fantasy" that failed to acknowledge the centrality of racial politics, especially in its portrayal of the New York City draft riots of 1863 as a backdrop to revenge and love. "The draft riots (among other things, a four-day pogrom directed against the city's African Americans) are to *Gangs* what the burning of Rome was to *Quo Vadis*."[79] Peter Hamill in the *New York Daily News* also dismissed the film as "a kind of baroque slasher movie, dripping with blood, glittery with knives and axes. The real story is better."[80] Scorsese, however, was not the only one blind to how the film marginalized racial politics. Christopher Shannon wrote that "Scorsese's recent film *The Gangs of New York* takes us back to a time when religion, not race, set the terms for ethno-cultural conflict in America."[81] The ideology of hyphen-nationalism was quite strong if a white ethnic historian viewed the years between 1846 and 1863 depicted in the film—a period defined by slavery, the abolitionist movement, and the American Civil War—as a time that religion, not race, set the terms for social group conflict in the United States.

The failure of *Gangs of New York* as a historical drama can be linked to what Gallagher calls the "immigrant tales" of white ethnics.[82] Scorsese began his career as an "unmeltable ethnic," where his Italian American identity resonated as a particular experience and social identity. As Scorsese experienced his own success and assimilation into mainstream America, however, his identification with his Italian American roots was less essential to his artistic identity.[83] In other words, as Scorsese adjusted to his new white racial identity, the collective "immigrant tale" acted as the historical memory that bound him to his fellow white ethnics and to a new hyphen-nationalist American identity. The ideological lens of hyphen-nationalism and its Ellis Island myth constructed in his public story a historical memory—both personal and fictional—that focused on the white ethnic experience as defining the core of the American experience.

We're All "New Immigrants" Now

Scorsese's public story is a perfect incarnation of hyphen-nationalism. The iconic Italian American filmmaker celebrated for his untarnished portrayal of the Italian American experience and the darker side of the American Dream is transformed by the turn of the century into the iconic American filmmaker celebrating the American experience as the story of new immigrants making the American experiment progress to a more perfect union. While Scorsese's public story began with the trope of unmeltable Italian Americans, at the turn of the century it shifted to the trope of white ethnics who suffered terrible harms and injustices on first arriving to the Promised Land but who over time became the backbone of the American nation. And it is this rags-to-riches history of new immigrants that defines the American experience not only for Scorsese but also for all enamored by the Ellis Island myth. As Scorsese made clear in 2003:

> It seems that the concept of America being open to immigrants, different cultures, different races, different religions, is now somewhat accepted. . . . The first generation usually struggles just to make ends meet, but the second generation finds itself going to school and taking advantage of the system. That's what makes this country great, what makes this experiment in democracy so interesting, it's never finished, it's always in the works.
>
> —MARTIN SCORSESE, INTERVIEW (2003)[84]

In the twenty-first century, Scorsese's America had become an experiment in democracy. It no longer offered a false promise, but struggled to incorporate new social groups into the American Dream. His films had not abandoned the darker aspects of this struggle, whether ethnic conflict in *Gangs of New York* (2002) or ethnic criminals in *The Departed* (2006). But now Scorsese emphasized how such moments were more a part of the past of white ethnics rather than their present. The height of hyphen-nationalism in his public story came on April 24, 2004. Scorsese received an Ellis Island Family Heritage Award from the Statue of Liberty–Ellis Island Foundation at the Ellis Island Immigration Museum. The award was established in 2001 with the inauguration of the American Family Immigration History Center that celebrated this "Nation of Immigrants."

> What does the statue symbolize for us today? . . . Is it a reminder? Or is it a promise? . . . The ideal of liberty often seems so far from us, almost unreachable. But somehow it never disappears, because it represents the best in us, the best we can hope for ourselves and for others.
>
> —MARTIN SCORSESE, LADY BY THE SEA (2004)[85]

Coinciding with Scorsese's Ellis Island Family Heritage Award was the debut of his documentary *Lady by the Sea: The Statue of Liberty* (2004) on the History Channel. The documentary was made to support the reopening of the Statue of Liberty after its closure following September 11, 2001. While not a major work in his oeuvre, the film speaks to a moment when Scorsese's ideological trajectory and public story as a white ethnic connected more clearly with the forces at play in the institutional "regime" Jacobson argues established and maintained the new hyphen-nationalism.[86] As Meryl J. Irwin argues, the Ellis Island myth had already established itself in a series of previous documentaries in the 1990s.[87] All these documentaries, as well as *Lady by the Sea*, tended more toward what Jacobson calls the liberal-pluralist expression of the White Ethnic myth. It becomes obvious in comparing Scorsese's narration in the documentary to the White Ethnic myth in his public story that the director shaped the documentary to fit his liberal view of the great American experiment. Guided by the Ellis Island myth of new immigrants, Scorsese brings together strikingly different histories under the American experiment the Lady by the Sea symbolized.

The documentary begins by reminding viewers that the statue was originally presented at the time of its inauguration in 1886 as a celebration of the freeing of American slaves. Over time, however, the documentary argues, the statue came to symbolize liberty as an American ideal—an ideal that at times excluded certain groups, including the freed African Americans slaves it originally celebrated. In bringing in the history of the Chinese Exclusion Act, the new immigrants, the Jim Crow South, the rejection of Jews fleeing Nazi Germany, the civil rights movement, the women's and gay rights movements, the rejection of Haitian refugees, and the plight of undocumented Mexican workers, the documentary emphasizes Scorsese's conception of the American experience as a series of struggles for inclusion in the promise of the American Dream. Each generation has its own "Nativists" and "Irish Immigrants" battling over who can lay claim to this dream. As Irwin argues, the new narrative found in Ellis Island documentaries allows white ethnic Americans of all generations to "become non-white-immigrants by passing back through the door."[88]

Several experts in the documentary, however, emphasis the radical *differences* in the experiences of racial minorities compared to European ethnics in the American experience. Yet Scorsese frames the documentary as a celebration of the ideal symbolized by the Statue of Liberty. In essence, all the various struggles become part of the American experiment. We have all become new immigrants or their descendants now, struggling to find the fulfillment of the ideals symbolized in the statue.[89] At his most liberal, multicultural best, Scorsese falls into the fundamental color blindness of the hyphen-nationalism of the White Ethnic myth: the erasure of *white privilege*.[90] This erasing of fundamental difference is apparent in how all the various social histories in the film are framed as a *shared experience* of all ethnic and racial minorities at some point in an America that "did not always open our doors to everyone." Scorsese says in *Lady by the Sea* that the statue "stands for the idea that the United States is not just a home for refugees, but a home for liberty, equality, and for justice." So, in the end, in Scorsese's public story, we are all fighting for a more perfect union. As he told Liane Hansen in 2007, "I mean, the whole country is, sort of, an experiment. I think an experiment still in the making. And we'll always be an experiment in that way—freedom and assimilation of different ethnic groups all living together in different cultures."[91]

The ideology of the White Ethnic myth in Scorsese's public story resonates with another observation of Jacobson on the power of hyphen-nationalism. Jacobson argues that this myth explains contemporary struggles of inclusion into the American Dream by constructing a historical memory where the 1960s represent the arrival of nonwhite "immigrants" to America.[92] The Immigration and Nationality Act of 1965 and the Civil Rights Act of 1964 mark this moment in the myth. In this rendering of American history, African Americans, Latinos, Asians, and other nonwhite ethnics only arrived as "free" immigrants in the 1960s. And like the new immigrants before them, they confronted the intolerance of contemporary Nativists, who Scorsese never points out includes many white ethnics. Even though African Americans, Chinese, Mexicans, and other "immigrants" actually populate the 1860s America of *Gangs of New York* or the twentieth-century America of Scorsese's immigrant grandparents and second-generation parents, somehow the starkly different paths of these minorities compared to white ethnics over the last 150 years doesn't quite register in Scorsese's public story.

The "Off-White" Auteur and Negotiating Hegemonic Masculinity

While I agree *Raging Bull* puts masculinity in crisis, I don't think it offers a radical critique of either masculinity or violence, even though it is profoundly disturbing. The film's attitude to violence is ambiguous. On one hand, it is validated as an essential component of masculinity, making possible resistance to a corrupt and repressive social system. On this level violence is seen as inseparable from desire, and is celebrated. On the other, the tragic scenario of *Raging*

> *Bull* demands that the hero be shown to be a guilty victim of his
> transgressive desires: his violence is so excessive, so self-destructive
> that it has to be condemned.
> —PAM COOK, "MASCULINITY IN CRISIS," SCENE (1982)[93]

Robert De Niro plays real-life boxer Jake La Motta in Martin Scorsese's *Raging Bull* (1980). Mirroring La Motta's own self-portrayal in his autobiography, De Niro plays La Motta as a violent, hypermasculine male.[94] La Motta's uncontrollable jealousy, and violent behavior out of the ring toward women and men, leads to his ultimate downfall. Pam Cook points not only to the film's ambiguous relation to this violence, especially toward women, but also to her own ambivalent love-hate relationship to the film as her "own cinéphiliac obsession with the film" was "far from exhausted."[95] Ambivalence, praise, and controversy over the portrayal of masculinity in Scorsese's films have plagued his public story. Even scholars' attempts at interpreting his films have led to interpretations of his portrayal of masculinity that range from it being critically deconstructive, to confusingly ambivalent, to deeply problematic.[96] A defining characteristic of Scorsese's oeuvre certainly has been the prominence of hypermasculine male characters, and for some critics, one-dimensional female characters. It is hard to ignore such an obsession over hypermasculinity as somehow irrelevant to understanding what Scorsese claims were very *personal* films. As an auteur director, he has been fascinated his entire career with violent, hypermasculinity to an extent some critics felt bordered on troubling tendencies in his own male imagination, rather than healthy critical examinations. The ambiguity Pam Cook noted in *Raging Bull* speaks volumes to how Scorsese's films and public story revealed the power of hegemonic masculinity at a time when white ethnic males faced a crisis over challenges to their previously taken-for-granted privileges and power since the civil rights and feminist movements of the 1960s and early 1970s. As Christina Marie Newland argues, the off-white hypermasculine world many of Scorsese's male characters inhabit of social marginalization, broken dreams, and tragic endings, act to portray hegemonic masculinity as a tragedy for these white ethnic males, rather than for the women and men who suffered from these characters' destructive ways.[97]

> But it is already possible to wonder what next year will make of "Taxi
> Driver," a box-office smash, brutal and perplexing, one of the most re-
> soundingly disliked films (in the Hollywood community) I can remem-
> ber, and one of the most coldly admired. . . . "Taxi Driver" remains a

powerful work, provocative in the sense of provoking strong responses both ways, a film skillful and personal.

—CHARLES CHAMPLIN, LOS ANGELES TIMES (1976)[98]

While Scorsese with his first feature films received accolades for his gritty portrayal of the mean streets of New York City, he also quickly elicited criticism over his obsession with violent hypermasculine men as well as his portrayal of women and minorities. Scorsese's mixed reviews often revolved around critics' and audiences' responses and interpretations of the violent hypermasculine men that have populated his films up to the present. The first such mixed reviews occurred early in his career with the film *Taxi Driver* (1976). As Charles Champlin admits, many critics, while admiring the artistry of this film, were struck by its sordid world and ultraviolent, blood-soaked ending. With the vigilante film *Death Wish* (1974) released only two years earlier, it was difficult not linking these two films about an urban landscape of sordid sin, crime, and an avenging angel of death. Patricia Patterson and Manny Farber in *Film Comment* noted in their review of *Taxi Driver* the "odes to Masculine Means" celebrated in this and other vigilante films in the early 1970s. They noted the *Taxi Driver*'s world "in which all the barely differentiated women are professional manipulators of men; black people as animalistic sinisters who get the sexual goods and call the sexual shots; the lower class patronized as animals feeding on each other," while the protagonist "floats around the world—a lean, long-legged loner in cowboy boots who strides down the center of the street, knowing he cuts a striking figure."[99] Richard Combs also argued in the *Monthly Film Bulletin* that this film's "strong streak of misogyny and racist sentiment . . . often seems to be floating through the film, unattached to the protagonists."[100]

I know this guy Travis. I've had the feelings he has, and those feelings have to be explored, taken out and examined. I know the feeling of rejection Travis feels, of not being able to make relationships survive. I know the *killing* feeling, of really being angry. . . . I look for a thematic idea running through my movies, and I see that it's the outsider struggling for recognition. . . . Travis Bickle, the taxi driver, is an outsider. And I realize that all my life *I've* been an outsider.

—MARTIN SCORSESE WITH GUY FLATLEY, NEW YORK TIMES (1976)[101]

In case anyone thought such prejudices and violent thoughts in the *Taxi Driver* were simply a reflection of his white male protagonist Travis Bickle,

Scorsese quickly put that idea to rest. As he told Guy Flatley, Scorsese identi-fied with this alienated and lonely taxi driver and his urges to strike back vio-lently at a world that rejected him. Remember, for Scorsese, all his films have been personal. As he told Gregg Kilday of the *Los Angeles Times* about *Taxi Driver*, "It's a very personal piece. It is almost as if I sat down and wrote a script myself, about bad feelings that I have about myself. . . . The picture just takes the idea of macho and takes it to its logical insane conclusion, graphically, pornographically, insane."[102] Such projections, in both senses of the word, of the insanely violent hypermasculine male would remain a Scorsese staple. With a film coda of a contented Travis Bickle, celebrated vigilante, driving once again on the streets of New York City, film critic Charles Champlin won-dered about "the ambiguous coda, with what seems to be a currently fashion-able and idiot theory that violence is good for what ails you, a rite of passage to maturity and mental health. Whether the film is saying this, or suggesting that society in its willful blindness is doomed to re-infect itself endlessly, is also unclear."[103] What eventually became clear is how the auteur director Scorsese would obsessively reinfect his films with such hypermasculine behavior.

> It's exceedingly violent as well as poetic and, finally, humane in the way of unsentimental fiction that understands that a life—any life—can only be appreciated when the darkness that surrounds it is acknowledged . . . he bellows, and then whimpers, "I'm not an animal." It's a risky moment that pays off. Though there's not one sequence in the film when he hasn't behaved like an animal, Jake, like all the rest of us, is the kind of animal who can ask a question.
>
> —VINCENT CANBY, NEW YORK TIMES (1980)[104]

> The most brutal thing about this foul-mouthed, face-breaking, consci-entiously misanthropic film is the dogged trust that assertiveness can overpower the claims of exploration or understanding. A raging bull is worshiped as the most noble of savages. Depicting such a creature is supposed to excuse all his violence and all of his creator's reluctance to examine the nature of the bull. Instead, the animal is seen caged . . . crying out, in extremis, that he is not an animal but a man.
>
> —DAVID THOMSON, FILM COMMENT (1981)[105]

Raging Bull remains for many critics the crowning achievement of Martin Scorsese as the great American independent auteur. The story of Italian American boxer Jake La Motta is visually stunning and emotionally unsettling. Vincent Canby and David Thomson show not only the polar opposite assessments found in this film's mixed reviews, but also how two noted film critics could interpret the same elements of the film—the constant brutal violence La Motta inflicted on all around him in his early life and his later declaration of humanity—in such starkly different ways. More important in understanding the power of the story about an off-white male boxer is how both Canby and Thomson are making *moral* interpretations of the film and its protagonist. Canby asks us to empathize with this brutally violent male boxer even as he admits that such empathy unfortunately must be based on "something far more mysterious" than the social milieu of the off-white, working-class Bronx.[106] Thomson on the other hand seems to tell us that the "something far more mysterious" is the hypermasculinity Scorsese fails to truly examine while simultaneously structuring empathy into a narrative that ends with a blotched, bloated, La Motta muttering "I could have been somebody" into the mirror of a nightclub dressing room. As Scorsese told Mary Pat Kelly, "he must be aware of certain things spiritually that we aren't, because our minds are too cluttered with intellectual ideas, and too much emotionalism. And because he's on that animalistic level, he may be closer to pure spirit. . . . That's the idea around the film, and that's what I like about it—that, and the idea of being born again."[107] Or as the biblical quote that ends *Raging Bull* reminds the viewers, "All I know is this: once I was blind and now I can see."[108] The off-white hypermasculine male seems to be redeemed in Scorsese's eyes.

Scorsese's next film featuring hypermasculine male characters was his critically acclaimed film *Goodfellas* (1990). Vincent Canby celebrated *Goodfellas* as "a breathless and brilliant new film" that was "both the politically most serious and most evilly entertaining movie yet made about organized crime."[109] And the film's authenticity, for Canby, came from its ordinariness around the brutal acts of its three main characters. Once again in a Scorsese visual roller-coaster ride, the violence in *Goodfellas* seems central to the lives of these gangsters yet not central to the interpretive frame of the story. As Leonard Quart pointed out in a positive review in *Cineaste*, "Scorsese himself avoids judging his characters or providing social or psychological explanations for their behavior. . . . Scorsese is at home with murderous rage—never romanticizing it, but treating it as a natural force that spews spontaneously and uncontrollably from his characters."[110] Of course, without social or psychological explanations, Quart falls prey to the common trope in hegemonic masculinity that violent hypermasculinity is simply a natural force—boys will be boys.[111] What Quart and other reviews suggest is that

Scorsese is not looking *critically* at hypermasculinity in any significant way. Nor is he in any way *deconstructing* it. In Scorsese's own comments and most reviews, such judgmental distance is an essence, and a powerful essence, of his style. As Tom Milne noted in *Monthly Film Bulletin*, Scorsese's "most *realistic* appraisal" of gangsters is "unconcerned with making excuses or moral judgments . . . *Goodfellas* sagely keeps its distance throughout, letting appearances speak for themselves."[112] But how does one balance a career-long obsession with violent hypermasculinity with this filmmaker supposedly holding back at examining it, let alone judging it. How does violent hypermasculinity speak for itself? This problem of supposed distance would reach new heights with Scorsese's next film, *Cape Fear* (1991).

> One of the key questions raised by feminist critics at the time concerned the director's collusion in the creation of a misogynist pop aesthetic. If Scorsese didn't know his sexual politics then, and was "innocently" working with genre, it's impossible to put forward such an argument in his defense today. . . . A rape movie? A film in which the camera acts as violator? Which opens with a series of shots of a young girl whose body is viewed with unequivocally violent intent? Dangerous territory indeed—but rest assured, this is *only* a film.
>
> —ANGELA MCROBBIE, SIGHT AND SOUND (1992)[113]

In referencing two of his first feature films, *Mean Streets* and *Taxi Driver*, film critic and feminist media scholar Angela McRobbie sets out a larger criticism of Martin Scorsese as one of the filmmakers behind the rise of hypermasculinity in Hollywood film. The graphic violence of rape depicted in *Cape Fear* stunned many viewers and critics, some audience members were said to have left in the middle of the film. But the film gained praise by others who seemingly had no problem with such brutal depictions of violence by a beefed-up, tattoo-laden Robert De Niro as the sociopath Max Cody. Jay Scott in the *Globe and Mail* exclaimed, "Martin Scorsese, without doubt the greatest living American director . . . has re-invented Cape Fear for the complicated, morally ambiguous nineties, a decade in which all too many families are post-nuclear. In so doing, he has created a psychologically dense, unbearably tense suspense masterpiece."[114] Scott noted four of Scorsese's hypermasculine films—*Mean Streets*; *New York, New York*; *Raging Bull*; and *Goodfellas*—as examples of this great director's work. Scott also did not feel compelled to warn readers that the film contained two violent rape scenes. Maybe McRobbie was right. Scorsese, along with other male filmmakers, had made the "misogynist pop aesthetics" of hypermasculinity in Hollywood film *normal.*

Scorsese's public story also showed how he hoped audiences saw violent hypermasculinity as normal. He told readers of the *New York Times*, "It's a picture about a man who wants revenge, and it's a lot of fun."[115] *Los Angeles Times* film critic Kenneth Turan certainly felt differently about this film. He called it "as sadistic as its star player."[116] But it was a personal film. Barbara De Fina, the film's producer and Scorsese's wife, told David Morgan of the *Los Angeles Times*, "I see a lot of him in the characters. I don't think he could live with making a movie that wasn't personal."[117] Strangely, De Fina does not say which characters she saw reflected in her husband. Scorsese, however, was clear on which character he was focused on as he placed the film as part of his over-two-decade fascination with hypermasculinity. "There is no doubt [De Niro and I] are attracted to similar characters that we've dealt with before; they're similar—they're not the same. There's different angles in each one. It's almost like trying to find out how many more sides you can find to a character like Travis or Max or Jake La Motta, or Jimmy Doyle."[118] In films constantly noted for their lack of judgment, their neutral distance, and their letting appearances speak for themselves, discerning the "sides" of violent hypermasculinity seems a somewhat problematic rationale for such a career-long obsession.

> A deafening silence surrounds the sexual politics of Scorsese's *Cape Fear.* Here we have—in a year which has already seen two widely publicised rape trials in the US—a violent rape movie in which women apparently collude in their own punishment at the hands of a rapist. Yet for the most part critics, even when shocked by the film's brutality, prefer to discuss it in formal and/or moral terms—as "cinema" or as a treatise on good and evil.
>
> **—PAM COOK, SIGHT AND SOUND (1992)**[119]

Why were Scorsese and De Niro so obsessed with reenacting violent hypermasculinity? And why was such hypermasculinity never condemned by them or the critics who praised their films and acting prowess? Pam Cook vehemently condemned the lack of reviews, positive or negative, that even mentioned the film had two brutal rapes. These silences suggest that such depictions in Hollywood film seemed unproblematic to most reviewers. As Mike Clark wrote in *USA Today*, "Martin Scorsese has monumentally refined 1962's *Cape Fear*, giving pulpy material imposing moral weight and the peerless cinematic pop he brought to *Goodfellas*. Because this superior remake is both lurid and psychologically complex, it immediately recalls *The Silence of the Lambs*. *Fear* deserves to duplicate *Lambs'* popularity."[120] For Pam Cook, what Clark saw as a film of moral heft and psychological debt, she saw as Scorsese's "most overtly feminophobic movie." And she added, "At the most, we can thank him for laying on the line with blistering clarity the way our culture devalues femininity as an alibi for male fears and desires."[121] For McRobbie and Cook, Scorsese had not only participated in the normalization of hypermasculinity in film but also in the reproduction of the very gender ideological constructs that obscure any critical understanding of it, from violence being a natural, irrepressible part of masculinity to women as a threat to such hegemonic masculine power.

Scorsese would continue to explore the various "sides" of violent hypermasculinity in subsequent films like *Casino* (1995), *Gangs of New York* (2002), *The Departed* (2006), and *The Wolf of Wall Street* (2013). As McRobbie suggests, maybe Scorsese saw the commercial value of his trope of hypermasculinity as a pop aesthetic. Some critics did note how Joe Pesci's sociopathic hypermasculine character in *Casino* seemed like simply a replay of his ultraviolent Tommy DeVito in *Goodfellas* (1990).[122] Directing the performance of hypermasculinity seemed to pay off with *The Departed* bringing in $290 million in box office and *The Wolf of Wall Street* grossing $392 million. As Jackson Katz argues, ultraviolent hypermasculinity has been a major staple of Hollywood film since the early 1970s.[123] While some scholars have linked this hypermasculinity to the Reagan era and the defeat of the United States in Vietnam,[124] hypermasculinity was as much a liberal masculinity as it was a conservative one. Martin Scorsese's public story presents him as a liberal. To film an antiwar protest in the late 1960s, for example, he joined a film collective that included another liberal auteur obsessed with hypermasculinity, Oliver Stone. And as we've seen, Scorsese's hyphen-nationalism was of the color-blind and gender-blind liberal variety.

"Raging Bull" is not simply the greatest boxing movie ever made. . . . He is the ultimate screen embodiment of raw Italian-American machismo at a certain moment in the ever-shifting melting pot of New York City. Blindly fighting his way to the top, then falling and stumbling into a shabby middle-age, undone by the same forces by which he rose, he is a potent tribal symbol who ultimately embarrasses his tribe. . . . "Raging Bull," like no movie before, personalizes the "Godfather" films'

Darwinian vision of an immigrant urban culture muscling its way up the lower rungs of the social ladder.

—STEPHEN HOLDEN, NEW YORK TIMES (2000)[125]

Stephen Holden's twentieth-anniversary review of *Raging Bull* (1980) was just two years before the release of *Gangs of New York* (2002). And it was just two years before Martin Scorsese announced to the world that he was an Italian American who was proud of the white ethnic American contribution to the American experience he shared with his other European American brethren. Holden's framing of *Raging Bull*'s Jake La Motta as the embodiment of new immigrant males' struggles up the social ladder allows us to see the colliding together of race and gender in the tales of off-white males in Scorsese's films and public story over his entire career. It speaks to a collective recouping of "otherness" in Scorsese's public story. In his films and public story, he and others have spoken to the white ethnic male of the past as a man who suffered a marginalization that not only made the American Dream a false promise written in pain and blood, but also made these males victims of a self-damaging hypermasculinity. As Charles Champlin wrote in the *Los Angeles Times* in 1980 about *Raging Bull*, a film centered on the brutal violence of Jake La Motta, "Scorsese in all his films has revealed a divided attitude toward the New York Italian-American subculture in which he arose, compassion for those who suffer along the mean streets, anger, shaded with despair, for the forces of the past—the paternalistic tradition, the church, the organized crime—that seem to him to stifle the possibilities of the young."[126] The off-white male as victim is a Scorsese specialty. And Scorsese's newest project, probably out by the time this book is published, will be *The Irishman*. A film about corrupt teamster Frank "The Irishman" Sheeran who is purported to have killed Jimmy Hoffa. And the film will star Robert De Niro, Joe Pesci, and Al Pacino: three Italian American actors who have given us iconic Hollywood performances of the ultraviolent, hypermasculine male.

Conclusion

Scorsese's brand and public story remained wedded for six decades to the autobiographical, personal, and sociohistorical in his films. This commitment to his brand as well as his self-image as a filmmaker led to the unique situation of a *public intellectual* negotiating his personal biographic journey as a highly acclaimed, richly rewarded, and upwardly mobile white ethnic male with his translation, along with others, of this journey in the narratives of the public story about his films and the American experience. With Scorsese's efforts to maintain his image as the authentic, personal, and epic visionary of American film closely following the evolution of American hyphen-nationalism, we see the miraculous conjoining of personal biography, preeminent storytelling, prophetic vision, public reception, and collective transcoding of the ideological formation that has driven this form of nationalism in the United States. We see at a personal level how Scorsese's life from a working-class Italian American in Little Italy to a rich, cosmopolitan American icon reflects the social journey Richard D. Alba argues leads to the twilight of ethnicity and the emergence of a European American identity.[127] And as France Winddance Twine and Charles A. Gallagher argue, white identity is about *biography* as *ideology*, and the transcoding of personal biography with broader discursive formations about whiteness and racial identity.[128] More important, however, is the power of a *collective* transcoding in memory, biography, sociohistorical commentary, criticism, and films of a narrative on the transformation of previously unmeltable-ethnic Americans into white European Americans in the public story of one of the most acclaimed American artists of the last half century.

While Scorsese was far more outspoken about how his biographical legend and films spoke to the Italian American and white ethnic American experience, he also interwove the *personal* and the *fictional* in his obsession with hypermasculinity. And given that such hypermasculinity was the province of his off-white male characters, whether Italian American or Irish American, it is hard to not recognize the link between ethnic identity and gender identity in his films and public story. Given how the ethnic revival occurred at the same time as second wave feminism, it is not surprising that in Scorsese's public story we find the recouping of loss in the racial and gender identities of this artist, as well as in the racial and gender identities of others who contributed to his story. We witness firsthand the commingling of a new white ethnic American identity with the rise of a new hypermasculinity in the popular imagination of America's new hyphen-nationalism. But even at its liberal best, many voices in Scorsese's public story leave unquestioned the recentering of the white ethnic male as defining the American experience, especially the hypermasculine white ethnic male. Ironically, the white ethnic male becomes both victim and hero in Scorsese's films and public story.

What is also striking about Martin Scorsese's public story is how, over an extended period of time, the *personal* and *biographical* of a celebrated intellectual intersected with the *public* and the *institutional*. Such a meshing of personal memory, creative imagination, and the institutional regimes of storytelling in print, film, television, and radio provides a detailed view of how the mechanisms of *whiteness*, *masculinity*, and *white-male privilege* do their ideological work. The purpose of my work, however, was not to isolate Scorsese for judgment or criticism, that is certainly not my role. Nor was it my intention to ignore the *immense* contribution he has made to American film and investigating the American experience. My work emphasizes his public story as a *collective* endeavor of various actors across public media and public sites from movie theaters, to newspapers, to film magazines, to film festivals, to award ceremonies, to the steps of the Ellis Island Immigration Museum in 2004. This collective public story is testament to the power embedded in the institutional and cultural regime of hyphen-nationalism in the United States and the power of hegemonic masculinity in the popular imagination. Such regimes work to obscure in personal memory, creative imagination, artwork, and public discourse the power and legacy of white male privilege.

American Rebels

REDUX

> Miles Davis makes you more of an artist. To help not take the road most traveled, take the other road. I always feel like he's telling me, "Trust your instinct and not try to please. Please yourself and that's the only way to please the artist gods."
>
> JOHN LEGUIZAMO, NEW YORK TIMES (2017)[1]

In 2017, John Leguizamo told the New York Times that the late Miles Davis inspires him to follow his own muse. Over twenty-five years after the trumpeter's death, the *idea* of Davis as an artistic rebel still resonates strongly for contemporary American artists like Leguizamo. Such an idea guided Leguizamo as an independent playwright and actor in his new play *Latin History for Morons*. The *idea* of Davis as a race man provocateur seems to inspire Leguizamo as well. This Latino artist in his *New York Times* interview positioned himself as a contemporary race man provocateur during a time in which many Latinos in America feel like strangers in their own land. His play was going to teach "morons" how Latinos have long contributed to the American experience. Leguizamo as artistic rebel and race man provocateur seems to have continued in the path that Davis forged in the last half of the twentieth century. Leguizamo, like both Davis and Scorsese, also has negotiated throughout his career a commitment to his art and an engagement with the culture industry. He has performed in major Hollywood films as well as independent films. He also has performed in network least objectionable programming (LOP) as well as more upscale non-network programming. And he has written and performed in award-winning plays. On the other hand, Leguizamo, like Davis and Scorsese, has presented hypermasculinity as well. As a Latino male actor, he has been occasionally called on to entertain audiences with hypermasculine characters like Benny Blanco in *Carlito's Way* (1993) and Ozzy Delvecchio in *Bloodline* (2015–17). The career of John Leguizamo clearly demonstrates that the main themes of autonomy, race, and gender that emerged in my look at the Heroic Age of American Art remain powerful forces in the structured meaningful activity of artists today.

In this conclusion, I first return to the three general themes of autonomy, race, and gender. I am not intending to provide some comprehensive summary of these themes, but more to provide brief comments on ideas elicited by the complex stories that emerged from these themes as I looked at the careers and public stories of Miles Davis and Martin Scorsese. Pierre Bourdieu's concept of Heroic Ages was presented in this book's introduction to set the context in which to explore in detail the cultural politics in American art during a period when artists encountered a far more open field in the meaning and practice of art. The most striking feature of my exploration was the power of race, ethnicity, class, and gender in defining the art and public stories of Davis and Scorsese. This book shows how the Heroic Age of American Art *invited* a robust cultural politics that moved beyond merely questions of artistic autonomy and artistic innovation, but also engaged different discursive fields and ideological formations as artists and others transcoded in their public stories broader cultural, social, and political issues. My work, however, not only helps us understand the past, but also speaks strongly to the present. So, in this conclusion I will share a few thoughts on what links the past and the present in the public stories of Miles Davis and Martin Scorsese. In particular, I will look at how the racial and gender imaginations and formations that informed the stories in this book remain as powerful, and as problematic, up to the present. I will then end this book with a final note on the special role *public stories* about art and artists have played, and will continue to play, in American cultural politics.

Autonomy in the Heroic Age

Box office is the undercurrent in almost all discussions of cinema, and frequently it's more than just an undercurrent. The brutal judgmentalism that has made opening-weekend grosses into a bloodthirsty spectator sport seems to have encouraged an even more brutal approach to film reviewing. . . . These firms and aggregators have set a tone that is hostile to serious filmmakers—even the actual name Rotten Tomatoes is insulting.

—MARTIN SCORSESE, HOLLYWOOD REPORTER (2017)[2]

It seems that auteurism and independence remain crucial motivating forces in the career of Martin Scorsese. Such an impression certainly appears in his contemporary public story as we are told of an artist still caught in a Sisyphean struggle for personal and artistic integrity. In an editorial in the *Hollywood Reporter*, Scorsese lambasts a brutal and shallow judgmentalism that he believes defines contemporary internet film criticism: a criticism, he argues, that is driven by a Hollywood box-office mentality. Scorsese is lamenting the brutal reviews of fellow auteur Darren Aronofsky's *Mother* (2017) in a cultural landscape he believes no longer supports the cinema that has defined independent film since the 1960s. His disgruntlement might also reflect the media framing of his highly personal film *Silence* (2016) as a box-office flop as opposed to another major artistic achievement in his long career. But then again, Scorsese made his Faustian bargain with Hollywood a long time ago. So, the constant balancing act between the logic of the Hollywood commercial aesthetic and the autonomous spirit of independent film remains a strong trope in his public story.

The genre communities I have addressed in looking at the music and film fields, where Miles Davis and Martin Scorsese made their art and had their public stories told, all claimed allegiance to autonomy, independence, and authentic creativity. And as Scorsese suggests in his editorial in the *Hollywood Reporter*, the structured meaningful activity in these independent genre communities seemed always to have the commercial culture industry as a large looming presence. All these genre communities, in some fashion, constantly confronted the question of their relationship to the major corporations who controlled the mass markets of music and film. Such positioning was made even more problematic by the difficulty of separating popular aesthetics and popular audiences from the industrial machinations and interests of the culture industry. Autonomous and independent music and film, however, have been able to directly connect with the popular through local scenes and subcultures who identify with experimental, underground, alternative, or indie music and film. It has been the seemingly vast gulf between local scenes, subcultures, art worlds, and the culture industry that have confounded autonomy-seeking artists, and also where avant-garde and indie producers and distributors have tried to build bridges. And so, one of the most important lessons to be learned is how since the beginning of the Heroic Age it has been the *bridges* and *opportunities* across these art fields that have allowed truly independent and innovative music and film to have a greater impact on a greater number of people. In part, I chose Davis and Scorsese precisely for how they had navigated such central concerns that dominated structured meaningful activities in modern jazz and independent film since the beginning of the Heroic Age of American Art. They both also succeeded in having a broad impact in their fields. And we can see that the successful navigation of such concerns continues up to the present whether in the careers of Steven Soderbergh, Ava DuVernay, Kamasi Washington, or Kendrick Lamar.

We have also seen that while these various independent genre communities had no love for the culture industry, they confronted a variety of distinctions that set them apart from one another and often led to rather contradictory or contentious meanings and practices. Such contradictions and contentions were even more complicated as autonomy, independence, rebellion, social relevance, or any other motivating ideas were defined differently by various artists and various genre communities. As a sociologist of art, I was disciplined not to make judgments on the contentious distinctions made by artists and genre communities in their structured meaningful activities during the Heroic Age. In other words, the intention of looking at the various *genre stories* told about music and film during the Heroic Age, and the conflicts and distinctions they generated, was not to suggest one was more valid or honest or critical than the other. I also did not pass judgments, because as an artist myself, I have too much respect for all the artists involved to make such a claim. I am sure, however, that my biases in favor of the popular still came out in my analysis, if only in me refusing to take seriously the claims made by various genre communities that the popular represented selling out or commercial pablum. But to claim avant-garde, neotraditional, fusion, or crossover jazz reflected or destroyed the true spirit of modern jazz was not the point in my work, nor to claim experimental film, independent film, or made-in-Hollywood film represented truly authentic and critical work. The point was how these genre communities set up ideas about making music and film that structured the meaningful activities in making and appreciating art.

I mentioned in the introduction to the book how structured meanings inform the actions, interpretations, appreciations, and emotions of those active in art fields. What we have seen in music and film during the Heroic Age is how powerful, durable, and malleable such ideas have been in the genre communities we encountered. Such powerful ideas, of course, brushed up against the constant demand to make some type of living and to survive as an avantgarde or independent artist. These powerful ideas also brushed up against the road to the culture industries and mass markets that provided more than just a living wage. However, we also discovered how ideas around autonomy, independence, and authentic creativity were shaped by other ideas informed by dynamics outside simply making music and film. The contentiousness over these powerful ideas, for example, clearly ratcheted up as the country was swept up in a series of political and cultural upheavals, suggesting a more profound revolution was happening beyond the world of music and film. One striking feature I found in the genre stories in the 1960s and early 1970s was how uninhibited artists and critics were in talking or writing at great length on the revolutionary, philosophical, political, and social significance of their genre communities and their art. It was at times mind-boggling how these revolutionary autodidacts would mix and match various political, philosophical, religious, historical, sociological, ethnomusicological, or whatever ideas that were in the air into their interviews, liner notes, or criticism. The 1960s and early '70s were indeed heady and contentious times.

One final note on the Heroic Age's quest for autonomy, independence, and innovation. It is somewhat ironic, or maybe simply a challenge, to address the concerns over autonomy, independence, creativity, and the power of the culture industries at a time when digital technology has been undermining the two juggernauts of commercial popular music and film. But outside of the severe decline in revenues in the recorded music market, what long-term effect the digital revolution will have on music and film is still unknown. What is clear, however, is when these industries suffered a similar chaotic transformation in the postwar period of the Heroic Age, revolutions in art generated a series of genre ideals that radically transformed American music and film. Yet no such artistic revolution has yet occurred in the latest chaotic transformation of these art fields. If the *opportunity space* is truly opening up for music and film, the jury is still out on whether the chaotic field will generate a new Heroic Era of artistic innovation and diversity.[3]

Race Consciousness in the Heroic Age

> We then enter the bebop age. Harlem jazz becomes very aggressive. Jimmy Doyle's good, but since he's white, he'll never be as good as someone like Charlie Parker or the other black musicians. He knows

that and it inhibits him. . . . He enjoys only relative success, no more than his type of music entitles him. . . . Where were they to go, these white jazzmen? Some exiled themselves to Europe. . . . Others turned to rock 'n' roll.

—MARTIN SCORSESE AT THE CANNES FILM FESTIVAL IN 1978[4]

Marsalis believes it is the conscious recognition in the minds of most white jazz players that they are not black that limits their ability and prevents them from getting "into the meat of the music."

—MITCHEL SEIDEL, DOWN BEAT (1982)[5]

Jimmy Doyle was a white tenor saxophone player in Martin Scorsese's 1977 film musical *New York, New York*. In the movie, Doyle struggled in the late 1940s and early '50s as a modern jazz musician. Scorsese believed that Doyle struggled in part because white musicians at the time did not have a chance against their black musician peers. As Miles Davis said in 1955, most white musicians simply could not swing. Wynton Marsalis was more in line with Scorsese, however, when in 1982 he suggested that white musicians were intimidated by black musicians and the jazz tradition. Of course, both Davis and Marsalis got tremendous heat for their comments, including accusations of racism.[6] It was easier, of course, for a white filmmaker like Scorsese to make such an argument than for Davis or Marsalis. In fact, Davis and Marsalis have been accused of being racist far more often than Scorsese. It is clear during the Heroic Age how the racial ideology and color-blind ideology of Jim Crow and New Jim Crow America translated the ideas of black and white artists through a white sensitivity that viewed such utterances from African Americans as more threatening and racist than from the mouths of whites.

Miles Davis and Wynton Marsalis as race-conscious musicians speaks volumes to how questions around aesthetics, tradition, genre, and the commercial culture industry were inseparable from questions around race and black art for African American artists during the Heroic Age and beyond. Black artists have struggled and rebelled through the meanings and practices of their art as well as in their public personas in Jim Crow and New Jim Crow America. Black artists have confronted a culture industry and high art institutions that have marginalized them as artists while simultaneously aiding in the co-optation of their art by white artists, critics, curators, entrepreneurs, and audiences. Race-conscious black artists also, especially in the interracial world of American music, have worked within a white dominated world where the white racial imagination has constantly lost in translation the meaning of their art, their words, and their actions. In this house of mirrors, however, the power of black art and Afro-modernism have given the world a breadth of art-making of incredible creative, cultural, and political dimensions. The power of African American music making especially has been remarkably enduring in American music, whether through spirituals, ragtime, jazz, gospel, rhythm and blues, funk, or rap music. Black artists have remained for over a century the vanguard of American music and an inspiration to artists around the world.

Miles Davis's iconic status in the African American community, however, was based on his unbridled commitment as a race man to challenging the dominant hegemony of Jim Crow and New Jim Crow America as it was with his accomplishments as a world-renowned jazz musician. Davis was certainly not alone as a black artist in challenging the racist regime of America as well as apartheid South Africa. What was remarkable was how Davis maintained until his death a concerted commingling of art, persona, and politics that refused to submit to the conservative forces driving America toward a New Jim Crow or denying the evil of apartheid South Africa. The neoconservative Wynton Marsalis in his art, persona, and politics distanced himself from contemporary politics and preferred to heap ridicule and disgust toward "ghetto" life and its music.[7] Marsalis simply reflected a conservative counterrevolution within the black community driven by a renewed politics of respectability. Davis, on the other hand, engaged the contemporary politics of the progressive African American community and embraced the concerns of the "ghetto" life and the sounds and words of its music. It is not by chance that Davis constantly complained about the new police state in the War on Drugs, whether talking about his numerous encounters with police (driving while black) or on his album *You're Under Arrest* (1985). Davis was watching and listening as the New Jim Crow was establishing itself across America. What is striking in his last studio albums, *You're Under Arrest* (1985), *Sun City* (1985), *Tutu* (1986), *Amandla* (1989), and *Doo-Bop* (1992), is how Davis was more overtly political in his music making than ever before. As his autobiography indicated, Davis seemed after six decades of life to have given up even more on the possibility that white people would give up their power and privilege without a fight. And *Doo-Bop* was clearly a musical tribute by Davis to a new Afro-modernist race music called hip-hop that would carry the mantle of a new black aesthetic and a new black cultural politics during the New Jim Crow era. Davis also acted as an inspiration to an emerging jazz-left cultural formation that incorporated the politics of the old Black Music movement with a more open and eclectic music making that engaged directly with contemporary politics and popular music.[8] A famous member of the jazz left, Cassandra Wilson, even released a tribute album, *Traveling Miles*, for Miles Davis in 1999.

The public story of Miles Davis also included the Crow Jim rants liberal white jazz critics and musicians had for over fifteen years. Such writings about reverse discrimination actually coincided with the most active years of the civil rights movement. It is clear that the white color-blind ideology and the white racial imagination in the jazz art world led to a lost-in-translation view of the music making of black musicians. Such social distance and biased translations transformed the liberatory power of race music into a bigoted black nationalism and confounded protests against persistent racial discrimination and racism through either a willful ignorance or a liberal acknowledgment of a Jim Crow music industry, but defense of a color-blind jazz art world. The power of this racial disjuncture was clear when in the 1980s and 1990s Wynton Marsalis also was accused of Crow Jim in his public story, beginning with his 1982 *Down Beat* interview and into his directorship of the Jazz at Lincoln Center in the 1990s. The power of the liberal color-blind ideology is evident in how all race men and race music, from the most radical avant-garde to the most traditional neoconservative, ruffled the feathers of many white critics and musicians. Marsalis might have also touched the sensitive bruises of white egos damaged during the heated days of radical black nationalism in the late 1960s and early 1970s. The racial minefield in jazz was certainly a difficult one to navigate as black musicians pursued their Afro-modernist agendas in an art world dominated by white critics, musicians, and audiences. But in the end, the Black Music movement was successful in gaining recognition and acceptance in the jazz art world, if unfortunately, not from the neotraditionalist running Jazz at Lincoln Center, and also passing the torch on to a new jazz left.[9]

Of course, it was the power of such a color-blind ideology that led Martin Scorsese to evolve from an unmeltable Italian American to hyphen-nationalist white ethnic American. His liberal color-blind ideology reimagined his own biography and the American experience as a series of struggles by immigrants to enter the American Dream and make America a more perfect union. In his public story, except for those damn Yankees and Nativists, we are all "new immigrants" waiting for our moment of assimilation. Of course, while the critique of color-blind ideology, including the liberal version presented in Scorsese's public story, remains important, the more recent rise to political relevance of a white supremacist alt right in America is certainly ever more disturbing. One can easily chart how the conservative color-blind ideology of racial resentment—the myth of African American *privilege* and the scourge of *reverse discrimination*—led to the joining of the conservative base of the Republican Party with an alt right that shares a similar racial resentment. More important, however, is how we need to acknowledge how the misconceptions inherent in the liberal color-blind ideology—the denial of the central importance of white privilege in contemporary America—opened up cultural and political opportunities for conservative color-blind ideology and white supremacy. The White Ethnic myth of European Americans defining the American experience, liberal or conservative, certainly has contributed to the racial framing of Make American Great Again. In many ways, Make American Great Again is a perfect expression of hyphen-nationalism in the United States.

The racial imagination was to play a vital part in the Heroic Ages of music and film. Both black and white racial imaginations engaged in the struggles to make autonomous, authentic, and critical art. But a major difference certainly pertained to the public stories of Miles Davis and Martin Scorsese. Davis and other black artists constantly confronted a white racial imagination that defined them as *black* and then demanded them to conform to a color-blind ideal that had no relationship to their experiences or motivations as artists, including the historical cultural appropriation of black music by white Americans. On the other hand, Davis and other black artists had a black race consciousness that always defined the structured meaningful activities of their art making. For Scorsese, in his public story during the ethnic revival and rise of hyphen-nationalism, his Italian American and white ethnic American identities and politics faced no similar opposing ethnic or racial imaginations. There was no ethnic minefield awaiting Scorsese, just a large demand in the white racial imagination for the celebration of symbolic ethnicity and a fascination for Italian Americans. Over time, Scorsese in his public story would embrace a new hyphen-nationalism and white ethnic American identity that obscured in personal memory, creative imagination, art, and public discourse the power and legacy of white privilege.

The Masculine Guise in the Heroic Age

He was the product of a masculine culture that aspired to be like a pimp, that embraced the cool performance styles of the players (pronounced "playas"), the "macks," the hustlers, who not only circulated in the jazz world but whose walk and talk also drew from the well of black music. . . . Pimps in African-American culture and

folklore are more than violent exploiters of women. They are masters of style, from the language and the stroll to the clothes and the wheels.
—ROBIN D. G. KELLEY ON MILES DAVIS, NEW YORK TIMES (2001)[10]

But instead of shattering or even seriously challenging those stereotypes, this breezy montage of interviews with pimps of varying ages in several American cities only reinforces them. . . . The movie bends over backward to be non-judgmental. But there is simply no getting around the reality that urban, street-level prostitution is a nasty game that exploits and degrades the women who get caught up in it.
—STEPHEN HOLDEN ON AMERICAN PIMP (2000)[11]

The attraction of what historian Robin D. G. Kelley calls the "pimp aesthetic" speaks volumes to the inescapable link between hypermasculinity, hipness, and the violent subordination of women. Kelley is not wrong about the fascination in popular culture with the urban pimp, especially the black urban pimp, although such a fascination reflects more the male gender imagination that dominates popular culture rather than Kelley's implied universal fascination. The documentary *American Pimp* (1999) by black filmmakers Albert and Allen Hughes, as Stephen Holden argued in the *New York Times*, lapsed into the same hagiography that lured Miles Davis into his supposed pimp aesthetic. And the convoluted interplay of black and white masculinity we found in the jazz art world with "virile" black musicians and "gentle" white musicians persists to the present. In the HBO show *The Deuce* (2017)—a show created by white producers David Simon and George Pelecanos about New York City's Forty-Second Street of the 1970s, also the backdrop to Scorsese's *Taxi Driver* (1973)—all the pimps are black except one white pimp who is shabbily dressed and too weak to handle his own women. It's hard being white and cool and tough. It is scary how persistent the white racial imagination is in its love-hate relationship with black hypermasculinity and its constant fear of white male castration. As James Baldwin lamented in his look at Norman Mailer, the famous white negro, in *Esquire* in 1961, "to be an American Negro male is also to be a kind of walking phallic symbol: which means that one pays, in one's own personality, for the sexual insecurity of others."[12] This racial and gender imagination during the Heroic Age certainly played out in the public story of Davis. And Martin Scorsese would tap into the American racial and gender imagination as well in his deep obsession with hypermasculinity. But Davis and Scorsese would engage hypermasculinity in quite different ways.

An obsession over masculinity permeated the jazz art world in which Miles Davis first made his career. But if a "pimp" hip masculinity existed in the black and white male gender imaginations in the jazz art world, it was only one aspect of these imaginations. Another form of masculinity was very prominent in the jazz art world. This was the white "playboy" masculinity found in men's magazines such as *Esquire*, *Cavalier*, and *Playboy*, where jazz was part of the soundscape of a white male fantasy of privilege and affluence littered with objects of consumption, including women. And Davis was portrayed in his public story as both a playboy and a Prince of Darkness. But if one reads carefully the public story of Davis, one senses that the playboy boxer was a far more important part of his male selfhood than the hypermasculine persona that emerged in the late 1960s and persisted until his death in interviews and his infamous autobiography. This is not to downplay the misogynistic talk and behavior revealed in his public story, but to highlight how *masculinity* was overdetermined in the jazz and pop music worlds in which Davis made his career. But its very over-determinedness also fed into its normalization. While white males grappled with their relation to black masculinity, black males were just as fascinated with aspects of white hegemonic masculinity.

While Miles Davis moved between various forms of masculinity from master artist to playboy to Prince of Darkness, his public story shows a certain complicity on his part to emphasize his hypermasculinity as he became more of a pop icon and entered the world of American popular music. While Sherrie Tucker and Ingrid Monson emphasize the commercial pressures in the jazz art world for black musicians to perform a certain black hypermasculinity,[13] American popular music was equally infused with a similar dynamic of black and white masculinity. Davis's public story shows how his performance of hypermasculinity became a core attraction to white music critics in the last two decades of his career. Like Michael Messner's analysis of sports where "wannabe" athletes enable the hypermasculinity of top athletes,[14] so music critics both read and enabled a hypermasculine Davis. What is quite striking in the public story of Davis is how his persona as a race man provocateur, which remained a major part of his presentation of self, was lost in translation and became part and parcel of his badass, hypermasculine persona. How we "remember" Miles Davis as an icon and celebrity has as much to do with his own words and behaviors as it does with their translation in the words of white critics and journalists. It is important to stress Davis's agency in the "Prince of Darkness" persona, but it must be emphasized that the public story we read to understand his hypermasculinity was predominantly written by white critics and journalists. So, we need to remain careful, and this is the case for any black male artist, to acknowledge that Davis's performance of masculinity was as much his act as it was the interpretation of white critics and journalists, or even black critics and journalists like Amiri Baraka or Alex Haley. What we must keep in mind is how the *male gender imagination*, like the *white racial imagination*, was shaping the public story of Miles Davis through *all* the males who wrote or voiced it.

> Scorsese refuses to pass judgment on any of his criminals. Their actions carry their own indictments. Better than anyone else now directing, Scorsese lets his audience relate to the characters as human beings caught in horrible, self-destructive webs of their own spinning. He allows us to ache with pity for odious sociopaths like Travis Bickle or Jake La Motta from "Raging Bull" (1980). They are terribly unhappy people.
>
> —RICHARD A. BLAKE, AMERICA (2006)[15]

Just as the *male gender imagination* interpreted the public figure of Miles Davis, it also has interpreted and identified with the fictional characters Scorsese has put up on the screen. Virtually all of Scorsese's iconic characters have been pure embodiments of hypermasculinity. Richard A. Blake in *America* was reviewing Scorsese's film *The Departed* (2006). The film was about Irish gangsters and police in Boston. According to Blake, the film was full of "breathless action and horrific violence."[16] So, having consumed the hypermasculine carnage of the film, Blake repeated almost verbatim the past themes in Scorsese's public story related to his hypermasculine films: the filmmaker passes no judgment, the action speaks for itself, and in the end, we should pity and empathize with the poor unhappy characters who are victims of their own hypermasculinity. Hypermasculinity became a misogynist pop aesthetic during the New Hollywood era with such films as *Straw Dogs* (1971), *Dirty Harry* (1971), *Death Wish* (1974), *Taxi Driver* (1976), and *Raging Bull* (1980), and continued during the Reagan era led by such cartoonish figures as Sylvester Stallone's John Rambo in *First Blood* (1982) and Chuck Norris's James Braddock in *Missing in Action* (1984).[17] And it continues up to the present in films like *Taken* (2009) and *Drive* (2011). Unlike most portrayals of Hollywood hypermasculinity, however, Scorsese's misogynist pop aesthetic has provided a more dramatic emotional payback. The more mindless, ultraviolent hypermasculinity of his characters, often enough directed at females, but sufficiently directed at other men, becomes a symptom of victimhood seeking redemption or leading to tragedy. The convoluted nature of this gender imagination at work is how film critics have consistently written about both victimhood *and* redemption for Scorsese's hypermasculine characters. Scorsese certainly touches a particular aspect of the male gender imagination that prefers to avoid sympathizing or understanding the pain others feel in the expression of hypermasculine violence, but feels compelled to sympathize with the male characters trapped in their self-destructive masculinity.

What the post–New Hollywood universe of hypermasculine films shows is how this misogynist pop aesthetic worked in multiple ways to render hegemonic masculinity normal, while also inoculating it from any critical examination by making its extreme expressions more often than not opportunities to sympathize with those who embody it. The heroism of hypermasculine protagonists defending themselves from invading aliens, enemy soldiers, sociopathic villains, or urban thugs normalized hypermasculinity as part of American hegemonic masculinity. As Jackson Katz argues, violence became naturalized and normalized within the regime of hegemonic masculinity. It even became a rite of passage or form of redemption.[18] But in Scorsese's films, the uglier reality of extreme hypermasculinity they supposedly revealed have not led ultimately to a critical examination of the true nature of hypermasculinity, nor empathy to its true victims. Instead, Scorsese's films have led him and most male film critics to identify with the actual perpetrators of hypermasculine violence and empathize with their plight. The male gaze, including Scorsese's, is allowed to experience hypermasculine violence guilt free as his films turn into morality tales of tragedy or redemption for their male characters. Whether hero or sociopath, the hypermasculine male more often than not is contained within the unquestioned normality of hegemonic masculinity in the popular male gender imagination.

Martin Scorsese's public story also brings to greater relief how the male gender imagination and white racial imagination acted in the dynamics of hegemonic masculinity in art and entertainment. In Scorsese's public story we saw the intermingling of the negotiation of ethnic, racial, and gender identities. Almost all of Scorsese's hypermasculine characters have been off-white ethnics. And as much as the portrayal of off-white ethnics since New Hollywood have constructed an indelible memory of the marginality and discrimination faced by European "new immigrant" communities, the hypermasculine off-white ethnic acts to place white ethnic males outside the hegemonic masculinity of Anglo-American power and privilege. Hypermasculinity becomes an act of rebellion as well as a symptom of victimhood for the marginal "outsider" white ethnic male. At the same time, however, Scorsese also feeds into the general misogynist pop aesthetic in Hollywood.

In other words, the hypermasculine off-white ethnic male acts ideologically in the construction of a hyphen-nationalist white ethnic mythology as well as in a gender ideology grappling with the loss of male power and privilege since second wave feminism. Scorsese's and others' "obsession" with hypermasculinity in his public story seems driven by not only their gender identities, but their ethnic and racial identities as well.

The gender imagination played a vital role in the Heroic Ages of music and film. Music and film played crucial roles in the popular male imagination's negotiation over masculinity during this period. Both Miles Davis and Martin Scorsese were complicit in performing or projecting hypermasculine images into the popular imagination. Both seemed obsessed with hypermasculine performances of selfhood or self-image, or hypermasculine projections of alter egos or warped ego ideals. The gender imagination also inescapably commingled with the racial imagination during this age. Such commingling was certainly obvious to James Baldwin when confronted with Norman Mailer's primitivist peon to the masculinity of jazz musicians in his fantasy as a "white negro."[19] And it also played out in how Davis had to negotiate his black masculinity under the purview of a white male imagination as well as a black male imagination. And for Scorsese, race and gender would coalesce around an off-white male projection of marginality and suffering that acted to obscure in the popular racial and gender imaginations white male power and privilege.

Looking Back to the Present

Hating Kanye West has long been an international pastime. . . . With Groundhog Day–like timing, West stuck his foot in his mouth earlier this year, decrying Beck's album of the year Grammy award. As was the case with when he protested against Taylor Swift's win in 2009, he again insisted Beyoncé was more deserving . . .

When you're rich and on top of the world, you start peeing on people, or molesting them, or killing them, or killing yourself. But what's truly crazy is that Kanye West hasn't done any of those things. In fact, . . . he's arguably the most critically beloved pop artist of the 21st century so far. . . . As a result, he occupies a bizarre place in the zeitgeist—absolutely beloved and absolutely reviled, simultaneously, sometimes, by the same people.

—BEN WESTHOFF, "THE ENIGMA OF KANYE WEST,"
THE GUARDIAN (2017)[20]

My album of the year was "Lemonade." So, a piece of me did die inside, as a Beyoncé Stan. I'm not going to lie. I was completely rooting for her. I voted for her. . . . She is my icon of my whole life. . . . I felt it was her time to win. My view is kind of what the fuck does she have to do to win album of the year . . . I love her.

—ADELE ON BEYONCÉ AT 2017 GRAMMY AWARDS (2017).[21]

Kanye West seems to be the contemporary embodiment of Miles Davis. The striking similarity between Ben Westhoff grappling with "The Enigma of Kanye West" in 2017 and Barbara Gardner's 1960 "The Enigma of Miles Davis" is almost surreal, if not ultimately depressing, in their verisimilitude five decades after the Civil Rights Act of 1964.[22] A celebrated creative force in popular music, West is as controversial in his public story as Davis was in his. It is the return of the race man provocateur as the enigmatic, angry, black male artist. Now echoes of Davis reverberate via Twitter with West asking, four months before the *Guardian* article on his enigmatic persona and celebrity, that "*Pitchfork, Rolling Stone, New York Times*, and any other white publication. Please do not comment on black music anymore."[23] All West's music, words, and behaviors, as contentious and as problematic as those of the "ill-tempered" Davis, are seemingly lost in translation as the social distance of race remains a permanent part of American music and society. Adele expressed a similar frustration over Beyoncé as West in a statement following her 2017 Grammy win for best album. Her album *24* beat out Beyoncé's *Lemonade*. Both West and Adele point to how a lot has not changed in American culture when it comes to the co-optation of black music as well as the position of black artists in the culture industry. Adele's statement, however, was treated more as an honest appraisal of the music industry than as a racist rant. One could only imagine how the press would have reacted if Beyoncé made the same argument. The point is how the racial ideology in the New Jim Crow America still translates the same ideas through a white racial lens that views such utterances from African Americans as more threatening and racist than from the mouths of whites. And if Miles Davis were still alive, he probably would have expressed sentiments similar to West's and Adele's. Davis walked out of the 1972 Grammy Awards when white jazz musician Bill Evans won best jazz performance over Davis and fellow black nominees Herbie Hancock, Dizzy Gillespie, and Roy Eldridge.[24] Maybe Davis was right, nothing ever changes in America when it comes to race.

I am not arguing that the racial order and the state of African Americans has not changed since the civil rights movement. But since such positive changes are often what a color-blind ideology tends to emphasize when confronted with the state of the African American community and black artists today, it might be best to emphasize how a lot has not changed in black-lives-matter and Oscars-so-white America. The same could be said for the state of the gender order today since second wave feminism. Since the positive changes for women and female artists in the United States is often what a gender-blind ideology tends to emphasize, it might be best to emphasize how a lot has not changed in pink-pussy-hat and me-too America. That a race-baiting, sexual predator, white supremacist now sits in the White House as president of the United States defending neo-Nazi demonstrators and pedophilic Republican senatorial candidates, we might want to reconsider what progress in racial and gender equality we truly have attained. Michelle Alexander presents a stunning in-depth analysis of how a New Jim Crow America has reconstructed a new racial order in which most African Americans remain segregated as a subordinate caste in the United States.[25] Meanwhile, since the Great Recession, many middle-class and working-class African Americans and Latinos have seen their post–civil rights gains fall to the wayside.[26] While women have advanced in certain professional fields, most previous male domains, from politics to business to entertainment, remain areas of male privilege and power.[27] Economic, political, and social gender inequality persists, while rape culture and hypermasculinity remain threats to the well-being of women.[28] Looking back to the careers and public stories of Miles Davis and Martin Scorsese seems to say as much about the present and it does about the past.

Adele also noted how Beyoncé was "making such relevant music" that deeply affected her and so many other "Beyoncé Stans" (hard-core fans of the artist).[29] Beyoncé's music video albums *Lemonade* (2016) and *Beyoncé* (2013) are just as critically acclaimed for their feminist and black-lives-matter politics as for their artistic achievements. But Beyoncé is not the first race woman to speak to the misogyny and racism permeating American society. She is following what Angela Davis shows was a grand tradition among female African American singers from Bessie Smith to Billie Holiday to Nina Simone to Abbey Lincoln to Aretha Franklin to Queen Latifah to Lauryn Hill.[30] And Kanye West is just following the race men of African American music from Duke Ellington to Miles Davis to Max Roach to Chuck Berry to James Brown to Gil Scott-Heron to Chuck D to Jay-Z. A cultural, social, and political Afro-modernism continues to define African American female and male artists into the twenty-first century. Whether Adele's passionate support of Beyoncé, or the rise to fame of Eminem, Daddy Yankee, and Matisyahu to the sound of hip-hop and reggae, Afro-modernism also continues to define the American and global landscape of popular music. And Afro-modernism continues to be co-opted by white musicians and singers as well. When white rappers Macklemore and Ryan Lewis beat critically acclaimed black rapper Kendrick Lamar for best new artist in 2014, it was another déjà vu moment in American music.

Back to Adele, Beyoncé, West, and the Grammys. Black artists have certainly advanced beyond their segregated place in the music market and industry since Davis walked out of the Grammy Awards ceremony in 1972.[31] In fact, in response to Davis and many other black artists' complaints about the 1972 Grammys, Roberta Flack won the 1973 best record award for "The First Time I Ever Saw Your Face." And Stevie Wonder was to win best album in 1974, '75, and '77. Yet, while Beyoncé has won twenty-two Grammy Awards, only four were crossover wins in categories outside R&B, Urban Contemporary, and Rap. Her first crossover wins were in 2010, ten years after her first win with Destiny's Child. Adele received her first top award her debut year with best new artist in 2009. She has since won fifteen Grammy Awards. So, since 2009 Adele has won thirteen Grammy Awards in the top categories of best new artist, pop vocal performance, album, vocal album, and song, while Beyoncé has won only three top categories in best pop vocal performance, song, and music video. And then there is Kanye West, winner of twenty-one Grammy Awards. Quite a record, except none of his awards were crossovers into the top Grammy categories. The internationally acclaimed pop star West is relegated to mere rap artist in the eyes of the American music industry. As Adele might say, what the fuck does West have to do! Miles Davis must be turning in his grave.

> After weeks of continuously unfolding abuse scandals, men have become, quite literally, unbelievable. . . . Men arrive at this moment of reckoning woefully unprepared. Most are shocked by the reality of women's lived experience. Almost all are uninterested or unwilling to grapple with the problem at the heart of all this: the often ugly and dangerous nature of the male libido. . . . The masculine libido and its accompanying forces and pathologies drive so much of culture and politics and the economy, while remaining more or less unexamined, both in intellectual circles and in private life.
>
> —STEPHEN MARCHE, NEW YORK TIMES (2017)[32]

Hypermasculinity is not just the preserve of the present occupant of the White House. It turns out, as journalist Stephen Marche argues in "The

Unexamined Male Libido," America has "discovered" that hypermasculinity permeates every social institution in the United States, while men willfully leave unexamined the breadth and scope of its impact. Marche is also clear how such hypermasculinity is not the preserve of any one group of males whether based on class, race, or political persuasion. It is all-pervasive and systematically ignored. Well, systematically ignored as a social problem, not systematically ignored in the hegemonic masculinity that continues to pervade popular culture. But Marche is wrong about one thing, hypermasculinity is not about libido. It is about male identity, power, and privilege in a world driven by an always susceptible hegemonic masculinity. Marche argues that it's a mix of both power and sexuality, which masculinity obviously is, but hegemonic masculinity is a specific expression of sexuality and gender identity centered on male power and privilege. And as much as Martin Scorsese's public story shows how white racial identity has doubled down since the civil rights era from the ethnic revival to a new hyphen-nationalism, recent events only point to how male gender identity has also doubled down from the hypermasculinity of New Hollywood to the gun-toting rise of the NRA.[33] During the Trump campaign, the presence of the B word along with open expressions of violent harm toward Hillary Clinton revealed that an ugly misogyny had woven itself into the American political psyche as much as an equally ugly racism. It seems as if Scorsese's vigilante Travis Bickle in *Taxi Driver*, who looked out at an urban landscape of fallen women and depraved African American men, had finally found his true brethren in the campaign to Make America Great Again.

> What I really want to say is that it is really hard sometimes for women in music. It's like a f——ing boys club that we just can't get into. . . . I tried for so long, I just really wanted to be taken seriously as a musician for my intelligence more than my body ever in this business. You don't always feel like when you're working that people believe that you have a musical background, that you understand what you're doing because you're a female.
>
> **—LADY GAGA AT BILLBOARD'S WOMEN IN MUSIC (2015)[34]**

I have always firmly believed that every director should be judged solely by their work, and not by their work based on their gender. Hollywood is supposedly a community of forward thinking and progressive people yet this horrific situation for women directors persists. Gender discrimination stigmatizes our entire industry. Change is essential. Gender neutral hiring is essential.

—KATHRYN BIGELOW, TIME (2015)[35]

But hypermasculinity is only an extreme expression, unfortunately far too common an extreme expression, of sexism that has permeated the culture industries. Lady Gaga's blast against the music industry was not the first attack by women musicians, singers, and songwriters about the misogyny of the American music industry. Female pop star Kesha Sebert's failed efforts to be released from a contract with successful record producer Dr. Luke, who abused her mentally and physically over several years, demonstrated the depth of gender discrimination in the industry.[36] And Kathryn Bigelow was also not alone in criticizing a film industry rampant with gender discrimination.[37] The ACLU in 2015 "sent three letters to the federal government . . . asking for an investigation into institutionalized sexism in the industry."[38] And in 2017, a strong and vocal #MeToo movement emerged, agitating for not only a radical change in the gender politics of the culture industry but also radical change in gender relations in all aspects of American life.

In some ways, we return to the issue I introduced at the beginning of the book of moving from the messiness of life, culture, and history into the hoped-for clarity of a sociological imagining of the structures and patterns that permeate American society and culture. But besides the way sociologists "translate" the world, we have found that the messiness of social life is also translated in the real world in distinctly different ways depending on who is doing the interpretation. In this case, it is how from this messiness certain individuals and groups have focused on the exceptional moments when individuals seem to have broken down the racial and gender boundaries that define our social order. Or in this messiness they have focused on when racial or gender barriers have been significantly transformed for the better by law or culture. It's this translation of the messiness of social life and history that feeds color-blind and gender-blind ideologies that seek to ignore how the racial formation and gender formation in the United States have shown themselves to be quite resilient. And how such translation allows color-blind and gender-blind ideologies to ignore how New Jim Crow and New Sexist America can reverse what progress minorities and women have made.

I bring in the present state of race and gender relations not to make some quick and simple diagnosis of how little the racial and gender orders have changed. But because the *present* and the *past* inform each other. They have haunted me since I began this project. The present has haunted me since Michelle Alexander's 2010 *The New Jim Crow* and 2013s Black Lives Matter shocked me from my comfortable position as a "critical" sociologist who studied and taught on the racial formation but enjoyed the social distance of the privilege and experience of a white ethnic sociologist that afforded me the luxury of an ivory tower radicalism. The present also shocked me from my comfortable position as a "pro-feminist" sociologist who studied and taught on the gender formation, but watched as rape culture still pervaded college campuses where supposedly liberal academia reigns. Or watched as an accomplished, brilliant, and thoughtful female presidential candidate was framed as a bitch and criminal to the political advantage of her opponent. Or watched the uncovering of a systemic problem of misogyny and hypermasculinity in the news, arts, and entertainment world I study for a living. This present has forced me to constantly reassess my reading of Miles Davis and Martin Scorsese. But the past in the public stories I read also informed how I read the present. How I read the public story of Kanye West as race man provocateur or Kesha Sebert as heroic rebel against hypermasculine oppression in the music industry. How I read film producer Harvey Weinstein as serial sexual predator or Ryan Gosling as a hypermasculine hero in *Drive* (2011). In reading the past, I have seen more clearly how the *normalization* of the white racial imagination and male gender imagination, and the racism and misogyny driving them, is not a vestigial remnant of this past, but a defining part of the present. The present and the past speak to the historical continuities of the racial and gender formations, and more importantly, to their resilience in the face of major social movements against them and their perpetuation under the guise of color-blind and gender-blind liberal ideologies.

A Final Note on Public Stories

There's nothing original in this tale and there's ample evidence, beyond West, that humans were not built to withstand the weight of celebrity. But for black artists who rise to the heights of Jackson and West, the weight is more, because they come from communities in desperate need of champions. Kurt Cobain's death was a great tragedy for his legions of fans. Tupac's was a tragedy for an entire people. When brilliant black artists fall down on the stage, they don't fall down alone.
—TA-NEHISI COATES, "I'M NOT BLACK, I'M KANYE,"
THE ATLANTIC (2018)[39]

In 2018, black writer Ta-Nehisi Coates presented a thoughtful rumination in *The Atlantic* on Kanye West's recent fall from grace. The singer-songwriter's controversial "Donald Trump is a fellow dragon energy brother" tweet on April 25, 2018, ignited a firestorm of criticism and dismay. Like many black writers who grappled with the fall from grace of Miles Davis three decades earlier, Coates entered West's public story not to present any final judgment on West, but to use the moment to join the ongoing *cultural politics* that had always been part of the public story of this "god in his time" artist for almost twenty years.[40] Coates's various reflections were less about the controversial tweet and more about the cultural significance and enigmas of artists like Kanye West and Michael Jackson as well as on the nature of fame, African American identity and self-esteem, America since November 2016, and the myths Americans tell themselves to hide the ugly truths about our racist sins, past and present. In his engagement in Kanye West's public story, Coates was effortlessly transcoding across a wide set of discursive fields and ideological formations, which is what has made him an award-winning writer. While not all artists' public stories have elicited as vibrant a cultural politics as Kanye West, many have *invited* such transcoding about art, artists, art fields, and their cultural, social, and political significance. And this book was about how the public stories of Miles Davis and Martin Scorsese represented major *collective* and *public* expressive spaces for these artists and others to grapple not only with American music and film but also with currents running through American society and politics.

I introduced Michael Ryan and Douglas Kellner's concept of "transcoding" because these authors were tackling a similar aspect of art, entertainment, and politics that I confronted in my discovery of the complex and multifaceted nature of Miles Davis's and Martin Scorsese's art and public stories.[41] While Ryan and Kellner were interested in Hollywood films' transcoding of other discursive fields, I was struck by how much the public stories of these two iconic artists were more than just about their art worlds and the groundbreaking art they created. Their artistic rebellion, creativity, and innovation were certainly part of their public stories, but from the very beginning far more was going on, even in terms of the cultural politics of music and film, let alone the cultural politics of American society. The complex and diverse storytelling I discovered certainly resonated with Tricia Rose's recent work on the ideological discourses she argues defined the "hip-hop wars."[42] But the most powerful aspect of the transcoding found in Davis's and Scorsese's public stories is how it bridged the most micro of personal biography to the most macro of social, political, and historical commentary with everything in between. These public stories even elicited the racial and gender imaginations of storytellers as they commented on the "virility" of black male musicians like saxophonist Sonny Rollins or the "redemption" of ultraviolent hypermasculine protagonists like boxer Jake La Motta.

Observers of art, media, and society are always seeking answers to how individuals and communities articulate the contours of seemingly distant ideological formations found in political discourse or social commentary. They also are seeking answers to how personal imaginations, memories, and biographies transcode such formations. I have shown how public stories in art are special discursive fields, or public expressive spaces, that connect different fields and formations as they transcode their meanings into stories about art, artists, and art fields. As individuals actively transcode different fields and formations in their everyday lives, conversations, and personal memories, they bring this transcoding into the *cultural politics* of American art. They do it not only in art and entertainment but also in the constant exchanges about art and society found in the public stories *about* artists and their art. Whether telling stories about Miles Davis, Martin Scorsese, Wynton Marsalis, Steven Soderbergh, John Leguizamo, Kathryn Bigelow, Ava DuVernay, Beyoncé, Adele, or the enigmatic Kanye West, such public stories invite artists, critics, journalist, writers, and others to join in a collective conversation about the most personal facets of their lives to the most political currents of American life. And, of course, such public stories invite a collective conversation about American art and entertainment as well.

ACKNOWLEDGMENTS

I would like to thank the members of the Colgate Sociology and Anthropology Reading Group, especially Carolyn L. Hsu, Elana Shever, Alicia Simmons, and Chris Henke, who helped me during the initial thinking and writing on this project. They helped to set me in the right direction. I also appreciate the positive feedback I received at several panels for the International Sociological Association Sociology of Art Research Committee. The Colgate Research Council was also generous in providing several grants to support my research. I also would like to thank the Institute for Jazz Studies at Rutgers University, Newark, especially archivist Tad Hershorn, who provided access to their archives and supportive advice. Finally, Michelle Bigenho has been a constant support throughout this project both personally and intellectually. Her thoughtful comments on my book gave me the confidence to remain true to myself in completing my vision of this project. Thanks Michelle!

NOTES

Introduction

1. László Benedek, dir., *The Wild One* (Columbia Pictures, 1953).

2. Peter Bart, "A Prisoner of the System," *New York Times*, October 23, 1966, X13. See also Ezra Goodman, "*Champion* Producer," *New York Times*, April 10, 1949, X4.

3. See Paul Lopes, "The Heroic Age of American Avant-Garde Art," *Theory and Society* 44, no. 3 (July 2015): 219–49.

4. Boris Tomaševskij, "Literature and Biography," in *Readings in Russian Poetics: Formalist and Structuralist Views*, ed. L. Matejka and K. Pomorska (Ann Arbor: University of Michigan Press, 1978), 47–55; also on biographical legend see Robert Kapsis, *Hitchcock: The Making of a Reputation* (Chicago: University of Chicago Press, 1992).

5. Ron Eyerman, "Toward a Meaningful Sociology of the Arts," in *Myth, Meaning, and Performance: Toward a New Cultural Sociology of the Arts*, ed. R. Eyerman and L. McCormick (Boulder, CO: Paradigm, 2006), 13–34.

6. Pierre Bourdieu, *The Rules of Art: Genesis and Structure of the Literary Field* (Stanford, CA: Stanford University Press, 1992).

7. Lopes, "Heroic Age of American Avant-Garde Art."

8. Vera L. Zolberg, *Constructing a Sociology of the Arts* (Cambridge: Cambridge University Press, 1990).

9. Judith R. Blau, "The Disjunctive History of U.S. Museums, 1869–1980," *Social Forces* 70, no. 1 (1991): 87–105.

10. Paul DiMaggio, "Cultural Boundaries and Structural Change: The Extension of the High Culture Model to Theater, Opera, and the Dance, 1900–1940," in *Cultivating Differences: Symbolic Boundaries and the Making of Inequality*, ed. M. Lamont and M. Fournier (Chicago: University of Chicago Press, 1992), 21–57.

11. Philip H. Ennis, *The Seventh Stream: The Emergence of Rock-n-Roll in American Popular Music* (Middletown, CT: Wesleyan University Press, 1992).

12. Richard A. Peterson, "Why 1955? Explaining the Advent of Rock Music," *Popular Music* 9, no. 1 (1990): 97–115.

13. Peterson, "Why 1955?"; Ennis, *Seventh Stream*; Paul Lopes, *The Rise of a Jazz Art World* (Cambridge: Cambridge University Press, 2002); Richard Maltby, *Hollywood Cinema*, 2nd ed. (Malden, MA: Blackwell, 2003).

14. Peterson, "Why 1955?"

15. DiMaggio, "Cultural Boundaries and Structural Change."

16. Lopes, "Heroic Age of American Art."

17. On genre communities and genre ideals see Jennifer C. Lena, *Banding Together: How Communities Create Genres in Popular Music* (Princeton, NJ: Princeton University Press, 2012).

18. Susan Sontag, *Against Interpretation, and Other Essays* (1966; reprint, New York: Picador, 2001).

19. Sontag, *Against Interpretation*, 303.

20. Sontag, *Against Interpretation*, 303–4.

21. John Nickel, "Disabling African American Men: Liberalism and Race Message Films," *Cinema Journal* 44, no. 1 (Fall 2004): 25–48; Bosley Crowther, "Kirk Douglas Plays the Hero in 'Champion,' Film of Ring Lardner's Fight Story," *New York Times*, April 11, 1949, 29.

22. Michael Omi and Howard Winant, *Racial Formation in the United States* (New York: Routledge and Paul Kegan, 1986); Michael Omi and Howard Winant, *Racial Formation in the United States*, 3rd ed. (New York: Routledge, 2014).

23. Omi and Winant, *Racial Formation in the United States*.

24. Nickel, "Disabling African American Men."

25. Eduardo Bonilla-Silva, *Racism without Racists: Color-Blind Racism and the Persistence of Racial Inequality in the United States* (Lanham, MD: Rowman and Littlefield, 2003).

26. Jesse Washington, "King 'Content of Character' Quote Inspires Debate," Associated Press, January 20, 2013, LexisNexis Academic, date accessed, June 6, 2018.

27. Bonilla-Silva, *Racism without Racists*.

28. Michelle Alexander, *The New Jim Crow: Mass Incarceration in the Age of Colorblindness* (New York: New Press, 2010).

29. Alexander, *New Jim Crow*.

30. Sarah Shannon, Christopher Uggen, Melissa Thompson, Jason Schnittker, and Michael Massoglia, "Growth in the U.S. Ex-felon and Ex-prisoner Population, 1948 to 2010," Population Association of America Annual Meeting (2011), http://paa2011.princeton.edu/papers/111687, date accessed, June 6, 2018.

31. Mike Hill, ed., *Whiteness: A Critical Reader* (New York: New York University Press, 1997); Ashley W. Doane and Eduardo Bonilla-Silva, eds., *White Out: The Continuing Significance of Racism* (New York: Routledge, 2003); France Winddance Twine and Charles A. Gallagher, eds., *Retheorizing Race and Whiteness in the 21st Century* (New York: Routledge, 2012).

32. Herman Gray, *Cultural Moves: African Americans and the Politics of Representation* (Berkeley: University of California Press, 2005).

33. Ronald Radano and Philip V. Bohlman, *Music and the Racial Imagination* (Chicago: University of Chicago Press, 2000), 1.

34. Radano and Bohlman, *Music and the Racial Imagination*, 5.

35. Eric Lott, *Love and Theft: Blackface Minstrelsy and the American Working Class* (Oxford: Oxford University Press, 1993).

36. Radano and Bohlman, *Music and the Racial Imagination*, 8.

37. Herman Gray, "Black Masculinity and Visual Culture," *Callaloo* 18, no. 2 (1995): 401–5; Jon Panish, *The Color of Jazz* (Jackson: University of Mississippi Press, 1997); Robin D. G. Kelley, "New Monastery: Monk and the Jazz Avant-Garde," *Black Music Research* 19, no. 12 (1999): 135–68; Eric Porter, *What Is This Thing Called Jazz: African American Musicians as Artists, Critics, and Activists* (Berkeley: University of California Press, 2002); Nichole T. Rustin, "*Cante Hondo*: Charles Mingus, Nat Hentoff, and Jazz Racism," *Critical Sociology* 32, no. 2–3 (2006): 309–31; Ingrid Monson, "The Problem with White Hipness: Race, Gender, and Cultural Conceptions in Jazz Historical Discourse," *Journal of the American Musicological Society* 48, no. 3 (1995): 396–422.

38. Paul Lopes, *The Rise of a Jazz Art World*.

39. Gray, *Cultural Moves*, 19.

40. Nickel, "Disabling African American Men." See also Bosley Crowther, "*Home of the Brave*, at Victoria," *New York Times*, May 13, 1949, 29; Bosley Crowther, "Screen: A Very Forceful Drama," *New York Times*, September 25, 1958, 29.

41. Isaac Julien, dir., *Baadasssss Cinema* (New York: New Video, 2002).

42. Richard D. Alba, *Ethnic Identity: The Transformation of White America* (New Haven, CT: Yale University Press, 1990); Mary C. Waters, *Ethnic Options: Choosing Identities in America* (Berkeley: University of California Press, 1990); Matthew Frye Jacobson, *Whiteness of a Different Color: European Immigrants and the Alchemy of Race* (Cambridge, MA: Harvard University Press, 1998); David R. Roediger, *Working toward Whiteness: How America's Immigrants Became White* (New York: Basic Books, 2005).

43. Matthew Frye Jacobson, *Roots Too: White Ethnic Revival in Post–Civil Rights America* (Cambridge, MA: Harvard University Press, 2006).

44. Barbara J. Risman, *Gender Vertigo: American Families in Transition* (New Haven, CT: Yale University Press, 1998).

45. Barbara J. Risman, "Gender as Social Structure: Theory Wrestling with Activism," *Gender and Society* 18, no. 4 (2005): 429–50; on the intersectionality of race, class, sexuality, and other forms of inequality also see Patricia Hill Collins, *Black Feminist Thought: Knowledge, Consciousness, and the Politics of Empowerment* (New York: Routledge, 1991).

46. R. W. Connell, *Masculinities* (Berkeley: University of California Press, 1995).

47. R. W. Connell and James W. Messerschmidt, "Hegemonic Masculinity: Rethinking the Concept," *Gender and Society* 19, no. 6 (2005): 829–59.

48. Michael A. Messner, *Taking the Field: Women, Men, and Sports* (Minneapolis: University of Minnesota Press, 2002).

49. Michael Ryan and Douglas Kellner, *Camera Politica: The Politics and Ideology of Contemporary Hollywood Film* (Bloomington: Indiana University Press, 1988), 12–13.

50. John Thornton Caldwell, *Production Culture: Industrial Reflexivity and Critical Practice in Film and Television* (Durham, NC: Duke University Press, 2008).

51. Robert E. Kapsis, "Reputation Building and the Film Art World: The Case of Alfred Hitchcock," *Sociological Quarterly* 30, no. 1 (1989): 15–35; Robert E. Kapsis, *Hitchcock: The Making of a Reputation*; Tomaševskij, "Literature and Biography."

52. France Winddance Twine and Charles A. Gallagher, "The Future of Whiteness: A Map of the 'Third Wave,'" in Twine and Gallagher, *Retheorizing Race and Whiteness in the 21st Century*, 1–20.

53. Lopes, *Rise of a Jazz Art World*.

54. Pierre Bourdieu, *The Field of Cultural Production* (New York: Columbia University Press); Bourdieu, *Rules of Art*.

55. Priscilla Parkhurst Ferguson, "A Cultural Field in the Making: Gastronomy in 19th-Century France," *American Journal of Sociology* 104, no. 3 (1998): 597–641; Shyon Baumann, "Intellectualization and Art World Development: Film in the United States," *American Sociological Review* 66 (June 2001): 404–26.

56. Herman Gray, *Watching Race: Television and the Struggle for "Blackness"* (Minneapolis: University of Minnesota Press, 1995); Sherrie A. Inness, *Tough Girls: Women Warriors and Wonder Woman in Popular Culture* (Philadelphia: University of Pennsylvania Press, 1998); Ron Becker, *Gay TV and Straight America* (New Brunswick, NJ: Rutgers University Press, 2006).

57. Tricia Rose, *Hip Hop Wars: What We Talk About When We Talk About Hip Hop—and Why It Matters* (New York: Basic Books, 2008); Ryan and Kellner, *Camera Politica*.

58. Twine and Gallagher, "Future of Whiteness."

Chapter 1: Miles Davis: Jazz, Race, and Negotiating the Popular

1. Leonard Feather, "A Man and His Music," *Los Angeles Times*, September 30, 1991, F1.

2. Steve Dollar, "Whispered Words with Wynton Marsalis," *Atlanta Journal and Constitution*, January 13, 1991, LexisNexis Academic, date accessed, December 1, 2017.

3. On race music, black professional musicians, and jazz see Paul Lopes, *The Rise of a Jazz Art World* (Cambridge: Cambridge University Press, 2002); Eric Porter, *What Is This Thing Called Jazz: African American Musicians as Artists, Critics, and Activists* (Berkeley: University of California Press, 2002).

4. For James Reese Europe's call for a "Negro Music" see Ron Welburn, "James Reese Europe and the Infancy of Jazz Criticism," *Black Music Research* 7 (1987): 35–44.

5. Herman Gray, *Cultural Moves: African Americans and the Politics of Representation* (Berkeley: University of California Press, 2005).

6. Gray, *Cultural Moves.*

7. Barry Ulanov, "Miles and Leo," *Metronome*, July 1947, 19.

8. Leonard Feather, "New Horns for Old," *Metronome Jazz 1950*, January 1950, 23.

9. Nat Hentoff, "Miles: A Trumpeter in the Midst of a Big Comeback Makes a Very Frank Appraisal of Today's Scene," *Down Beat*, November 2, 1955, 13.

10. Ralph Gleason, "Rhythm Section: Miles Davis, Tops Small Group Stylist," *Milwaukee Journal*, October 11, 1958, Institute of Jazz Studies (hereafter IJS) file.

11. Martin Williams, "Miles Davis: A Man Walking," *Saturday Review*, November 10, 1962, 55.

12. Ross Russell, "Miles Davis: Miles in the Sky," *Jazz and Pop*, January 1969, 49, 50.

13. Jack Chambers, *Milestones: The Music and Times of Miles Davis* (New York: Da Capo Press, 1998).

14. Hentoff, "Miles: A Trumpeter in the Midst of a Big Comeback Makes a Very Frank Appraisal of Today's Jazz Scene," 13–14.

15. Charles Mingus, "An Open Letter from Charlie Mingus," *Down Beat*, November 30, 1955, 12–13.

16. Frank Alker, *The Miles Davis Reader: Interviews and Features from Down Beat Magazine* (New York: Hal Leonard Books, 2007), 44–46.

17. On the general disdain for jazz critics held by jazz musicians see John Gennari, *Blowin' Hot and Cool: Jazz and Its Critics* (Chicago: University of Chicago Press, 2006).

18. Ralph Gleason, *Miles Davis in Person—Friday Night at the Blackhawk, San Francisco, Vol. II* (Columbia, 1961), liner notes.

19. Nat Hentoff, "The Murderous Modes of Jazz," *Esquire*, September 1960, 89.

20. Lopes, *Rise of a Jazz Art World.*

21. "Legendary Miles at Monterey," *Sacramento Observer*, August 28, 1969, Ethnic News-Watch, date accessed, June 12, 2016.

22. Stanley Goldstein, "Miles Davis," *Playboy*, August 1960, IJS file; Marc Crawford, "Miles Davis: Evil Genius of Jazz," *Ebony*, January 1961, 70.

23. Gleason, *Miles Davis in Person.*

24. Joe Goldberg, *Jazz Masters of the Fifties* (New York: Macmillan, 1965), 82.

25. Bill Coss, "History of the Year," *Metronome Jazz 57*, January 1957, 12.

26. Guthrie P. Ramsey Jr., *Race Music: Black Cultures from Bebop to Hip-Hop* (Berkeley: University of California Press, 2003).

27. On the white racial lens and racial order see Jon Panish, *The Color of Jazz* (Jackson: University of Mississippi Press, 1997); Lopes, *Rise of a Jazz Art World*; Porter, *What Is This Thing*; Nichole T. Rustin. "*Cante Hondo*: Charles Mingus, Nat Hentoff, and Jazz Racism," *Critical Sociology* 32, no. 2–3 (2006): 309–31; Ingrid Monson, *Freedom Sounds: Civil Rights Call Out to Jazz and Africa* (Oxford: Oxford University Press, 2007).

28. John Hammond, "The Tragedy of Duke Ellington, the "Black Prince of Jazz": A Musician of Great Talent Forsakes Simplicity for Pretension," *Down Beat*, November 1935, 1, 6.

29. John Tynan, "Les McCann and 'The Truth,'" *Down Beat*, September 15, 1960, 20.

30. On the use of terms like *soul* and *funk* as signifiers of black ownership of black culture see Robin Kelley, *Yo' Mama's Disfunktional! Fighting the Culture Wars in Urban America* (Boston: Beacon, 1997).

31. Nat Hentoff, "Jazz Messengers Blazing a Spirited Trail," *Down Beat*, February 22, 1956, 10.

32. Don DeMichael, "Inside the Cannonball Adderley Quartet," *Down Beat*, June 8, 1961, 19+.

33. Sonny Rollins, *Freedom Suite* (Riverside, 1958), liner notes.

34. Nat Hentoff, "The New Faces of Jazz," *The Reporter*, August 17, 1961, 52.

35. Margo Guryan, *Max Roach: Percussion Bitter Sweet* (Candid, 1961), liner notes.

36. Guryan, *Max Roach*.

37. Monson, *Freedom Sounds*.

38. Robin D. G. Kelley, "Dig They Freedom: Meditations on History and the Black Avant-Garde," *Lenox Avenue* 3 (1997): 13–27.

39. George Hoefer, "Ornette Coleman," *Down Beat*, January 7, 1960, 40.

40. Billy Taylor, "Progressive Jazz," *Down Beat*, March 7, 1956, 11.

41. On the melding of different trends in modern jazz and other music in Black Music see Ronald M. Radano, *New Musical Figurations: Anthony Braxton's Cultural Critique* (Chicago: University of Chicago Press, 1993); Kelley, "Dig They Freedom"; Porter, *What Is This Thing Called Jazz*.

42. LeRoi Jones, "The Jazz Avant-Garde," *Metronome*, September 1960, 9.

43. Victor Schonfeld, *Rufus* (Fontana, 1963), liner notes.

44. Bill Quinn, "Marion Brown: Topside Underground," *Down Beat*, February 6, 1967, 14+.

45. Steve Young, *The New Wave in Jazz: New Black Music* (Impulse, 1965), liner notes.

46. Nat Hentoff, "The New Jazz—Black, Angry, and Hard to Understand," *New York Times*, December 25, 1966, A10.

47. Porter, *What Is This Thing Called Jazz*.

48. Terry Martin, "Caught in the Act: Roscoe Mitchell," *Down Beat*, September 7, 1967, 28+.

49. Archie Shepp, "Archie Shepp Speaks Bluntly," *Down Beat*, December 16, 1965, 11+.

50. Robert Osterman, "They Don't Call It Jazz," *National Observer*, June 7, 1965.

51. LeRoi Jones, *Black Music* (New York: William and Morrow, 1967), 189, 210–11.

52. Michael Patterson, "Archie Shepp," *Black World*, November 1973, 89.

53. A. B. Spellman, "Deeper Than Jazz," *New Republic*, May 11, 1968, 37+.

54. Bill Smith, "Unit Structures: Cecil Taylor," *Coda*, March 1975, 2+.

55. Valerie Wilmer, "Milford Graves," *Coda*, September 1976, 8+.

56. Robert Levin, "The Third World: Archie Shepp II," *Jazz and Pop*, December 1970, 12.

57. John Tynan, "Take Five," *Down Beat*, November 23, 1961, 40; Leonard Feather, "Feather's Nest," *Down Beat*, February 15, 1962, 40; "The Jazz Avant-Garde: Pro and Con," *Music '65*, January 1966, 88+; LeRoi Jones, "Loft Jazz," *Down Beat*, May 9, 1963, 13–14.

58. Jones, "Loft Jazz"; John Litweiler, *The Freedom Principle: Jazz after 1958* (New York: Da Capo Press, 1984).

59. "Declaration by the Avant-Garde," *Music '64*, January 1965, 70.

60. Robert Palmer, "The New Jazz Wave," *Saturday Review*, October 27, 1979, 48.

61. "Ebony Black Music Poll: The Winners for 1974," *Ebony*, February 1974, 44, 46.

62. Leonard Feather, "Miles Lives, Music Lives, Life Goes On . . ." *Melody Maker*, September 12, 1970, 26.

63. Mike Hennessey, "Jazz Is Holding Its Own," *Jazz and Pop*, December 1970, 24+.

64. Don Heckman, "Jazz-Rock," *Stereo Review*, November 1974, 75.

65. Chambers, *Milestones*.

66. Heckman, "Jazz-Rock," 76.

67. Leonard Feather, "Blindfold Test: Miles Davis," *Down Beat*, June 18, 1964, 31.

68. "Top LPs & Tapes," *Billboard*, June 23, 1973.

69. "A Flourish in Jazz," *Time*, July 7, 1976, 38+.

70. Nat Freedland, "Cross Over the Bridge from Jazz to Pop," *Billboard*, June 23, 1973, 54.

71. Heckman, "Jazz-Rock," 75.

72. Barry Tepperman, "Record Review: Miles Davis," *Coda*, January 1976, 27.

73. Dan Morgenstern, "Miles in Motion," *Down Beat*, January 3, 1970, in Alker, *Miles Davis Reader*, 95.

74. Leonard Feather, "Blindfold Test: Clark Terry," *Down Beat*, January 20, 1972, 30.

75. "People Are Talking About," *Jet*, July 30, 1970, 16+.

76. Leonard Feather, "The Name of the Game," *Down Beat*, October 15, 1970, 11.

77. Leonard Feather, "The Definitive Miles Davis," *Penthouse*, June 1972, 18+.

78. Jane Ennis, "Miles Smiles," *Melody Maker*, January 9, 1973, 43+.

79. Don DeMichael, "Jazz's Picasso Puts It in Black and White," *Rolling Stone*, December 13, 1969, 23+.

80. Al Aronowitz, "Rock Is a White Man's Word, Says Miles," *Melody Maker*, October 17, 1970, 44.

81. DeMichael, "Jazz's Picasso," 23+.

82. Frederick Murphy, "Miles Davis: The Monster of Modern Music," *Encore*, July 21, 1975, 50.

83. Murphy, "Miles Davis: The Monster of Modern Music," 50.

84. Ennis, "Miles Smiles," 43+.

85. Greg Hall, "Miles: Today's Most Influential Contemporary Musician," *Down Beat*, July 18, 1974, 16+.

86. Phyl Garland, "Ebony Music Poll: The Winners for 1976," *Ebony*, June 1976, 62.

87. Vernon Frazier, "Don Pullen," *Coda*, October 1976, 2+.

88. Bret Primack, "Blindfold Test: Lester Bowie," *Down Beat*, May 17, 1976, 33.

89. Bill Coles, *Miles Davis: The Early Years* (1974; New York: Da Capo Press, 1994), 104–5.

90. "A Silver Newport with All the Wonderful Mixed Up Jazz," *Time*, July 10, 1978, 82+.

91. Albert Goldman, "Eclectic Plus Ethnic Plus Electric Equals Fusion," *Esquire*, October 1977, 44, 56.

92. David Lee, "Weather Report: Mr. Gone," *Down Beat*, January 11, 1979, 22.

93. "Concert Review: Weather Report," *Down Beat*, February 22, 1979, 39.

94. Neil Tesser, "Weather Report: Heavy Weather," *Down Beat*, May 19, 1977, 23.

95. Bob Rosenthal, "Weather Report," *Down Beat*, February 1981, 14+.

96. A. James Liska, "Grover Washington Jr. The Midas Touch," *Down Beat*, April 1983, 14+.

97. A. James Liska, "Interview: Wynton and Branford Marsalis," *Down Beat*, December 1982, 14+.

98. Chris Albertson, "Wynton Marsalis' Impressive Debut Album Promises Well for the Future of Jazz," *Stereo Review*, May 1982, IJS file.

99. Hollie I. West, "Wynton Marsalis: Blowing His Own Horn, Speaking His Own Mind," *Jazz Times*, July 1983, IJS file.

100. Howard Mandel, "The Wynton Marsalis Interview," *Down Beat*, July 1984, 16+.

101. Mandel, "The Wynton Marsalis Interview."

102. Stanley Crouch, *Wynton Marsalis* (Columbia, 1982), liner notes.

103. On Crouch as neoconservative critic see Stanley Crouch, *Notes on the Hanging Judge* (Oxford: Oxford University Press, 1990).

104. Stanley Crouch, "Bringing Atlantis Up to the Top," *Village Voice*, April 16, 1979, 65, 67; Stanley Crouch, "The King of Constant Repudiation," *Village Voice*, September 3, 1979, 20+.

105. See Gray, *Cultural Moves*, 32–51.

106. Stanley Crouch, *Standard Time, Volume One* (Columbia, 1987), liner notes.

107. Wynton Marsalis, "Why We Must Preserve Our Jazz Heritage," *Ebony*, February 1986, 159.

108. Evelyn Brooks Higginbotham, *Righteous Discontent: The Women's Movement in the Black Baptist Church, 1880–1920* (Cambridge, MA: Harvard University Press, 1993).

109. Wynton Marsalis, "In Defense of Standards," *Keynote* (December 1984): IJS file.

110. John Lahey, "The New Jazz Tradition," *Coda*, December 1984, 10+.

111. John Pareles, "Jazz Swings Back to Tradition," *New York Times*, June 17, 1984, SM22+; John Pareles, "Youth Puts Vigor in Jazz: Young Players Enliven Jazz," *New York Times*, September 9, 1984, H33.

112. John Ephland, "Musical Harvest," *Down Beat*, December 1990, 6.

113. Liska, "Interview: Wynton & Branford Marsalis."

114. "47th Annual Readers' Poll," *Down Beat*, December 1982, 18+.

115. "46th Annual Readers' Poll," *Down Beat*, December 1981, 20+.

116. On Davis's last decade of music making see George Cole, *The Last Miles: The Music of Miles Davis, 1980–1991* (Ann Arbor: University of Michigan Press, 2005).

117. Leonard Feather, "Miles Davis Concert—The Prince Has Gone," *Los Angeles Times*, September 28, 1981, G1.

118. Stephen Brunt, "Miles Davis and His Music Cut through Affections," *Globe and Mail*, June 20, 1985, E4.

119. West, "Wynton Marsalis."

120. In Steve Bloom, "The Hottest Lips in America," *Rolling Stone*, November 8, 1984, IJS file.

121. Stanley Crouch, "Play the Right Thing," *New Republic*, February 12, 1990, IJS file.

122. Gary Giddins, "The Young Jazzman of Our Dreams," *Village Voice*, October 16, 1984, IJS file.

123. Greg Tate, "Stagolee vs. the Proper Negro," *Village Voice*, September 1984, in Greg Tate, *Flyboy in the Buttermilk: Essays on Contemporary America* (New York: Simon and Schuster, 1992), 51.

124. Gray, *Cultural Moves*, 32–51.

125. Robin Tolleson, "Miles Davis: *Doo-Bop*," *Down Beat*, August 1992, 37.

126. Samuel A. Floyd Jr., *The Power of Black Music: Interpreting Its History from Africa to the United States* (Oxford,: Oxford University Press, 1995).

127. Gray, *Cultural Moves*, 32–73.

128. Gray, *Cultural Moves*, 52–73.

Chapter 2: Martin Scorsese: Rival Narratives of Autonomy in American Film

1. Andrew Lewis Conn, "The Adolescents of Martin Scorsese," *Film Comment*, May/June 1998, 24–27.

2. Pia Farrell, "France Lionizes U.S. Director Scorsese," *Hollywood Reporter*, October 7, 1991, LexisNexis Academic, date accessed, November 9, 2017.

3. Andrew Sarris, "Notes on the Auteur Theory in 1962," *Film Culture* 27 (Winter 1962–63): 1–9; Andrew Sarris, *The American Cinema: Directors and Directions, 1929–1968* (New York: Dutton, 1968).

4. D. K. Holm, *Independent Cinema* (Harpenden, UK: Kamera Books, 2008), 12.

5. Pierre Bourdieu, *Distinction* (Cambridge, MA: Harvard University Press, 1984).

6. Richard Maltby, *Hollywood Cinema*, 2nd ed. (Malden, MA: Blackwell, 2003).

7. Bernard Weinraub, "Martin Scorsese, Attracted to Excess, Still Taking Risks," *New York Times*, November 27, 1995, C11.

8. Timothy Rhys, "Martin Scorsese' Comfortable State of Anxiety," *MovieMaker*, Fall 2002, 60.

9. Sarris, "Notes on the Auteur Theory"; Sarris, *American Cinema*.

10. Peter Biskind, *Easy Riders, Raging Bulls* (New York: Simon and Schuster, 1998), 16; Shyon Baumann, *Hollywood Highbrow: From Entertainment to Art* (Princeton, NJ: Princeton University Press, 2007).

11. Amy Taubin, "Martin Scorsese's Cinema of Obsession," in *Martin Scorsese Interviews*, ed. P. Brunette (Jackson: University Press of Mississippi, 1999), 138.

12. Martin Scorsese and Michael Henry Wilson, *A Personal Journey with Martin Scorsese through American Movies* (New York: Hyperion, 1997), 17.

13. Elaine Dutka, "I Am the Movies I Make," *Los Angeles Times*, February 22, 1997, F1.

14. Ian Christie, "The Illusionist," *Sight and Sound*, January 2012, 36.

15. Michiku Kakutani, "Scorsese's Past Colors His New Film," *New York Times*, February 13, 1983, 23.

16. Phillips McCandlish, "From Little Italy to Big-Time Movies," *New York Times*, October 18, 1973, 64.

17. Hal Hinson, "Scorsese, Master of the Rage," *Washington Post*, November 24, 1991, C01.

18. Peter Biskind and Susan Linfield, "Chalk Talk," in Brunette, *Martin Scorsese Interviews*, 108.

19. Anthony DeCurtis, "The Rolling Stone Interview: Martin Scorsese," *Rolling Stone*, November 1, 1990, 108.

20. Guy Flatley, "He Has Often Walked 'Mean Streets,'" *New York Times*, December 16, 1973, 169.

21. Jack Mathews, "Paradise Lost, Wise Guy Style," *Los Angeles Times*, November 19, 1995, 8.

22. DeCurtis, "Rolling Stone Interview," 107.

23. Rhys, "Martin Scorsese's Comfortable State of Anxiety," 60.

24. T. Anderson, dir., "Hollywood Style," *American Cinema* (New York Center for Visual History, KCET Los Angeles, and BBC, 1995), DVD, 00:10:05–00:11:30.

25. Rick Tetzeli, "The Vision Thing," *Fast Company*, December/January 2011, 106.

26. Esther B. Fein, "Martin Scorsese: The Film Director as Local Alien," *New York Times*, September 29, 1985, H19.

27. Roger Copeland, "An Avant-Gardist Toys with the Past," *New York Times*, March 7, 1976, D13.

28. Rudolf Arnheim, "Art Today and the Film," *Art Journal* 25, no. 3 (Spring 1966): 242.

29. Maya Deren, "Cinematography: The Creative Use of Reality," *Daedalus* 89, no. 1 (1960): 167.

30. Sheldon Renan, *An Introduction to the American Underground Film* (New York: E. P. Dutton, 1967), 83–103.

31. P. Adams Sitney, "Structural Film," *Film Culture* 47 (1969): 1.

32. Susan Sontag, *Against Interpretation* (New York: Noonday Press, 1966), 5, 11.

33. Hans Richter, "The Film as an Original Art Form," *Art Journal* 10, no. 2 (1951): 19–23.

34. Maya Deren, "Cinema as an Art Form," *New Directions* 9 (1946): 115–18.

35. Fred Wellington, "Film '65—Thirteen Panel Discussions," *Film Culture* 40 (1966): 27.

36. Jonas Mekas, *Movie Journal: The Rise of the New American Cinema, 1959–1971* (New York: Macmillan, 1972), 1–2.

37. Jonas Mekas, "Cinema of the New Generation," *Film Culture* 21 (1960): 8–9.

38. Geoff King, *American Independent Cinema* (New York: I. B. Tauris, 2005), 8.

39. Gregory Markopoulos, "Toward a New Narrative Film Form," *Film Culture* 31 (1963): 15–16; Annette Michelson, "Film and the Radical Aspiration," *Film Culture* 42 (1966): 34–42.

40. Richard Schickel, "The Movies Are Now High Art," *New York Times*, January 5, 1969, SM32–44; Ernest Callenbach, "Movie Journal," *Film Quarterly* 26, no. 2 (Winter 1972/73): 49–51.

41. Mekas, *Movie Journal*, 220.

42. Bourdieu, *Distinction*.

43. Maya Deren, *Essential Deren*, ed. B. R. McPherson (Kingston, NY: McPherson, 2005), 10–11.

44. Wellington, "Film '65," 27.

45. Mekas, "Cinema," 19.

46. Deren, "Cinema as an Art Form," 112.

47. Mekas, *Movie Journal*, 200.

48. Stan Brakhage, *Essential Brakhage: Selected Writings on Filmmaking*, ed. B. R. McPherson (Kingston, NY: McPherson, 2001), 144.

49. Wellington, "Film '65," 27.

50. Karel Reisz, "Experiment at Brussels," *Sight and Sound*, Summer 1958, 232.

51. Brakhage, *Essential Brakhage*," 12.

52. James Peterson, *Dreams of Chaos, Visions of Order: Understanding the American Avant-Garde Cinema* (Detroit: Wayne State University Press, 1994), 1–2.

53. Mekas, *Movie Journal*, 339.

54. Mekas, *Movie Journal*, 15.

55. Peter Decherney, *Hollywood and the Culture Elite: How the Movies Became American* (New York: Columbia University Press, 2005), 181–82.

56. Todd Bayma, "Art World Culture and Institutional Choices: The Case of Experimental Film," *Sociological Quarterly* 36, no. 1 (1995): 90–91; Paul Arthur, "Unseen No More? The Avant-Garde on DVD," *Cineaste* 32, no. 1 (2006): 6–13; Rebecca M. Alvin, "A Night at the Movies: From Art House to 'Microcinema,'" *Cineaste* 32, no. 3 (2007): 4–7; Kathryn Ramsey, "Economics of the Film Avant-Garde and Strategies in the Circulation of Films, Ideas, and people," *Jump Cut* 52, Summer 2010, date accessed, September 19, 2017; David Andrews, "The Two Avant-Gardes," *Jump Cut* 52, Summer 2010, date accessed, September 19, 2017.

57. Decherney, *Hollywood and the Culture Elite*, 202–3.

58. Ramsey, "Economics of the Film Avant-Garde"; Andrews, "Two Avant-Gardes."

59. David Ansen, "Hollywood Goes Independent," *Newsweek*, April 6, 1987, 64; Janet Maslin, "Is a Cinematic New Wave Cresting?" *New York Times*, December 13, 1992, H1; John Fried, "Rise of the Indie," *Cineaste* 19, no. 4 (1993): 38–40; Patrick Goldstein, "New New Wave," *Los Angeles Times*, December 12, 1999, C8.

60. Emanuel Levy, *Cinema of Outsiders: The Rise of American Independent* (New York: New York University Press, 1999); Greg Merritt, *Celluloid Mavericks: A History of American Independent Film* (New York: Thunder's Mouth Press, 2000); Peter Biskind, *Down and Dirty Pictures: Miramax, Sundance, and the Rise of Independent Film* (New York: Simon and Schuster, 2004); Geoff King, *American Independent Cinema* (New York: I. B. Tauris, 2005); Yannis Tzioumakis, *American Independent Cinema: An Introduction* (New Brunswick, NJ: Rutgers University Press, 2006).

61. Pauline Kael, "Are Movies Going to Pieces?" *Atlantic Monthly*, November 1964, date accessed, November 2, 2014.

62. Baumann, *Hollywood Highbrow*.

63. L. Hirschberg, "The Directors: Two American Film Makers Who Live Outside the Law," *New York Times*, November 16, 1997, SM90.

64. Kael, "Are Movies Going to Pieces."

65. Leonard Quart, "'I Still Love Going to the Movies': An Interview with Pauline Kael," *Cineaste* 25, no. 2 (2000): 8–13.

66. David Paletz, "Judith Crist: An Interview with a Big-Time Critic," *Film Quarterly* 22, no. 1 (1968): 28.

67. Sarris, "Notes on the Auteur Theory in 1962," 5–6.

68. Pierre Bourdieu, *The Field of Cultural Production* (New York: Columbia University Press, 1993).

69. John Cassavetes, "What's Wrong with Hollywood," *Film Culture* 19 (1959): 4–5.

70. Sheila Benson, "Cassavetes Left His Imprint on a Generation of Film Makers," *New York Times*, February 6, 1989, G2.

71. Renan, *An Introduction to the American Underground*," 42, 99–100.

72. King, *American Independent Cinema*, 2.

73. Mekas, *Movie Journal*, 10–11.

74. "Cinema: The $40,000 Method," *Time*, March 24, 1961.

75. "Hollywood: The Shock of Freedom," *Time*, December 12, 1967.

76. Schickel, "The Movies Are Now High Art."

77. Richard Schickel, *Conversations with Scorsese* (New York: Knopf, 2011), 72.

78. Schickel, *Conversations with Scorsese*, 97.

79. Stephen Farber, "Has Martin Scorsese Gone Hollywood," *New York Times*, March 30, 1975, 79.

80. Fred Kaplan, "Alice Doesn't Live Here Anymore," *Cineaste* 7, no. 1 (January 1975): 32–34; Karyn Kay and Gerald Perry, "*Alice Doesn't Live Here Anymore*: Waitressing for Warner's," *Jump Cut* 7, May/July 1975, 5–7.

81. Dan Georgakas, "Raging Bull," *Cineaste* 11 (December 1980): 28–30.

82. Vincent Canby, "Never Forget: Money Plays the Star Role in Hollywood," *New York Times*, May 13, 1984, A17.

83. Stephen Farber, "Five Horsemen after the Apocalypse," *New York Times*, July 1, 1985, 32.

84. Farber, "Five Horsemen after the Apocalypse," 32.

85. Peter Steven, ed., *Jump Cut: Hollywood, Politics, and Counter-Cinema* (New York: Praeger, 1985), 15–16.

86. "Editorial: The Cineaste in Society," *Cineaste* 3, no. 3 (Winter 1969/70): 2.

87. Chuck Kleinhans, "Reading and Thinking About the Avant-Garde," *Jump Cut* 6, March/April 1975, 21–25.

88. Steven, *Jump Cut*, 23.

89. Susan Sontag, "A Century of Cinema," *Parnassus* 22, no. 1–2 (January 1997).

90. Lawrence Van Gelder, "She Champions the Cause of Independent Film," *New York Times*, April 18, 1982, H15.

91. King, *American Independent Cinema*.

92. King, *American Independent Cinema*; Tzioumakis, *American Independent Cinema: An Introduction*.

93. Merritt, *Celluloid Mavericks*.

94. Frederick Wasser, *Veni, Vidi, Video: The Hollywood Empire and the VCR* (Austin,: University of Texas Press, 2001).

95. Davis Ansen, "Hollywood Goes Independent," *Newsweek*, April 6, 1987, LexisNexis Academic, date accessed, September 17, 2014.

96. Duane Byrge, "Redford Sees Indie 'Revolution,'" *Hollywood Reporter*, January 26, 1994, date accessed, November 9, 2017.

97. Janet Maslin, "Is a Cinematic New Wave Cresting?" *New York Times*, December 13, 1992, H1.

98. Janet Maslin, "Who's Who Among the New Hot Film Makers," *New York Times*, December 13, 1992, H26.

99. John Fried, "Rise of the Indie: An Interview with Hal Hartley," *Cineaste* 19, no. 4 (January 1993): 38.

100. Patrick Goldstein, "The New New Wave," *Los Angeles Times*, December 12, 1999, C8.

101. Biskind, *Down and Dirty Pictures*; Peter Biskind, "Inside Indiewood," *The Nation*, March 16, 2000, https://www.thenation.com/article/inside-indiewood, date accessed, November 13, 2017

102. Will Cohu, "*Pulp Fiction* Changed It All," *Daily Telegraph*, August 22, 2004, LexisNexis Academic, date accessed, November 10, 2017.

103. Tim Robey, "The Rise and Rise of Indiewood," *The Telegraph*, September 6, 2004, LexisNexis Academic, date accessed, November 10, 2017.

104. "Goodfellas," Box Office Mojo, http://www.boxofficemojo.com/movies/?id=goodfellas .htm, date accessed, November 13, 2017.

105. Biskind, "Inside Indiewood."

106. Maslin, "Is a Cinematic New Wave Cresting?"

107. Biskind, *Down and Dirty Pictures*.

108. Michael Cieply, "For Independent Filmmakers, Final Cut Is Now Just Step One," *New York Times*, August 13, 2009, A1.

109. Paul Elie, "Redemption," *New York Times*, November 27, 2016, SM45+.

110. Gavin Smith, "The Art of Vision: Martin Scorsese's *Kundun* Interview," *Film Comment*, January/February 1998, 22.

111. Biskind, "Inside Indiewood."

112. "History," *Film Independent*, https://www.filmindependent.org/spirit-awards/history, date accessed, November 10, 2017.

113. Farber, "Has Martin Scorsese Gone Hollywood?"

114. Maltby, *Hollywood Cinema*.

115. Dutka, "I Am the Movies I Make."

116. Pamela McClintock, "Why Martin Scorsese's Next Movie Will Cost More Than $125M," hollywoodreporter.com, March 1, 2017, LexisNexis Academic, date accessed, June 13, 2018.

117. Dutka, "I Am the Movies I Make."

118. Steven Soderbergh, "The State of Cinema," San Francisco International Film Festival, April 13, 2013.

119. McClintock, "Why Martin Scorsese's Next Movie."

120. Ron Eyerman, "Toward a Meaningful Sociology of the Arts," in *Myth, Meaning, and Performance: Toward a New Cultural Sociology of the Arts*, ed. R. Eyerman and L. McCormick (Boulder, CO: Paradigm, 2006), 16–20.

Interlude

1. See Boris Tomaševskij, "Literature and Biography," in *Readings in Russian Poetics: Formalist and Structuralist Views*, ed. L. Matejka and K. Pomorska (Ann Arbor: University of Michigan Press, 1978), 47–55; Robert Kapsis, *Hitchcock: The Making of a Reputation* (Chicago: University of Chicago Press, 1992).

2. On intersectionality see Kimberlé Williams Crenshaw, "Mapping the Margins: Intersectionality, Identity Politics, and Violence against Women of Color," *Stanford Law Review* 43 (1991): 1241–99; Patricia Hill Collins, *Black Feminist Thought: Knowledge, Consciousness, and the Politics of Empowerment* (New York: Routledge, 1991).

Chapter 3: Miles Davis: The Unreconstructed Black Man in Modern Jazz

1. James McBride, *Kill 'em and Leave: Searching for James Brown and the American Soul* (New York: Spiegal and Grau, 2016), 10.

2. "How Hip-Hop Failed Black America," Questlove, *New York Magazine*, May 6, 2014, http://www.vulture.com/2014/05/questlove-hip-hop-failed-black-america-part-3-black-loses -cool.html, date accessed, May 30, 2016.

3. Leonard Feather, "That Birdland Beating," *Melody Maker*, September 9, 1959, IJS file; Miles Davis, *Miles: The Autobiography* (New York: Simon and Schuster, 1989).

4. Joel Dinerstein, *The Origins of Cool in Postwar America* (Chicago: University of Chicago Press, 2017).

5. "Post-Bopper," *Time*, January 20, 1958, 65; Nat Hentoff, "Miles Davis: Last Trump," *Esquire*, March 1, 1959, 88–90.

6. Daniel Goleman, "Black Scientists Study the 'Pose' of the Inner City," *New York Times*, April 21, 1992, C7. See also Richard Majors and Janet Mancini Billson, *Cool Pose: The Dilemmas of Black Manhood in America* (New York: Lexington Books, 1992).

7. Michael Omi and Howard Winant, eds., *Racial Formation in the United States* (New York: Routledge and Kegan Paul, 1986), 12.

8. Quincy Troupe, *Miles and Me* (Berkeley: University of California Press, 2000), 167.

9. Herman Gray, "Black Masculinity and Visual Culture," *Callaloo* 18, no. 2 (1995): 401–2.

10. Greg Tate, "Preface to a One-Hundred-and-Eighty Volume Patricide Note: Yet Another Few Thousand Words on the Death of Miles Davis and the Problem of the Black Male Genius," in *Black Popular Culture*, ed. Gina Dent (New York: New Press, 1998), 244–45.

11. Sherrie Tucker, "Big Ears: Listening for Gender in Jazz Studies," *Current Musicology* 71–73 (Spring 2001–Spring 2002): 390.

12. Brooks Johnson, "Racism in Jazz," *Down Beat*, October 6, 1966, 15.

13. Archie Shepp, "Archie Shepp Speaks Bluntly," *Down Beat*, December 16, 1965, 11.

14. Leonard Feather, "Jazz Is Neither Negro or White," *New York Daily News*, December 8, 1957, IJS file; Nat Hentoff, "Racial Prejudice Works Both Ways," *Harper's*, June 1959, IJS file; William Russo, "Recording Reports: Jazz," *Saturday Review*, November 14, 1959, 54+; John Tynan, "Les McCann and 'The Truth,'" *Down Beat*, September 15, 1960, 20+; Gene Lees, "Afterthought," *Down Beat*, October 13, 1960, 53; Leonard Feather, "The Racial Undercurrent," *Music 61*, January 1961, 44+; Don DeMichael, "Inside the Cannonball Adderley Quintet, Part I," *Down Beat*, June 8, 1961, 19+; "Racial Prejudice in Jazz," *Down Beat*, March 12, 1962, 20+; "Crow Jim," *Time*, October 19, 1962, 58+; "Racial Prejudice in Jazz, Part II," *Down Beat*, March 29, 1962, 22+; "A Need for Racial Unity in Jazz," *Down Beat*, April 11, 1963; 16+; Don Cerulli, "Crow Jim: No Gigs for Ofays," *Rogue*, January 1964, 54+; Nat Hentoff, "The Playboy Panel: Jazz Today and Tomorrow," *Playboy*, February 1964, 29–38, 56–58, 139–42; John S. Wilson, "Jazz, Black and White," *New York Times*, August 14, 1966, 320.

15. Otis Ferguson, *H.R.S. Rag*, October 1938; Barry Ulanov, "Crow Jim," *Metronome*, May 1949, 42; "Crow Jim Is as Bad as Jim Crow," *Down Beat*, March 9, 1951, 10.

16. Nat Hentoff, "Miles: A Trumpeter in The Midst of a Big Comeback Makes a Very Frank Appraisal of Today's Jazz Scene," *Down Beat*, November 2, 1955, 13–14; Charles Mingus, "An Open Letter from Charlie Mingus," *Down Beat*, November 30, 1955, 12–13.

17. "Slugging of Miles Davis," *Down Beat*, October 1, 1959, 11.

18. Alex Haley, "The Swinging Life of Miles Davis," *Climax*, May 1961, 38–39; Alex Haley, "The Two Faces of Miles Davis," *Negro Digest*, August 1961, 83.

19. Joe Goldberg, *Jazz Masters of the Fifties* (New York: Macmillan, 1965), 64.

20. Barbara Gardner, "The Enigma of Miles Davis," *Down Beat*, January 7, 1960, 20–21.

21. Bill Coss, "The Hot and the Cool," *Metronome Jazz 1958*, January 1958, 74.

22. Nat Hentoff, "What's Happening to Jazz," *Harper's Magazine*, April 1, 1958, 32.

23. Charles Chaplin, "Where Is This Thing Called Jazz?" *Los Angeles Times*, June 25, 1965, C8.

24. Alex Haley, "Miles Davis: A Candid Interview with the Jazz World's Premier Iconoclast," *Playboy*, September 1962, 57.

25. Julian Adderley, "My Experience with Miles Davis," *New York Amsterdam News*, January 1, 1960, IJS file.

26. John Rockwell, "To Miles Davis and Fans, a Concert Is Just Part of the Whole Story," *New York Times*, September 15, 1974, 56.

27. Wayne Svoboda, "A Rare Appearance of Miles Davis May Actually Include Miles Davis," *Wall Street Journal*, July 1, 1981, IJS file.

28. Frederick Murphy, "Miles Davis: The Monster of Modern Music," *Encore*, July 21, 1975, IJS file.

29. Gardner, "Enigma of Miles Davis," 23.

30. Sascha Burland and Robert Reisner, "The Midnight Horn," *Nugget*, December 1958, IJS file.

31. "Jazz: The Loneliest Monk," *Time*, February 28, 1964, http://content.time.com/time /subscriber/article/0,33009,873856,00.html, date accessed, June 21, 2018.

32. Leonard Feather, "Musing with Miles," *Melody Maker*, June 6, 1964, 12.

33. Haley, "Miles Davis," 57.

34. Stanley Goldstein, "Miles Davis," *Playboy*, August 1960, 106.

35. John Gennari, *Blowin' Hot and Cool* (Chicago: University of Chicago Press, 2006); Ingrid Monson, *Freedom Sounds: Civil Rights Call Out to Jazz and Africa* (Oxford: Oxford University Press, 2007); Eric Porter, *What Is This Thing Called Jazz? African American Musicians as Artists, Critics, and Activists* (Berkeley: University of California Press, 2002).

36. Gardner, "Enigma of Miles Davis," 20–21.

37. Chris Albertson, "The Unmasking of Miles Davis," *Saturday Review*, November 27, 1971, 13.

38. Goldstein, "Miles Davis," 39, 78.

39. Don Cerulli, "Crow Jim: No Gigs for Ofays," *Rogue*, January 1964, 54+; Nat Hentoff, "The Playboy Panel: Jazz—Today and Tomorrow," *Playboy*, February 1964; "'Negro Artists Exploited' Mingus Urges Investigation," *Toronto Daily Star*, October 31, 1964, IJS file; Don Heckman, "What Next for Jazz," *Down Beat*, January 1965, 32+; Martin Williams, "No Work in U.S. for Ornette," *Down Beat*, June 30, 1966; David A. Hunt, "Black Voice Lost in White Superstructure," *Coda* (February 1974): 12+.

40. "Etiquette of Race Relations," *Ebony*, December 1949, 78.

41. John Rockwell, "To Miles Davis and Fans, a Concert Is Just Part of the Whole Story," *New York Times*, September 9, 1974, 56.

42. Don DeMichael, "Jazz's Picasso Puts It in Black and White," *Rolling Stone*, December 13, 1969, 23+.

43. Goldstein, "Miles Davis."

44. Marc Crawford, "Miles Davis: Evil Genius of Jazz," *Ebony*, January 1961, 70.

45. "Miles Davis Rips Record Firm for Bias," *Jet*, January 7, 1970, 42.

46. Stephen Davis, "My Ego Only Needs a Good Rhythm Section," *Real Paper*, March 21, 1973, 13.

47. Crawford, "Miles Davis: Evil Genius of Jazz," 69.

48. Davis, *Miles: The Autobiography*, 375.

49. Crawford, "Miles Davis: Evil Genius of Jazz," 70.

50. Robin D. G. Kelley, "'We Are Not What We Seem': Rethinking Black Working-Class Opposition in the Jim Crow South," *Journal of American History* 80, no. 1 (June 1993): 76.

51. Kelley, "We Are Not What We Seem," 76.

52. Miles Davis, "A Self-Portrait," *Esquire*, March 1962, 72.

53. Goldstein, "Miles Davis," 106.

54. George Pitts, "George Pitts Sez," *New Pittsburgh Courier*, August 25, 1962, 15.

55. Haley, "Miles Davis," 57+, IJS file.

56. Crawford, "Miles Davis," 69.

57. Miles Davis with Leonard Feather, *Down Beat*, July 2, 1964.

58. Quincy Troupe, "Miles Styles I," *Spin*, November, 1985, 74.

59. DeMichael, "Jazz's Picasso," 23+.

60. Jimmy Saunders, "Miles Davis: Get Up with It," *Playboy*, April 1975, 100.

61. DeMichael, "Jazz's Picasso."

62. Hubert Saal, "Miles of Music," *Newsweek*, March 23, 1970, 35.

63. Murphy, "Miles Davis."

64. Leonard Feather, "The Definitive Davis," *Penthouse*, July 1972, 114, 120.

65. Albertson, "Unmasking," 13.

66. Jack Hamilton, *Just around Midnight: Rock and Roll and the Racial Imagination* (Cambridge, MA: Harvard University Press, 2016).

67. Nat Hentoff, "The New Jazz—Black, Angry, and Hard to Understand," *New York Times*, December 25, 1966, A10.

68. Michael Watts, "Miles Davis," in *Today's Sounds: A Melody Maker Book*, ed. Ray Coleman (London: Hamlyn, 1973), 123.

69. David Breskin, "Searching for Miles," *Rolling Stone*, September 29, 1983.

70. Ingrid Monson, "The Problem of White Hipness: Race, Gender, and Cultural Conceptions in Jazz Historical Discourse," *Journal of the American Musicological Society* 48, no. 3 (1995): 396–422; Jon Panish, *The Color of Jazz* (Jackson: University of Mississippi Press, 1997); Nichole T. Rustin, "*Cante Hondo*: Charles Mingus, Nat Hentoff, and Jazz Racism," *Critical Sociology* 32, no. 2–3 (2006).

71. Monson, "Problem with White Hipness"; Panish, *The Color of Jazz*; Rustin, "*Cante Hondo*"; Gray, "Black Masculinity"; Robin D. G. Kelley, "New Monastery: Monk and the Jazz Avant-Garde," *Black Music Research* 19, no. 12 (Autumn 1999): 135–68.

72. Bill Coss, "The Hot and the Cool," *Metronome Jazz 1958*, January 1958, 83.

73. Monson, "Problem with White Hipness;" Panish, *The Color of Jazz*; Rustin, "*Cante Hondo*."

74. Whitney Balliett, "Musical Events: Jazz Concert," *New Yorker*, May 27, 1961, IJS file.

75. Leonard Feather, "The Real Miles Davis," *Melody Maker*, September 17, 1960, 59.

76. Frank Alkyer, ed., *The Miles Davis Reader* (New York: Hal Leonard Books, 2007), 201–4.

77. George Goodman Jr., "Miles Davis: 'I Just Pick Up My Horn and Play,'" *New York Times*, June 28, 1981, 12.

78. Martin Williams, "The Man in the Green Shirt," *Independent* (London), October 6, 1991, LexisNexis Academic, date accessed, July 16, 2013.

79. Bill Coss, "Miles Davis Is Nature's Boy," *Metronome Jazz 1958*, January 1958, 42.

80. Nat Hentoff, "Miles Davis: The Last Trump," *Esquire*, March 1959, 88.

81. Nat Hentoff, "Miles Davis," *International Musician*, February 1961, IJS file.

82. Martin Williams, "Miles Davis: A Man Walking," *Saturday Review*, November 10, 1962, 54.

83. John S. Wilson, "Miles Davis Joins Evans in Concert," *New York Times*, May 20, 1961, 13.

84. Ralph Gleason, "Miles Davis Projects from the Blues into the Purest Form of Jazz," *San Francisco Chronicle*, April 2, 1961, IJS file.

85. Crawford, "Evil Genius of Jazz," 76.

86. John Palcewski, "The Miles Davis: A Semi-Affectionate Reminiscence," *Cavalier*, May 1969, in Paul Maher Jr. and Michael K. Dorr, eds., *Miles on Miles: Interviews and Encounters with Miles Davis* (Chicago: Lawrence Hill Books, 2009), 48.

87. Jane Ennis, "Miles Smiles," *Melody Maker*, January 9, 1973, 17.

88. bell hooks, "Feminism Inside: Toward a Black Body Politic," in *Black Male: Representations of Masculinity in Contemporary American Art*, ed. Thelma Goodman (New York: Whitney Museum of American Art, 1994), 128.

89. Peter Benchley, "New Sounds from Miles Davis," *Reporter Dispatch* (Newsweek Features Service), July 22, 1970, IJS file.

90. Troupe, "Miles Styles I," 73.

91. Ken Franckling, "Miles Davis at Age 60: All He Wants Is Respect," *Sun Times*, May 18, 1986, IJS file.

92. Hentoff, "Miles Davis."

93. Palcewski, "The Miles Davis," 46.

94. Rita Reif, "Miles Davis's Home Is a Study in Curves," *New York Times*, July 18, 1970, 26.

95. Harriet Choice, "Miles Davis, Solo: Brews Concocted and Broods Begotten," *Chicago Tribune*, January 20, 1974, E3.

96. Goldstein, "Miles Davis," 107.

97. Palcewski, "The Miles Davis," 46.

98. Leonard Feather, "The Definitive Miles Davis," *Penthouse*, June 1972, 33.

99. Amiri Baraka, "Miles Davis," *New York Times*, June 16, 1985, SM24, 43, 45, 48, 50.

100. Rustin, "*Cante Hondo.*"

101. Nick Kent, "Lighting Up with the Prince of Darkness," *The Face*, May 1986, in Maher and Dorr, *Miles on Miles*, 264.

102. Clive Davis, "Jarring Jazz Notes," *The Times*, March 3, 1990, LexisNexis Academic, date accessed, July 16, 2013.

103. Davis, *Miles: The Autobiography*, 362, 405, 407–8.

104. Jonathan, "Miles: The Autobiography," *Washington Post*, October 1, 1989, LexisNexis Academic, date accessed, July 16, 2013.

105. Davis, *Miles: The Autobiography*, 54.

106. Davis, *Miles: The Autobiography*, 402.

107. Jack Chambers, "Back from the Wallow," *Globe and Mail*, December 30, 1989, LexisNexis Academic, date accessed, July 16, 2013.

108. Pearl Cleage, *Mad at Miles: A Blackwoman's Guide to Truth* (Southfield, MI: Cleage Group, 1990), 13–14.

109. "New Book, 'Mad at Miles: A Blackwoman's Guide to Truth,'" *Michigan Citizen*, February 23, 1991. Ethnic NewsWatch, date accessed, June 12, 2016.

110. Robin D. G. Kelley, "A Jazz Genius in the Guise of a Hustler," *New York Times*, May 13, 2001, AR1.

111. Tucker, "Big Ears," 389.

112. hooks, "Feminism Inside: Toward a Black Body Politic."

113. Clyde Taylor, "The Game," in *Black Male: Representations of Masculinity in Contemporary American Art*, ed. Thelma Golden (New York: Whitney Museum of American Art, 1994), 169.

114. Greg Tate, "Silence, Exile, and Cunning," *Village Voice*, October 15, 1991, 90.

115. Lewis MacAdams, *The Birth of the Cool: Beat, Bebop, and the American Avant-Garde* (New York: Free Press, 2001); John Leland, *Hip: The History* (New York: Harper Perennial, 2004); Dinerstein, *Origins of Cool.*

116. John Szwed, *So What: The Life and Times of Miles Davis* (New York: Simon and Schuster, 2002), 403.

Chapter 4: Martin Scorsese: A Sojourn from Italian American to White Ethnic American

1. Except for the section "The 'Off-White' Auteur and Negotiating Hegemonic Masculinity," this chapter was originally published as Paul Lopes, "The Power of Hyphen-Nationalism: Martin Scorsese's Sojourn from Italian American to White Ethnic American," *Social Identities: Journal for the Study of Race, Nation, and Culture* 23, no. 5 (2017): 562–78.

2. Richard Schickel, *Conversations with Scorsese* (New York: Knopf, 2011), vii–viii.

3. Matthew Frye Jacobson, *Roots Too: White Ethnic Revival in Post–Civil Rights America* (Cambridge, MA: Harvard University Press, 2006).

4. Boris Tomaševskij, "Literature and Biography," in *Readings in Russian Poetics: Formalist and Structuralist Views*, ed. L. Matejka and K. Pomorska (Ann Arbor: University of Michigan Press, 1978); also on biographical legend see Robert Kapsis, *Hitchcock: The Making of a Reputation* (Chicago: University of Chicago Press, 1992).

5. Marc Raymond, *Hollywood's New Yorker: The Making of Martin Scorsese* (Albany: State University of New York Press, 2013).

6. Thomas J. Ferraro, *Feeling Italian: The Art of Ethnicity in America* (New York: New York University Press, 2005).

7. Laura Mulvey, "Visual Pleasure and Narrative Cinema," *Screen* 16, no. 3 (1975): 6–18.

8. Ellis Cashmore, *Martin Scorsese's America* (Cambridge: Polity Press, 2009).

9. Matthew Frye Jacobson, *Whiteness of a Different Color: European Immigrants and the Alchemy of Race* (Cambridge, MA: Harvard University Press, 1998); David R. Roediger, *Working toward Whiteness: How America's Immigrants Became White* (New York: Basic Books, 2005); Jacobson, *Roots Too*.

10. Jacobson, *Roots Too*.

11. Monica McDermott and Frank L. Samson, "White Racial and Ethnic Identity in the United States," *Annual Review of Sociology* 31 (2005): 245–61.

12. Richard D. Alba, *Ethnic Identity: The Transformation of White America* (New Haven, CT: Yale University Press, 1990); Mary C. Waters, *Ethnic Options: Choosing Identities in America* (Berkeley: University of California Press, 1990).

13. Alba, *Ethnic Identity*, 293.

14. Alba, *Ethnic Identity*, 293.

15. George Lipsitz, *The Possessive Investment in Whiteness: How White People Profit from Identity Politics* (Philadelphia: Temple University Press, 1998); Howard Winant, "White Racial Projects," in *The Making and Unmaking of Whiteness*, ed. B. B. Rasmussen, E. Klinenberg, I. J. Nexica, and M. Wray (Durham, NC: Duke University Press, 2001), 97–112; Eduardo Bonilla-Silva, *Racism without Racists: Color-Blind Racism and the Persistence of Racial Inequality in the United States* (Lanham, MD: Rowman and Littlefield, 2003); Ashley W. Doane and Eduardo Bonilla-Silva, eds., *White Out: The Continuing Significance of Race* (New York: Routledge, 2003); Jacobson, *Roots Too*; Rona Tamiko Halualani, "Abstracting and De-Racializing Diversity: The Articulation of Diversity in the Post-Race Era," in *Critical Rhetorics of Race*, ed. M. G. Lacy and K. A. Ono (New York: New York University Press, 2011), 247–63.

16. Winant, "White Racial Projects"; Jacobson, *Roots Too*.

17. Bonilla-Silva, *Racism without Racists*.

18. Thomas K. Nakayama and Robert L. Krizek, "Whiteness: A Strategic Rhetoric," *Quarterly Journal of Speech* 81 (1995): 291–309; Ruth Frankenberg, "The Mirage of an Unmarked Whiteness," in Rasmussen, Klinenberg, Nexica, and Wray, *Making and Unmaking of Whiteness*, 72–96; Troy Duster, "The 'Morphing' Properties of Whiteness," in Rasmussen, Klinenberg, Nexica, and Wray, *Making and Unmaking of Whiteness*, 113–37; Jenifer Guglielmo and Salvatore Salerno, *Are Italians White? How Race Is Made in America* (New York: Routledge, 2003); France Winddance Twine and Charles A. Gallagher, "The Future of Whiteness: A Map of the 'Third Wave,'" in *Retheorizing Race and Whiteness in the 21st Century*, ed. France Winddance Twine and Charles A. Gallagher (New York: Routledge, 2012), 1–20.

19. Michael G. Lacy and Kent A. Ono, introduction to Michael G. Lacy and Kent A. Ono, eds., *Critical Rhetorics of Race* (New York: New York University Press, 2011), 1–17.

20. Twine and Gallagher, "Future of Whiteness," 9.

21. Lee Lourdeaux, *Italian and Irish Filmmakers in America: Ford, Capra, Coppola, and Scorsese* (Philadelphia: Temple University Press, 1990).

22. Jonathan J. Cavallero, *Hollywood's Italian American Filmmakers: Capra, Scorsese, Savoca, Coppola, and Tarantino* (Urbana: University of Illinois Press, 2011).

23. Gene D. Phillips, *Godfather: The Intimate Francis Ford Coppola* (Lexington: University Press of Kentucky, 2004).

24. Robert Casillo, "Four Italian American Directors on the Theme of Their Ethnicity: 1990–2007," in *Mediated Ethnicity: New Italian-American Cinema*, ed. G. Muscio, J. Sciorra, G. Spagnoletti, and A. J. Tamburri (New York: John D. Calandra Italian American Institute, 2010), 103–15.

25. Guy Flatley, "He Has Often Walked 'Mean Streets,'" *New York Times*, December 16, 1973, 169.

26. Vincent Canby, "Screen: A First Feature," *New York Times*, September 9, 1969, 39.

27. Paul Lieberman, "A Pair of Ringmasters: To Scorsese, They Were Always Mean Streets," *Los Angeles Times*, December 8, 2002, E1.

28. For a review of literature on American urban ethnic communities see Robert Casillo, *Gangster Priest: The Italian-American Cinema of Martin Scorsese* (Toronto: University of Toronto Press, 2006).

29. Thomas J. Ferraro, *Feeling Italian: The Art of Ethnicity in America* (New York: New York University Press, 2005).

30. Michael Novak, *The Rise of the Unmeltable Ethnics* (New York: Macmillan, 1972). For symbolic ethnicity see Richard A. Alba, *Italian Americans: Into the Twilight of Ethnicity* (Englewood Cliffs, NJ: Prentice-Hall, 1985).

31. Les Keyser, *Martin Scorsese* (New York: Twayne, 1992), 4.

32. Esther Fein, "Martin Scorsese: The Film Director as Local Alien," *New York Times*, September 29, 1985, H19.

33. David Resin, "Playboy Interview: Martin Scorsese," *Playboy*, April 1991, 57–72, 161.

34. Michael Henry, "The Passion of St. Martin Scorsese," trans. and ed. Mary Pat Kelly in Mary Pat Kelly, *Scorsese: The First Decade* (Pleasantville, NY: Redgrave, 1980), 149.

35. Richard Combs, "Hell Up in the Bronx," *Sight and Sound*, Spring 1981, 132.

36. Michael Henry Wilson, *Scorsese on Scorsese* (Paris: Cahiers du cinéma, 2011), 28.

37. Jeremy Janes, "Beyond Ethnic Parody," *Los Angeles Times*, November 5, 1972, S24.

38. Paul Zimmerman, "Mean Streets," in Mary Pat Kelly, *Scorsese: The First Decade*, 177.

39. David Denby, "Mean Streets: The Sweetness of Hell," *Sight and Sound*, Winter 1973/74, 48.

40. Kevin Thomas, "Coming of Age in Little Italy," *Los Angeles Times*, October 25, 1973, D1.

41. Tom Milne, "Mean Streets," *Monthly Film Review*, January 1, 1974, 103.

42. Jeremy Janes, "Movies: Martin Scorsese—Beyond Ethnic Parody," *Los Angeles Times*, November 5, 1972, S24.

43. Tom Burke, "'Mean Streets' Leads Scorsese up New Avenues," *Los Angeles Times*, June 9, 1974, 01.

44. Flatley, "He Has Often Walked," 169.

45. Foster Hirsch, "Why Feel Sorry for These Hoods," *New York Times*, December 30, 1973, 65.

46. Casillo, *Gangster Priest*.

47. Andrew M. Greely, "TV's Italian Cops: Trapped in Old Stereotypes," *New York Times*, July 27, 1975, X1.

48. Mark Kermode, "The Dark Side of Scorsese's Films," *Observer*, November 21, 2011, 8, Infotrac Newsstand, date accessed, March 16, 2016.

49. "Scorsese's Catholic Artistry," *America*, March 5, 2007, 4.

50. Richard R. Blake, "Tibetan Poetry," *America*, April 11, 1998, 20–21.

51. Paul Elie, "Redemption," *New York Times*, November 27, 2016, SM45.

52. Cashmore, *Martin Scorsese's America*, 8.

53. Michiko Kakutani, "Scorsese's Past Colors His New Film," *New York Times*, February 13, 1983, H1.

54. Janes, "Beyond Ethnic Parody"; Marjorie Rosen, "New Hollywood: Martin Scorsese Interview," *Film Comment*, March/April 1975, 42–46; P. Brunette, ed., *Martin Scorsese Interviews* (Jackson: University Press of Mississippi, 1999); Ian Christie and David Thompson, *Scorsese on Scorsese* (London: Faber and Faber, 2003).

55. Cavallero, *Hollywood's Italian American Filmmakers*.

56. Larissa M. Ennis, "Off-White Masculinity in Martin Scorsese's Gangster Films," in *A Companion to Martin Scorsese*, ed. A. Baker (Malden, MA: John Wiley and Sons, 2015), 173–94.

57. Linda Mizejewski, "Movies and the Off-White Gangster," in *American Cinema of the 1990s: Themes and Variations*, ed. C. Holmlund (New Brunswick, NJ: Rutgers University Press, 2005), 24–44.

58. Meryl J. Irwin, "'Their Experience Is the Immigrant Experience': Ellis Island, Documentary Film, and Rhetorically Reversible Whiteness," *Quarterly Journal of Speech* 99, no. 1 (2013): 74–97.

59. Frank Tomasulo, "Italian Americans in Hollywood Cinema: Filmmakers, Characters, Audiences," *Voices in Italian Americana* 7, no. 1 (1996): 65–77; Cavallero, *Hollywood's Italian American Filmmakers*.

60. Richard Maltby, *Hollywood Cinema* (Malden, MA: Blackwell Publishing, 2003).

61. Jacobson, *Roots Too*.

62. Lieberman, "A Pair of Ringmasters," E1.

63. "Martin Scorsese on New York's Five Point Intersection," AFI Docs May 2010, AFI Docs Channel, YouTube, http://youtu.be/Ym4geoT5QOg, date accessed, December 2, 2014.

64. Martin Scorsese, "A Box Filled with Magic," *Newsweek*, June 22, 1998, 50–52.

65. Ingrid Sischy, "'Gangs of New York': An Exclusive Portfolio and Interview with Martin Scorsese," *Interview*, December/January 2003, 109.

66. Flatley, "He Has Often Walked," 169.

67. "Director Martin Scorsese," *Fresh Air*, National Public Radio and WHYY-FM, Philadelphia, January 27, 2003.

68. *A Personal Journey with Martin Scorsese through American Film*, DVD, Martin Scorsese and Henry Wilson, dir. (1995; Burbank, CA: Buena Vista Entertainment, 2012).

69. Martin Scorsese, "The Leading Man," *Rolling Stone*, May 15, 2003, 89.

70. Matt R. Lohr, "Irish American Identity in the Films of Martin Scorsese," in *A Companion to Martin Scorsese*, ed. A. Baker (Malden, MA: Wiley and Son, 2015), 214–36.

71. Jonathan J. Cavallero, "Issues of Race, Ethnicity, and Television Authorship in *Martin Scorsese Presents the Blues* and *Boardwalk Empire*," in Baker, *A Companion to Martin Scorsese*, 214–36.

72. Gavin Smith, "Battle Royale," *Film Comment*, January/February 2003, 2.

73. Ian Christie, "Manhattan Asylum," *Sight and Sound*, June 2003, 21–22.

74. "Cannes," *Hollywood Reporter*, May 21, 2002, LexisNexis Academic, date accessed, November 8, 2017.

75. Christie and Thompson, *Scorsese on Scorsese*, 266.

76. Kevin Baker, "An Immigrant's Tale That Scratches off History's Veneer," *Los Angeles Times*, December 29, 2002, E12.

77. Ann Hornaday, "Urban Mythmaker: Director Scorsese Creates an Old New York of Blood and Grit," *Washington Post*, December 18, 2002, Style C1.

78. Jami Bernard, "Scorsese and the Age of Violence Set in a Lowdown Downtown, Period Drama Takes a Stab at History," *New York Daily News*, December 20, 2002, 61.

79. J. Hoberman, "Once Upon a Time in Fantasyland: Vice City," *Village Voice*, December 24, 2002, 102.

80. Peter Hamill, "Trampling City's History," *New York Daily News*, December 15, 2002.

81. Christopher Shannon, "Catholicism as the Other," *First Things* 139 (January 2004): 46.

82. Charles Gallagher, "Playing the White Ethnic Card: Using Ethnic Identity to Deny Contemporary Racism," in *White Out: The Continuing Significance of Race*, ed. A. W. Doane and E. Bonilla-Silva (New York: Routledge, 2003), 145.

83. Casillo, "Four Italian American Filmmakers."

84. Sischy, "Gangs of New York," 109.

85. Martin Scorsese, *Lady by the Sea: The Statue of Liberty*, the History Channel, 2004.

86. Jacobson, *Roots Too*.

87. Irwin, "Their Experience Is the Immigrant Experience."

88. Irwin, "Their Experience Is the Immigrant Experience," 92.

89. Scorsese had already expressed this equivalency between white and nonwhite immigrants in *The Neighborhood* (2001), a short film about Little Italy he made in commemoration of 9/11. See Cavallero, *Hollywood's Italian American Filmmakers*.

90. Jacobson, *Roots Too*.

91. "Scorsese on the Immigrant Experience on Film," *Weekend Edition*, NPR, June 10, 2007.

92. Jacobson, *Roots Too*.

93. Pam Cook, "Masculinity in Crisis? Pam Cook on Tragedy and Identification in 'Raging Bull,'" *Scene* 23, no. 3–4 (September 1982): 39.

94. Jake La Motta with Joseph Carter and Peter Savage, *Raging Bull: My Story* (Englewood Cliffs, NJ: Prentice-Hall, 1970).

95. Cook, "Masculinity in Crisis?"

96. Steven G. Kellman, ed., *Perspectives on RAGING BULL* (New York: G. K. Hall, 1994); Kevin J. Hayes, ed., *Martin Scorsese's Raging Bull* (Cambridge: Cambridge University Press, 2005).

97. Christina Marie Newland, "Martin Scorsese's *Raging Bull*, Italian American Masculinity, and the American Dream," *Film Matters*, Spring 2013, 20–25.

98. Charles Champlin, "Post-Oscar Scripts—Melodies That Linger On," *Los Angeles Times*, April 11, 1976, S1.

99. Patricia Patterson and Manny Farber, "Taxi Driver: The Power and the Gory," *Film Comment*, May/June 1976, 26–30.

100. Richard Combs, "Taxi Driver," *Monthly Film Bulletin*, January 1976, 201.

101. Guy Flatley, "Martin Scorsese's Gamble," *New York Times*, February 8, 1976, SM9.

102. Gregg Kilday, "Scorsese Virtuoso of Urban Angst," *Los Angeles Times*, March 14, 1976, V32.

103. Charles Champlin, "Time Bomb Ticks toward Bloodbath in 'Taxi Driver,'" *Los Angeles Times*, February 22, 1976, K28.

104. Vincent Canby, "Robert De Niro in 'Raging Bull,'" *New York Times*, November 14, 1980, C11.

105. David Thomson, "The Director as Raging Bull," *Film Comment* (January/February 1981), in *Film Comment*, May/June 1998, 56.

106. Canby, "Robert De Niro in 'Raging Bull.'"

107. Kelly, *Scorsese*, 32.

108. Martin Scorsese, dir., *Raging Bull* (United Artists, 1980).

109. Vincent Canby, "A Cold-Eyed Look at Mob's Inner Workings," *New York Times*, September 19, 1990, C11.

110. Leonard Quart, "Goodfellas," *Cineaste* 18, no. 2 (1991): 44.

111. Jackson Katz, *Tough Guise 2* (San Francisco: Kanopy Streaming, 2016).

112. Tom Milne, "Goodfellas," *Monthly Film Bulletin*, December 1990, 357.

113. Angela McRobbie, "Cape Fear," *Sight and Sound*, March 1992, 39.

114. Jay Scott, "Film Review Goodfellas," *Globe and Mail*, September 21, 1990, LexisNexis Academic, date accessed, November 21, 2017.

115. Marcelle Clements, "Celebrating Suffering," *Los Angeles Times*, November 10, 1991, H5.

116. Kenneth Turran, "Scorsese's Way with a Badfella," *Los Angeles Times*, November 13, 1991, F1.

117. David Morgan, "Back to Cape Fear," *Los Angeles Times*, February 17, 1991, N7–8.

118. Morgan, "Back to Cape Fear."

119. Pam Cook, "Scorsese's Masquerade," *Sight and Sound*, April 1992, 14.

120. Mike Clark, "Scorsese's 'Cape Fear' Hits with Brutal Force," *USA Today*, November 13, 1991, 5D.

121. Cook, "Scorsese's Masquerade."

122. Bernard Weinraub, "Martin Scorsese, Attracted to Excess, Still Taking Risks," *New York Times*, November 27, 1995, C11; Jack Mathews, "Paradise Lost, Wise Guy Style," *Los Angeles Times*, November 19, 1995, 8.

123. Katz, *Tough Guise 2*.

124. Douglas Kellner, *Media Culture: Cultural Studies, Identity, and Politics between the Modern and the Postmodern* (New York: Routledge, 1995).

125. Stephen Holden, "After 20 Years Still Comes Out Swinging," *New York Times*, August 4, 2000, E23.

126. Charles Champlin, "Portraits of the American Experience," *Los Angeles Times*, November 9, 1980, G5.

127. Richard D. Alba, *Italian Americans: Into the Twilight of Ethnicity* (Englewood Cliffs, NJ: Prentice-Hall, 1985); Alba, *Ethnic Identity*.

128. Twine and Gallagher, "Future of Whiteness."

Conclusion

1. Sopan Deb, "This Music Shaped a Broadway Show," *New York Times*, November 12, 2017, AR8.

2. Martin Scorsese, "Martin Scorsese on Rotten Tomatoes, Box Office Obsession and Why 'Mother!' Was Misjudged," *Hollywood Reporter*, October 10, 2017, LexisNexis Academic, date accessed, November, 20, 2017.

3. Paul DiMaggio, "Cultural Boundaries and Structural Change: The Extension of the High Culture Model to Theater, Opera, and the Dance, 1900–1940," in *Cultivating Differences: Symbolic Boundaries and the Making of Inequality*, ed. M. Lamont and M. Fournier (Chicago: University of Chicago Press, 1992), 21–57.

4. Michael Henry Wilson, "Cannes, May 1978," *Scorsese on Scorsese* (Paris: Cahiers du cinéma, 2011), 70–71.

5. Mitchel Seidel, "Profile: Wynton Marsalis," *Down Beat*, January 1982, 52+.

6. On accusations of racism against Wynton Marsalis see Terry Teachout, "The Color of Jazz," *Commentary*, September 1995, 50–53.

7. With his 2007 album, *From the Plantation to the Penitentiary*, Marsalis does criticize the criminal justice system as a new system of slavery but continues to focus most of his anger, as he did two decades earlier, on decadent hip-hop and ghetto street culture. See Bill Milkowski, "Wynton Marsalis: Wynton Throws the Gauntlet," *Jazz Times*, April 2007, https://jazztimes.com/features/wynton-marsalis-wynton-throws-down-the-gauntlet, date accessed, November 27, 2017.

8. Herman Gray, *Cultural Moves: African Americans and the Politics of Representation* (Berkeley: University of California Press, 2005), 52–73.

9. Gray, *Cultural Moves*, 52–73; Tom Piazza, "Lincoln Center and Its Critics Swing Away," *New York Times*, January 16, 1994, H26.

10. Robin D. G. Kelley, "Miles Davis: The Chameleon of Cool; a Jazz Genius in the Guise of a Hustler," *New York Times*, May 13, 2001, AR1.

11. Stephen Holden, "From Blaxploitation Stereotype to Man on the Street," *New York Times*, June 9, 2000, E17.

12. James Baldwin, "The Black Boy Looks at the White Boy Norman Mailer," *Esquire*, May 1961, 102+.

13. Ingrid Monson, "The Problem of White Hipness: Race, Gender, and Cultural Conceptions in Jazz Historical Discourse," *Journal of the American Musicological Society* 48, no. 3 (1995): 396–422; Sherrie Tucker, "Big Ears: Listening for Gender in Jazz Studies," *Current Musicology* 71–73 (Spring 2001–Spring 2002): 375–408.

14. Michael Messner, *Taking the Field: Women, Men, and Sports* (Minneapolis: University of Minneapolis Press, 2002).

15. Richard A. Blake, "God's Lonely Men," *America*, November 13, 2006, 30.

16. Blake, "God's Lonely Men," 29.

17. Douglas Kellner, *Media Culture: Cultural Studies, Identity, and Politics between the Modern and the Postmodern* (New York: Routledge, 1995).

18. Jackson Katz, *Tough Guise 2* (San Francisco: Kanopy Streaming, 2016).

19. Norman Mailer, *The White Negro* (San Francisco: City Lights Books, 1957).

20. Ben Westhoff, "The Enigma of Kanye West," *The Guardian*, June 25, 2017, LexisNexis Academic, date accessed, November, 26, 2017.

21. "Grammys 2017: Adele on Rooting for Beyoncé," https://www.youtube.com/watch?v=xVosZQZ58wo, date accessed, November 25, 2017.

22. Barbara Gardner, "The Enigma of Miles Davis," *Down Beat*, January 7, 1960.

23. Karen Mizoguchi, "Keeping Up with Kanye West's Twitter Rants: Tells 'White Publications' 'Please Do Not Comment on Black Music Anymore,'" *People Celebrity*, http://people.com/celebrity/kanye-west-takes-to-twitter-again-rants-about-tidal-and-ex-slaves/, date accessed, November 26, 2017.

24. "Blacks Win 17 Grammy Awards, but Miles Davis, Motown Execs Walk Out," *Jet*, March 30, 1972, 70; "Grammy Awards 1972," *Awards Shows*, http://www.awardsandshows.com/features/grammy-awards-1972-221.html, date accessed, November 25, 2017.

25. Michelle Alexander, *The New Jim Crow: Mass Incarceration in the Age of Colorblindness* (New York: New Press, 2010).

26. Dedrick Asante-Muhammed, Chuck Collins, Josh Hoxie, and Emanuel Nieves, *The Ever-Growing Gap: Without Change, African American and Latino Families Won't Match White Wealth for Centuries* (Washington, DC: Institute for Policy Studies, 2016).

27. Mary Evans, *The Persistence of Gender Inequality* (Malden, MA: Polity Press, 2017).

28. Cynthia Hess, Jessica Milli, Jeff Hayes, and Ariane Hegewisch, *The Status of Women in the States: 2015* (Washington, DC: Institute for Women's Policy Research, 2015).

29. "Grammys 2017: Adele on Rooting for Beyoncé."

30. Angela Davis, *Blues Legacies and Black Feminism: Gertrude Ma Rainy, Bessie Smith, and Billie Holiday* (New York: Pantheon Press, 1998).

31. https://www.grammy.com, date accessed, November 15, 2017.

32. Stephen March, "The Unexamined Brutality of the Male Libido," *New York Times*, November 25, 2017, SR2.

33. Katz, *Tough Guise 2*.

34. Karen Mizoguchi, "Lady Gaga Calls the Music Industry a 'F—king Boys Club' in Emotional Speech: 'It's Really Hard for Women,'" *People*, December 12, 2015, http://people.com/celebrity/lady-gaga-calls-music-industry-a-f-king-boys-club, date accessed, November 27, 2017.

35. Eliana Dockterman, "Kathryn Bigelow: We Must End Gender Discrimination in Hollywood," *Time*, May 12, 2015, http://time.com/3856444/kathryn-bigelow-aclu-sexism-hollywood/?iid=sr-link2, date accessed, November 28, 2017.

36. Hannah Ellis-Petersen, "Kesha: Leading the Fight against Sexism at the Music Industry's Core," *The Guardian*, February 27, 2016, LexisNexis Academic, date accessed, November 28, 2017.

37. Stacy L. Smith, Marc Choueiti, and Stephanie Gall, *Asymmetrical Academy Awards 2: Another Look at Gender in Best Picture Nominated Films from 1977 to 2010* (2011), Report for Annenberg School for Communication and Journalism, University of Southern California, Los Angeles.

38. Smith, Choueiti, and Gall, *Asymmetrical Academy Awards*.

39. Ta-Nehisi Coates, "I'm Not Black, I'm Kanye," *The Atlantic*, May 7, 2018, https://www .theatlantic.com/entertainment/archive/2018/05/im-not-black-im-kanye/559763/, date accessed, June 15, 2018.

40. Coates, "I'm Not Black, I'm Kanye."

41. Michael Ryan and Douglas Kellner, *Camera Politica: The Politics and Ideology of Contemporary Hollywood Film* (Bloomington: Indiana University Press, 1988), 12–13.

42. Tricia Rose, *Hip Hop Wars: What We Talk About When We Talk About Hip Hop—and Why It Matters* (New York: Basic Books, 2008).

INDEX

abstraction, 10, 79

ACLU. *See* American Civil Liberties Union

Adderley, Julian "Cannonball," 38, 57, 116, 122

Adderley, Nat, 42

Adele, 190–92, 197

aesthetic of the real, 71–72, 84–86, 90, 98

aesthetics, types of, in American film, 71–72

African Americans: in American film industry, 17; blackness as constructed by, 15–17; infra-political in lives of, 124–25, 144; masculinity associated with, 16, 111, 132, 133, 135, 143, 186, 189; purported racism of, 112–13, 120, 126–27, 129–30, 183; racial etiquette for, 13, 17, 109–11, 114, 118–22, 125, 144

Afro-modernism, 40–43, 68–69, 113, 182–83, 191–92

Alba, Richard D., 149

Albertson, Chris, 60, 121, 129

Alexander, Michelle, 14, 191; *The New Jim Crow*, 195

Allen, Woody, 95

Allied Artists (film studio), 11

alternative rock, 11

Altman, Robert, 95

America (magazine), 155

American Civil Liberties Union (ACLU), 194

American Dream, 106, 148, 156–57, 162–65, 173, 183

American film: aesthetic types in, 71–72; digital technology and, 180; genre communities of, 71, 100–101; in Heroic Age, 9–13; hypermasculinity and, 19, 193–94; public stories of, 101; race in relation to, 17–18; themes of, 71

American Film (magazine), 75

American Film Institute, 74

American music: digital technology and, 180; in Heroic Age, 9–13; hypermasculinity and, 19, 193–94; jazz's status in, 34; race in relation to, 15–17, 181–82; social distance in, 190

American Pimp (documentary), 185

Anders, Allison, 92, 95

Anderson, Paul Thomas, *The Master*, 99

antijazz, 49, 51, 56

Araki, Gregg, 92

Armstrong, Louis, 36, 38

Arnheim, Rudolf, 78

Aronofsky, Darren, *Mother*, 178

Art Ensemble of Chicago, 50

Asbury, Herbert, *Gangs of New York*, 160

Association for the Advancement of Creative Musicians, 49

Atlanta Journal and Constitution (newspaper), 32

The Atlantic (magazine), 196

Atlantic Monthly (magazine), 83–84

Atlantic Records, 44

audience-musician relationship in modern jazz, 115–16

auteurs: avant-garde–popular tensions for, 29; commercial challenges facing, 177–79; Scorsese as model of, 28, 71, 72–77, 96–99, 147, 150, 168

autonomy: of black music, 57; characteristic of avant-garde art, 4, 5, 8; Davis and, 28; in Heroic Age, 4–8, 177–80; independent film and, 28; Scorsese and, 28, 71, 73–74, 76, 96–99, 177–78. *See also* independence

avant-garde art: American, 2, 5–6; emergence of, 5; experimental film compared to, 77–79; ideas associated with, 5; journalistic references to, 7; pure aesthetic of, 71–72, 77–83; rejection of terminology of, by black musicians, 47; significance of, in American art field, 6

Ayler, Albert, 46, 47

Ayler, Donald, 47

Back to Africa movement, 127

Baker, Chet, 134

Baker, Kevin, 161

Baldwin, James, 185, 189

Balliett, Whitney, 133
Baraka, Amiri. *See* Jones, LeRoi
Bart, Peter, 1
Baumann, Shyon, 24, 84
bebop, 27–28, 35, 38, 40, 180. *See also*
    hard bop
Beck, 189
Becker, Ron, 24
Benson, George, 53
Bergson, Henri, 80
Bernard, Jami, 161–62
Berry, Chuck, 2, 191
Beyoncé, 189–92, 197
Bicentennial, of United States (1976), 157
Bigelow, Kathryn, 193–94, 197
Billboard (magazine), 52, 53, 193
biographical legends: collective nature
    of, 105; Davis, 20–22, 105–7, 109–45;
    defined, 3, 21, 105; Scorsese, 20–22, 75,
    106–7, 146–75. *See also* public stories
Birdland, New York City, 113
Biskind, Peter, 75, 93–95, 97; *Down and
    Dirty Pictures*, 83, 94
Black Arts Repertory Theater/School, New
    York City, 49
Black Lives Matter, 195
Black Mountain College, 9
Black Music movement, 45–50, 57, 59–63,
    68–69, 182–83
black nationalism, 41, 42, 44, 46, 66, 182–83
blackness: African American construction
    of, 15–17; bebop and, 28; Davis and,
    16–17, 66–67, 111–14, 121–24, 129–30,
    138–39, 145, 182; free jazz and, 44–46,
    48–49; hard bop and, 42–43; and hyper-
    masculinity, 107; modern jazz in relation
    to, 16, 28; neoconservative commentary
    on, 66–67; sexuality associated with, 185;
    white construction of, 15
Black Panthers, 66, 136
Blake, Richard A., 187
Blakey, Art, 40
Blau, Judith R., 6
blaxploitation film, 17
"Blindfold Test" (*Down Beat* column), 37
blockbusters, 71, 89, 92–93, 95, 97
Bloodline (television series), 177
Bohlman, Philip V., 15–16
Bonilla-Silva, Eduardo, 14, 149
Boone, Pat, 2, 11
Borden, Lizzie, 92
Bourdieu, Pierre, 2, 4, 5, 8, 24, 71, 80,
    84–85, 177
Bowie, David, 131

Bowie, Lester, 57, 59
Brakhage, Stan, 10, 81, 82
Brando, Marlon, 1–2, 159
Breskin, David, 131
British Film Institute, 74
Brown, James, 48, 55, 123, 128, 137, 191
Brown, Marion, 45, 130
Brubeck, Dave, 37, 45, 113
Brunt, Stephen, 65
Buñuel, Luis, 74
Burland, Sascha, 118
Burnett, Charles, *Killer of Sheep*, 90

Cage, John, 10
Caldwell, John Thornton, 20
Canby, Vincent, 89, 168–69
Capitol Records, 35, 36
Captain America: The First Avenger (film), 97
Carlito's Way (film), 177
Carmichael, Stokely, 2
Carpenter, John, *Halloween*, 11
Cashmore, Ellis, 156
Casillo, Robert, 150–51
Cassavetes, John, 85–87, 98; *A Child Is
    Waiting*, 86; *Faces*, 87; *Love Streams*, 87;
    Shadows, 86; *Too Late Blues*, 86
Catholicism, 155–59
Cavalier (magazine), 135, 137, 138, 186
Cavallero, Jonathan J., 156
Cerulli, Don, 133
Chambers, Jack, 142
Champlin, Charles, 166–67, 168, 173
Chicago Sun Times (newspaper), 136–37
Chicago Tribune (newspaper), 137
Choice, Harriet, 137
Christie, Ian, 160
Chuck D, 191
Cieply, Michael, 95
Cimino, Michael, 150–51
Cineaste (magazine), 88, 90, 92, 169
Cinecom, 91
Cinemablend (online magazine), 96, 97
cinema verité, 86
Civil Rights Act (1964), 165, 190
Clapton, Eric, 56
Clark, Mike, 171
Clarke, Shirley, 87; *The Connection*, 86
classical music, 13, 35, 39, 41, 44, 61, 69
Cleage, Pearl, 142–43
Cleaver, Eldridge, 66
Climax (magazine), 114
Clinton, Hillary, 193, 195
Coates, Ta-Nehisi, 195–96
Cobain, Kurt, 195

Coda (magazine), 48, 53, 57, 63
Coen, Joel and Ethan, 92
Cohen, Leonard, 131
Cohu, Will, 93, 94
Cole, Bill, 57
Coleman, Ornette, 37, 44–45, 49, 61; *The Shape of Jazz to Come*, 44
Collective Black Artists, 50
collectives, for Black Music, 49
color-blind ideology, 14–16, 40, 111, 112, 119, 129, 149, 160, 164–65, 172, 181, 183–84, 191, 194–95
Coltrane, John, 38, 45–46, 48, 53, 122
Columbia Pictures, 1
Columbia Records, 36, 38, 123
Combs, Richard, 153, 167
commercial aesthetic, 71–72, 88, 90, 93, 94, 98, 100
commercialism: Black Music's failure, 48–50; Davis and, 29, 32, 38–39, 52–53, 55–56, 64–65, 69, 122; fusion jazz and, 57; Hollywood film and, 71–72; modern jazz and, 38–39; Scorsese and, 29, 88–89, 98, 172
Conn, Andrew Lewis, 70
Connell, R. W., 18–19
conservative ideology, 183–84
Cook, Pam, 165–66, 171–72
cool jazz, 35, 40, 132–34
coolness, 67, 109, 110–11, 114, 118–19, 131–34, 136, 138–39, 143–45, 184
Cooper, Karen, 90
Copland, Roger, 77
Coppola, Francis Ford, 77, 89, 95, 150–51; Godfather trilogy, 151, 154, 155, 172–73
Corea, Chick: *Light as a Feather*, 52
Corman, Roger: *Boxcar Bertha*, 12, 87, 156; *Swamp Women*, 11
Coss, Bill, 40, 115–16, 132–34
countercinema, 89–90
Craven, Wes, *A Nightmare on Elm Street*, 11
Crawford, Marc, 124, 126
Crist, Judith, 84
crossover jazz, 51–53, 56–57, 59–65, 68–69
Crouch, Stanley, 61–63, 66
Crow Jim, 112–13, 120, 126–27, 129–30, 132, 141, 183
The Crusaders, 52, 53, 56
cultural politics: of Heroic Age, 5, 13, 105, 177; in public stories, 20, 23, 24; race music and, 43. *See also* politics

Daddy Yankee, 191
Daedalus (magazine), 78
Dali Lama, 155

Dash, Julie, 92
Davis, Angela, 191
Davis, Miles, 31–69; achievements of, 33–34; autobiography of, 66, 111, 123, 138–43, 182; and autonomy, 28; awards and honors for, 56–57, 64, 65, 117, 183; biographical legend of, 20–22, 105–7, 109–45; biographies of, 57; and blackness, 16–17, 66–67, 111–14, 121–24, 129–30, 138–39, 145, 182; and boxing, 114, 119, 135; commercial success of, 32, 38–39, 52–53, 55–56, 64–65, 69, 122; coolness of, 67, 109, 110–11, 114, 118, 132, 134, 136, 138–39, 143–45, 184; criticisms of, 53–58, 64–66; death of, 31, 32, 34; early career of, 34–39; as enigma, 106, 111, 114–15, 117, 120, 123, 125–26, 131, 138, 145, 190; as "evil genius," 106, 110, 115, 131, 138, 140; and gender, 3–4, 106–7; genre communities relevant to, 27; heroin addiction of, 35, 135, 142, 144; hipness of, 67, 69, 114, 118, 132, 134–36, 138–40, 142; and hypermasculinity, 19–20, 131–40, 142, 144–45, 184–87, 189; income of, 38, 50, 122; as innovator, 35–38, 50–57; interviews with, 37, 54–56, 65–66, 116, 125–29, 135; Marsalis compared to, 32–33, 67; misinterpretations and misunderstandings of, 106, 111, 116, 118, 125–26, 132, 136, 138, 145, 186, 187; as model of middlebrow genre, 13; as model rebel, 2–3, 67–68, 111, 136, 176; musical style of, 133–34; personality/public persona of, 33, 38, 110–11, 113–45; personal style of, 38, 67, 136–37; police interactions with, 110, 113, 136–37, 182; and politics, 68, 124–25, 132, 138, 182; and popular music, 38, 56, 64–65, 69; as Prince of Darkness, 65, 115, 120, 131, 133, 135–40, 142, 186; public story of, 20–22, 31–69, 106, 120–21, 123, 125–27, 132, 134–38, 141, 145, 183, 186–87, 196–97; quintet of 1960s, 36–37; and race, 3–4, 106, 109–45; as race man provocateur, 120, 124–31, 135–36, 138–42, 176, 182, 186; and race music, 17, 28, 40–44, 54–57, 68; social identity of, 3, 23, 115, 120; as unreconstructed black man, 106, 111, 122, 124–31, 144–45; as visionary artist, 32; West compared to, 189–92; and whites in music world, 37, 54–56, 113, 115, 120–30, 135–36, 141, 181; and women, 111, 137–40, 142–43, 186; youth of, 127, 135, 136–37, 142. *See also* Davis, Miles, albums of

Davis, Miles, albums of: *Amandla*, 68, 182; *Aura*, 65; *Bitches Brew*, 50, 52, 53, 55, 56, 135; *Doo-Bop*, 22, 68, 145, 182; *In a Silent Way*, 55; *Kind of Blue*, 36; *Miles Ahead*, 36; *On the Corner*, 56; *Porgy and Bess*, 36; *Sketches of Spain*, 36; *Star People*, 65; *Sun City*, 68, 182; *Tutu*, 65, 68, 182; *Walkin'*, 40; *We Want Miles*, 65; *You're Under Arrest*, 136–37, 182

Davis, Stephen, 123

Death Wish (film), 167, 187

DeCurtis, Anthony, 75

De Fina, Barbara, 171

DeMichael, Don, 56, 122, 128

Demme, Jonathan, 92

Denby, David, 154

De Niro, Robert, 166, 170–71, 173

De Palma, Brian, 150–51

Deren, Maya, 78, 79, 80

Desmond, Paul, 37, 113

Destiny's Child, 192

The Deuce (television show), 185

digital technology, 180

DiMaggio, Paul, 7–8

Dinerstein, Joel, 110, 145

Direct Cinema, 79, 80, 82, 86, 90

Dirty Harry (film), 187

Disney-Miramax, 94

Dixieland jazz, 38, 39

DIY (do-it-yourself), 86

Dollar, Steve, 32

Dolphy, Eric, 52

Down Beat (magazine), 35, 36, 37, 39, 41, 44, 47, 49, 53, 54, 56, 58–61, 64, 68, 112, 113, 114, 127, 133, 181, 183

Doyle, Jimmy, 180–81

Dr. Dre, 143

Drive (film), 187, 195

Dr. Luke, 194

Duel in the Sun (film), 75, 152

DuVernay, Ava, 179, 197

Eastwood, Clint, *Million Dollar Baby*, 98

Easy Mo Bee, 68

Ebony (magazine), 50, 56–57, 62, 121–24, 126–27, 135, 138

Edwards, James, 17

Eldridge, Roy, 190

Elie, Paul, 155–56

Ellington, Duke, 31, 38, 67, 191; *Reminiscing in Tempo*, 41

Ellis Island Family Heritage Award, 163

Eminem, 143, 191

Encore (magazine), 56, 117, 128

Ennis, Jane, 135

Ennis, Larissa M., 156

Ephland, John, 64

Esquire (magazine), 58, 110, 124–25, 134, 185, 186

ethnicity: hypermasculinity and, 148; non-white, 164–65; off-white, 157, 160, 166, 169, 173–74, 188–89; revival of, in 1960s, 17; Scorsese and, 3–4, 17, 77, 106, 146–75, 183–84, 188–89; unmeltable, 18, 106, 148, 153, 157, 162–63, 174; whiteness as, 17–18, 147–49, 157–75, 189, 193

Europe, James Reese, 33

Europe, jazz musicians in, 50, 112

European American identity, 15, 149, 151, 161, 173–74, 184

Evans, Bill, 190

Evans, Gil, 36, 113

experimental film: avant-garde art compared to, 77–79; genre community of, 71; genre ideals of, 9–10; vs. Hollywood, 79, 81, 85; independent film compared to, 77–80, 83–86; origins of, 78; personal nature of, 81; public story of, 78–83; pure aesthetic of, 77–85; reception of, 82–84; types of, 79

experimental music, 9–10

exploitation film, 10–12

Eyerman, Ron, 4, 101

Farber, Manny, 167

Farber, Stephen, 88, 96, 97, 98

Farrell, James T., 155

Fast Company (magazine), 76

Feather, Leonard, 31, 35, 37, 50–51, 54–55, 65, 119, 127–29, 133, 138

Fellini, Federico, 70

feminist perspective, 107

Ferguson, Priscilla Parkhurst, 24

Ferrara, Abel, 150–51

Fillmore East, New York City, 54

Fillmore West, San Francisco, 54

Film Comment (magazine), 70, 96, 167, 168

Film Culture (magazine), 80, 81

FilmDallas, 91

film distributors, 91

film festivals, 91

Film Forum, New York City, 90

Film Quarterly (journal), 82, 84

First Blood (film), 187

Five Spot jazz club, New York City, 44

Flack, Roberta, 192

Flatley, Guy, 75, 152, 155, 167–68

Floyd, Samuel A., Jr., 68

Fluxus, 9

Franckling, Ken, 136–37
Franklin, Aretha, 48, 191
Franklin, Carl, 92
Frazier, Vernon, 57
freedom, 43–46
free jazz, 36, 38, 39, 44–46, 48–49, 52
French New Wave. *See* New Wave cinema
funk, 31, 40, 42, 52
fusion jazz, 37, 50–63, 68–69

Gallagher, Charles A., 21, 24, 174
Gardner, Barbara, 114, 117, 190
Garvey, Marcus, 127
gender: in American society, 18, 107, 144–45,
    148, 184–89, 191; Davis and, 3–4, 106–7;
    discrimination in American film and
    music industries, 193–94; male gender
    imagination, 185–89; musical style and,
    133–34; Scorsese and, 3–4, 106–7. *See
    also* hypermasculinity; masculinity;
    women
gender-blind ideology, 172, 191, 194–95
gender imagination. *See* male gender
    imagination
genre communities: boundary maintenance
    performed by, 9; Davis and, 27; defined,
    9; Scorsese and, 27
Georgakas, Don, 88
Geto Boys, 68
Getz, Stan, 134
Giddins, Gary, 67
Gillespie, Dizzy, 133, 190
Gleason, Ralph, 36, 39, 133, 134
Globe and Mail (Canada; newspaper), 65,
    142, 170
Godard, Jean-Luc, 73
Goldberg, Joe, 39, 114
Goldman, Albert, 58
Goldstein, Patrick, 92, 93
Goldstein, Stanley, 120, 121, 125, 126, 137–38
Gomez, Nick, 92
Gone with the Wind (film), 98
Goodman, Benny, 36, 44
Good Will Hunting (film), 97
Gosling, Ryan, 195
Grammy Awards, 189–92
Graves, Milford, 48
Gray, Herman, 15, 24, 33, 67, 132
Greeley, Andrew M., 155
Greenberg, Clement, 77
Greenwich Village, New York City, 9, 79
Gross, Terry, 159
Guardian (London; newspaper), 189
Guryan, Margo, 43

Haley, Alex, 114, 116, 186
Hamill, Peter, 162
Hammond, John, 41
Hancock, Herbie, 52, 56–57, 190; *Head-
    hunters*, 52; *Mwandishi*, 52
Hansen, Liane, 165
Hanson, John, *Northern Lights*, 90
hard bop, 36, 39–45, 51, 132–33
Harpers (magazine), 112
Harris, Eddie, 53–54
Hawks, Howard, 73, 77
Heckman, Don, 51–52, 53
Hefner, Hugh, 2, 137
Hendrix, Jimi, 56, 130, 136
Hennessey, Mike, 51
Henry, Michael, 153–54
Hentoff, Nat, 35–36, 37, 42, 46, 116, 130,
    134, 137
Heroic Age of American Art: autonomy
    in, 4–8, 177–80; characteristics of, 6;
    cultural politics of, 5, 13, 105, 177; Davis
    and Scorsese illustrative of, 3; defined, 2;
    factors contributing to, 6–8; gender in, 18,
    107, 184–89; hypermasculinity in, 19–20,
    184–89; overview of, 5–8; race in, 107,
    180–84; themes of, 23; white identity in, 15
high art, 8–10
Hill, Lauryn, 191
Hinson, Hal, 75
hip-hop, 68, 69, 145, 182
hipness, 67, 69, 114, 118, 132, 134–36, 138–40,
    142, 144–45
Hirsch, Foster, 155
Hitchcock, Alfred, 21, 147
Hoberman, J., 162
Hoefer, George, 44
Hoffa, Jimmy, 173
Hoffman, Abbie, 2
Holden, Stephen, 172–73, 185
Holiday, Billie, 191
Hollywood: commercial aesthetic of, 71–72,
    88, 90, 93, 94, 98, 100; decline of, in
    1950s, 1–2; experimental film vs., 79, 81,
    85; genre community of, 71; hegemony
    of, 28, 71; hypermasculinity in films of,
    172, 187; independent film in relation to,
    4–5, 85–90, 92–95, 177–78; production
    value of films from, 98; and race, 17;
    Scorsese and, 71, 73, 88–89, 94, 96–99,
    101, 177–78. *See also* New Hollywood
Hollywood Reporter (newspaper), 161,
    177–78
Holm, D. K., 71
hooks, bell, 136

Hopper, Dennis, *Easy Rider*, 12

Hornaday, Ann, 161

Hughes, Albert and Allen, *American Pimp*, 185

Hughes, Howard, 75

hypermasculinity: in American film and music industries, 19, 193–94; in American society, 192–95; black, 107; Davis and, 19–20, 131–40, 142, 144–45, 184–87, 189; and ethnicity, 148; in Heroic Age, 19–20, 184–89; in Hollywood films, 172, 187; Leguizamo and, 177; rise of, 18–19; Scorsese and, 19–20, 148, 156, 165–75, 185, 187–89; violence linked to, 20, 144–45; white, 107

hyphen-nationalism, 17, 147–49, 157, 160, 162–65, 172, 174–75, 184, 189, 193

Ice-T, 66, 68

Imagism, 80

immigration. *See* new immigrants

Immigration and Nationality Act (1965), 165

improvisation, 45–46

Impulse Records, 46

Inception (film), 98

independence, 2, 6, 8, 28. *See also* autonomy

Independent Feature Project, 91

independent film: aesthetic of the real in, 71–72, 84–86, 90; avant-garde–popular tensions in, 12–13; Cassavetes and, 85–87; critical success of, 84; defining, 4; development of, 85–86; experimental film compared to, 77–80, 83–86; genre community of, 12, 71, 83; Hollywood in relation to, 4–5, 85–90, 92–95, 177–78; institutionalization of, 91–92; Kramer as participant in, 1; narrative in, 90; and politics, 89–90; *politique des auteurs* in, 73–74, 80; popular art in relation to, 12–13, 29, 84; Scorsese and, 28, 71, 73, 87–89, 96–99, 177–78; sociocultural themes of, 12; as structured meaningful activity, 4–5

Indiewire (online magazine), 96

Indiewood, 93–95, 99–100

infra-politics, 124–25, 132, 138, 144

Inness, Sherrie A., 24

institutional racism, 14, 149

International Musician (magazine), 134

intersectionality, 106–7

Irwin, Meryl J., 164

Isle of Wight Festival, 54

Italian American ethnicity, 18, 106, 146–48, 150–57, 159, 162–63, 173, 183

Italian Neorealism. *See* Neorealism

Jackson, Michael, 195–96

Jacobs, Ken, 77

Jacobson, Matthew Frye, 147, 148, 164–65

James, Jeremy, 154

Jay-Z, 109, 191

jazz: antijazz, 49, 51, 56; black rejection of, 47, 55–56, 128; commercial challenges of, 50; masculinity linked to, 132–34, 186; *Playboy* and, 137; as race music, 16, 28, 33, 40–41; status of, in American culture, 34, 69; traditionalist movement in, 32–33, 59–69; white appropriation of, 28, 40–41, 47, 111–12, 130, 141, 181–82. *See also* modern jazz

Jazz and Pop (magazine), 48, 51

Jazz at Lincoln Center, 34, 67, 183

Jazz Composers Guild, 49

jazz left, 182–83

Jazz Loft, 9, 49

Jazz Magazine, 130

Jazz Messengers, 42

jazz-rock fusion. *See* fusion jazz

Jazz Times (magazine), 61, 65

Jet (magazine), 54

Jim Crow, 14–15, 47, 105–6, 111, 114, 119–20, 124–30, 136, 140, 141–42, 144, 181–83. *See also* New Jim Crow

Johnson, Brooks, 112

Jones, LeRoi (later Amiri Baraka), 45, 47–48, 138, 186

Jones, Quincy, 60, 69

Julliard School of Music, 34

Jump Cut (magazine), 89–90

Jung, C. G., 80

Kael, Pauline, 83–84, 89

Kakutani, Michiko, 74–75, 156

Kapsis, Robert E., 21

Kasdan, Lawrence, 89

Katz, Jackson, 172, 188

Kazan, Elia: *America, America*, 159–60; *On the Waterfront*, 159

Kelley, Robin D. G., 43, 124, 132, 143–44, 184–85

Kellner, Douglas, 20, 24, 196

Kelly, Mary Pat, 169

Kent, Nick, 139–40

Kenton, Stan, 45

Kermode, Mark, 155

Keyser, Les, 153

Kilday, Gregg, 168

King, B. B., 56

King, Geoff, 90; *American Independent Cinema*, 83

King, Martin Luther, Jr., 2
Kool Jazz Festival, 65
Kopple, Barbara, *Harlan County U.S.A.*, 90
Kramer, Stanley, 1–2; *Champion*, 12; *The Defiant Ones*, 17; *Home of the Brave*, 12, 17
Kurosawa, Akira, 73

Lady Gaga, 193
Lahey, John, 63
Lamar, Kendrick, 179, 192
La Motta, Jake, 166, 168–69, 173, 197
Lang, Jack, 70
Lateef, Yusef, 46
Lee, Jeanne, 130
Lee, Spike, 66, 92
Leguizamo, John, 176–77, 197; *Latin History for Morons*, 176
Leland, John, 145
Lennon, John, 143
Less, David, 58
Levy, Emanuel, *Cinema of Outsiders*, 83
Lewis, John, 45
Lewis, Ramsey, 57
Lewis, Ryan, 192
liberalism: and color-blind ideology, 14, 16, 40, 111, 119, 127, 129, 149, 164–65, 172, 174, 181, 183–84, 191, 194–95; and gender-blind ideology, 172, 191, 194–95; masculinity associated with, 172, 174
Lieberman, Paul, 152, 157–58
Lincoln, Abbey, 43, 130, 191
Lincoln Center, New York City, 34, 82
Linfield, Susan, 75
Liska, A. James, 58–60, 64
Little Italy, New York City, 74–77, 146–47, 152–56, 158–59
Little Richard, 11
Los Angeles Filmex, 91
Los Angeles Times (newspaper), 31, 92, 93, 116, 152, 154, 157–58, 161, 166–67, 168, 171, 173
Lower East Side, New York City, 159
Lubiano, Wahneema, 15
Lucas, George, 95

MacAdams, Lewis, 145
Macklemore, 192
Mailer, Norman, 185, 189
Make America Great Again, 184, 193
male gender imagination, 185–89, 195
Malick, Terrence, 77
Maltby, Richard, 72, 98
Marche, Stephen, 192–93
Marley, Bob, 131

Marsalis, Wynton, 32–34, 36–38, 59–69, 181–83, 197; *From the Plantation to the Penitentiary*, 220n7; *Standard Time, Volume One*, 62
Martin, Terry, 47
Martin, Trayvon, 110
masculinity: black, 16, 111, 132, 133, 135, 143, 186, 189; hegemonic, 18–19, 107, 148, 166, 169, 172, 186, 188, 193; jazz linked to, 132–34, 186; in male gender imagination, 185–89, 195; and male privilege, 166, 175, 186, 188–89, 191, 193. *See also* hypermasculinity
Maslin, Janet, 92, 95
Matisyahu, 191
Mazursky, Paul, 95
McBride, James, 109, 110
McCall, Steve, 139
McCarthy, Joe, 2
McNamara, Robert, 2
McPherson, Bruce, 80
McRobbie, Angela, 170, 172
Mekas, Jonas, 80, 81, 82, 86
Melody Maker (magazine), 50–51, 55, 56, 119, 131, 135
Merritt, Greg, *Celluloid Mavericks*, 83
Messner, Michael A., 19, 186
#MeToo movement, 194
Metronome (magazine), 34, 35, 45
Metronome Jazz (magazine), 35, 39–40, 115, 132, 134
Michigan Citizen (newspaper), 143
middlebrow art, 12–13
Midler, Bette, 131
Milne, Tom, 154, 170
Milwaukee Journal (newspaper), 36
Mingus, Charles, 37, 45, 112, 130, 139, 143
Miramax, 91–95
misogyny, 111, 138–39, 140, 142–44, 167, 170–71, 186–88, 193–95
Missing in Action (film), 187
Mitchell, Roscoe, 47
modal jazz, 36
modern jazz: audience-musician relationship in, 115–16; avant-garde era of, 32–33; avant-garde–popular tensions in, 12–13; blackness in relation to, 16, 28; and commercialism, 38–39; contention and controversy in, 32–33, 50–69; financial struggles of musicians, 50; genre community of, 12; neoclassical, 32–33, 59–69; politics in relation to, 42–44; popular art in relation to, 29; race in relation to, 12–13, 16, 27–28, 180–81; social distance

modern jazz (*continued*)
in, 16–17, 106, 111, 113–14, 118–20, 183; sociocultural themes of, 12
Modern Jazz Quartet, 37, 45
Monk, Thelonious, 37, 119
Monson, Ingrid, 43, 118, 130–33, 186
Monthly Film Bulletin (journal), 167, 170
Montreal Film Festival, 91
Morgan, David, 171
Morgenstern, Dan, 53
Motown, 55, 128
MovieMaker (magazine), 74
multiculturalism, 149
Mulvey, Laura, 148
Murphy, Eddie, 66
Murphy, Frederick, 56, 117, 128
Murray, David, 64
Museum of Modern Art, New York City (MoMA), 82

NAACP. *See* National Association for the Advancement of Colored People
narrative, in film, 77–79, 90
The Nation (magazine), 95
National Association for the Advancement of Colored People (NAACP), 127
National Endowment for the Humanities (NEH), 91, 157
National Observer (magazine), 47
National Rifle Association (NRA), 193
Navarro, Fats, 133
Negro Digest (magazine), 114
Negro Music, 33
Nelson, Ozzie, 2
neo-bop. *See* hard bop
neoclassical jazz, 32–33, 59–69
neoconservatism, 32, 62, 66–67, 69, 182, 183
Neorealism, 87
Netflix, 100
New American Cinema, 28, 79, 81, 85–87, 90–91, 98, 100–101
New Hollywood, 28, 70, 73, 76, 83–85, 87, 89–90, 99–100, 150–51, 188, 193. *See also* independent film
new immigrants, 161–65, 173, 183, 188
New Jim Crow, 14–15, 69, 106, 111, 138, 142, 181–82, 190–91, 194–95
Newland, Christina Marie, 166
New Line Cinema, 91
New New Wave, 92, 94–95
Newport Jazz Festival, 35–36, 53
New Republic (magazine), 66
New Sexism, 194
Newsweek (magazine), 82, 91–92, 128, 158

Newton, Huey, 66, 136
New Wave cinema, 70, 76, 86, 87
The New Wave in Jazz (album), 46, 49
New York Amsterdam News (newspaper), 116
New York Daily News (newspaper), 161–62
New Yorker (magazine), 133
New York Film Festival, 79, 81, 82
New York Magazine, 109
New York Post (newspaper), 82
New York School, 86
New York Times (magazine), 112
New York Times (newspaper), 7, 46, 74–75, 77, 82, 88, 90, 92, 95, 117, 122, 130, 137, 138, 143, 152, 153, 155, 159, 167, 168, 171, 172–73, 176, 184–85, 192
New York University (NYU), 22, 76
Nilsson, Rob, *Northern Lights*, 90
Nolan, Christopher: *Batman Begins*, 93; *Dunkirk*, 98; *Insomnia*, 93; *Memento*, 93
Norris, Chuck, 187
North Beach, San Francisco, 9
Novak, Michael, 153
NRA. *See* National Rifle Association
Nugget (magazine), 118
NYU. *See* New York University

off-white ethnicity, 157, 160, 166, 169, 173–74, 188–89
Omi, Michael, 13–14, 110
Ornette Coleman Quartet, 44

Pacino, Al, 173
Palcewski, John, 135, 137, 138
Palmer, Robert, 49–50
Panish, Jon, 118, 131–33
Parker, Charlie "Bird," 31, 34, 37, 49, 65, 180
Patterson, Patricia, 167
Payne, Alexander, 95, 97
Peirce, Kimberly, 95
Pelecanos, George, 185
Penn, Arthur, *Bonnie and Clyde*, 87
Penthouse (magazine), 54–55, 128–29, 138
Pesci, Joe, 172, 173
Peterson, James, 82
Picasso, Pablo, 39
Pierson, John, 97
pimps, 144, 184–85
Pitts, George, 126
Playboy (magazine), 112, 116, 120, 126, 128, 137, 153, 186
poetic film, 79
Poitier, Sidney, 17
politics: black musicians and, 42–44, 112, 130, 191; countercinema and, 89–90;

Davis and, 68, 124–25, 132, 138, 182; independent film and, 89–90. *See also* cultural
politics; infra-politics
politique des auteurs, 73–74, 80
popular art: Black Music movement and,
47–48; Davis and, 38, 56, 64–65, 69; high
art in relation to, 8, 10; independent film
and, 12–13, 29, 84; institutional context
of, 7–8; modern jazz and, 12–13, 29;
rebellion in, 10–12; Scorsese and, 76
Porter, Eric, 46
Pound, Ezra, 80
Prestige Records, 36
productions value, 98
progressive jazz, 40, 44–45. *See also* free jazz
Pryor, Richard, 66
Public Broadcasting System (PBS), 91
Public Enemy, 66, 68
public intellectuals, 149–51, 173
public stories: of American film, 101; of
Davis, 20–22, 31–69, 106, 120–21, 123,
125–27, 132, 134–38, 141, 145, 183, 186–87,
196–97; defined, 2–3, 20; of experimental
film, 78–83; research method for, 21–22;
scholarly significance of, 24, 196–97; of
Scorsese, 18, 20–22, 70–101, 106, 147–66,
171–75, 178, 183, 188, 193, 196–97. *See also*
biographical legends
Pullen, Don, 57
pure aesthetic, 71–72, 77–85

Quart, Leonard, 169
Queen Latifah, 68, 191
Questlove (Ahmir Khalib Thompson), 109,
110, 114

race: American film in relation to, 17–18;
American music in relation to, 15–17,
181–82; in American society, 13–18, 191;
bebop in relation to, 27–28; Davis and,
3–4, 106, 109–45; in Heroic Age, 107, 180–
84; modern jazz in relation to, 12–13, 16,
27–28, 180–81; Scorsese and, 162, 164–65,
167; social distance based on, 16–17, 106,
111, 113–14, 118–22, 131–32, 183, 190; white
ethnicity and, 149. *See also* color-blind
ideology; Jim Crow; New Jim Crow
race music: Davis and, 17, 28, 40–44, 54–57,
68; hard bop as, 40–44; hip-hop and rap
as, 69; jazz as, 16, 28, 33, 40–41; neoclassical jazz musicians on, 61–63, 67; and
politics, 43
racial etiquette, for African Americans, 13,
17, 109–11, 114, 118–22, 125, 144

racial formation, 13–16, 105–6, 149, 194–95
racial imagination: gender imagination
linked to, 189; in Heroic Age, 184; masculinity and, 107, 148, 185–86; music and,
15–16, 41, 181–84; white, 41, 106, 111, 134,
144–45, 148, 181–85, 195
Radano, Ronald, 15–16
Ramsey, Guthrie P., Jr., 40, 42
rap music, 68, 69
Raymond, Marc, 147
Reagan, Ronald, 67, 172, 187
Real Paper (newspaper), 123
rebellion: in American art, 2; characteristic
of avant-garde art, 5; Davis as model of,
2–3, 67–68, 111, 136, 176; in 1950s, 1–2;
in popular art, 10–12; Scorsese as model
of, 2–3
Redford, Robert, 91
Reed, Lou, 9, 131
Reich, Steve, 10
Reisner, Robert, 118
Reisz, Karel, 82
Renoir, Jean, 73
Rensin, David, 153
The Reporter (magazine), 42
Republican Party, 184
reverse discrimination, 183, 184. *See also*
whiteness: and claims of black racism
Rhys, Timothy, 73, 74, 76
rhythm and blues, 48
Richter, Hans, 79
Risman, Barbara J., 18
Roach, Max, 38, 40, 42–43, 112, 130, 191;
Percussion Bitter Sweet, 43; *We Insist!
Freedom Now Suite*, 42, 43
Robbe-Grillet, Alain, 145
Robey, Tim, 93–94
rock and roll music, 10–12, 128, 130
rock music, 50–52, 54–56, 58, 66, 128, 130,
135, 141
Rockwell, John, 116–17, 122
Roediger, David R., 148
Rogosin, Lionel, *Come Back, Africa*, 86
Rolling Stone (magazine), 55, 56, 75, 122, 128,
130, 131, 159
Rolling Stones, 123
Rollins, Sonny, 40, 42–43, 61, 133, 197;
Freedom Suite, 42
Romero, George: *Dawn of the Dead*, 12;
Night of the Living Dead, 11
Rose, Tricia, 24, 196
Rosenthal, Bob, 58–59
Rufus (album), 45
Russell, David O., 95

Russell, Ross, 37
Rustin, Nichole T., 131–33, 139
Ryan, Michael, 20, 24, 196

Sacramento Observer (newspaper), 38
Saint Patrick's Cathedral, New York City, 157–59
Sanborn, David, 60
Sanders, Pharoah, 48
San Francisco Chronicle (newspaper), 134
San Francisco International Film Festival, 99–100
Sarris, Andrew, 71, 84, 89
Saturday Review (magazine), 36, 121
Saunders, Jimmy, 128
Sayles, John, 92
Scene (magazine), 165–66
Schickel, Richard, 146–47
Schonfeld, Victor, 45
Scorsese, Martin: aesthetic of the real in films by, 84–85, 98; affective connection to film, 75–76; as auteur, 28, 71, 72–77, 96–99, 147, 150, 168; and authenticity, 147, 154–55, 157, 169, 174; autobiographical character of films of, 74, 75, 149–50, 153, 157–58, 166–68, 171, 173–74 (*see also* personal-passion films of); and autonomy (*see* and independent/autonomous filmmaking); awards and honors for, 70, 74, 163; biographical legend of, 20–22, 75, 106–7, 146–75; and class, 77, 156; and commercialism, 88–89, 98, 172; and ethnicity, 17–18, 77, 106, 146–75, 183–84, 188–89; film knowledge of, 74–75, 152, 159; and gender, 3–4, 106–7; genre communities relevant to, 27; and Hollywood, 71, 73, 88–89, 94, 96–99, 101, 177–78; and hypermasculinity, 19–20, 148, 156, 165–75, 185, 187–89; and independent/autonomous filmmaking, 28, 71, 73–74, 76, 87–89, 96–99, 177–78; interviews with, 72–73, 75–76, 96, 99, 153–55, 157–61, 163, 165, 167–68, 171; Italian American ethnicity of, 18, 106, 146–48, 150–57, 159, 162–63, 173, 183; as model of middlebrow genre, 13; as model rebel, 2–3; on modern jazz, 180–81; as outsider-insider, 73–74, 76–77, 85, 96–99; personal-passion films of, 96–99, 155, 160 (*see also* autobiographical character of films of); and popular film, 76; as public intellectual, 149–51, 173; public story of, 18, 20–22, 70–101, 106, 147–66, 171–75, 178, 183, 188, 193, 196–97; reputation of, 70; social identity of, 3,
23, 162; victimhood/marginalization as theme in films of, 156–57, 160, 166–68, 173, 174, 187–88; violence in films of, 165–73, 187–88; and white ethnicity, 18, 106, 146–49, 151, 157–75, 183–84, 189; women in films of, 166–67, 170–72; youth of, 74–76, 146, 152–59. *See also* Scorsese, Martin, films of
Scorsese, Martin, films of: *Alice Doesn't Live Here Anymore*, 88, 153, 156; *The Aviator*, 75, 96; *Boardwalk Empire*, 147, 160; *Boxcar Bertha*, 12, 87, 156; *Cape Fear*, 96, 153, 170–72; *Casino*, 96, 155, 156, 159–60, 172; *Color of Money*, 153; *The Departed*, 96, 147, 155, 160, 163, 172, 187; *Gangs of New York*, 94, 96, 98, 147, 157–58, 160–63, 172, 173; *Goodfellas*, 94, 96, 101, 155, 156, 159–60, 169–70, 172; *Hugo*, 96, 97, 98; *The Irishman*, 97, 99, 100, 173; *Italianamerican*, 157; *Kundun*, 96, 98, 155; *Lady by the Sea: The Statue of Liberty*, 163–65; *The Last Temptation of Christ*, 96, 153, 160; *Mean Streets*, 75, 87–88, 98, 147, 152, 154–56, 170; *My Voyage to Italy*, 74; *The Neighborhood*, 219n89; *New York, New York*, 88, 159–60, 170, 181; *A Personal Journey with Martin Scorsese through American Movies*, 74, 159; *Raging Bull*, 75, 88–89, 153, 156, 165–66, 168–70, 172–73, 187; *Shutter Island*, 96; *Silence*, 22, 96–99, 98, 101, 155, 178; *Taxi Driver*, 88, 98, 153, 166–68, 185, 187, 193; *Who's That Knocking at My Door*, 87, 98, 152, 154; *The Wolf of Wall Street*, 96–99, 101, 156, 160, 172
Scott, James C., 124
Scott, Jay, 170
Scott-Heron, Gil, 191
Seattle Film Festival, 91
Sebert, Kesha, 194, 195
Seidel, Mitchel, 181
September 11, 2001 attacks, 164
Shannon, Christopher, 162
Sheeran, Frank "The Irishman," 173
Shepp, Archie, 38, 45–48, 60, 112, 130
Sight and Sound (journal), 74, 82, 160, 170, 171
The Silence of the Lambs (film), 172
Silver, Horace, 40
Silver, Joan Micklin, *Hester Street*, 90
Simon, David, 185
Simone, Nina, 191
Sinatra, Frank, 143
Singer, Bryan: *Public Access*, 93; *Usual Suspects*, 93; *X-Men*, 93

Sitney, P. Adams, 78
Skouras, 91
Smith, Bessie, 191
Smith, Gavin, 96, 160
Smith, Kevin, 95
social distance: in American society, 131–32, 190; in modern jazz, 16–17, 106, 111, 113–14, 118–20, 183
social identity: of Davis, 3, 23, 115, 120; of Scorsese, 3, 23, 162
Soderbergh, Steven, 99–100, 179, 197; *Lucky Logan*, 100
Sontag, Susan, 10, 78–79, 90
soul jazz. *See* hard bop
soul music, 47, 48
Specialty (record label), 11
Spellman, A. B., 48
Spielberg, Steven, 70, 73, 89, 95
Spin (magazine), 127, 136
sports, 19, 186
Stallone, Sylvester, 187
Statue of Liberty–Ellis Island Foundation, 163
Steinem, Gloria, 2
Stereo Review (magazine), 51–52, 53, 60
Stern, Bert, *Jazz on a Summer's Day*, 86
Steven, Peter, 89, 90
Stevens, Cat, 131
Stitt, Sonny, 40
Stone, Oliver, 92, 172
Stone, Sly, 56, 123
Straw Dogs (film), 187
structured meaningful activity, 4–5, 20
Sundance Film Festival, 91, 94–95
Sundance Institute, 91, 92
Svoboda, Wayne, 117
Swift, Taylor, 189
swing, 29
Szwed, John, 145

Taken (film), 187
Tarantino, Quentin, 92, 95; *Hateful Eight*, 99; *Pulp Fiction*, 93
Tate, Greg, 67, 111, 144, 145
Taubin, Amy, 74
Taylor, Cecil, 45, 48–49, 130
Taylor, Clyde, 144
Tchicai, John, 45, 49
Telegraph (London; newspaper), 94
Telluride Film Festival, 91
Tepperman, Barry, 53
Terry, Clark, 53–54
Tesser, Neil, 58
Thiele, Bob, 46

Thomas, Kevin, 154
Thomson, David, 168–69
Thor (film), 97
Threadgill, Henry, 64
Thurman, Uma, 93
Time (magazine), 52, 82, 87, 110, 119, 193–94
Today's Sounds (magazine), 130–31
Tolleson, Robin, 68
Tomaševskij, Boris, 3, 21
Toronto Film Festival, 91
Townsend, Robert, 92
Tracy, Jack, 35
transcoding, 20, 23, 24, 105, 148, 150, 174, 177, 196–97
Travolta, John, 93
Troupe, Quincy, 111, 127, 136
Truffaut, François, 74
Trump, Donald, 191, 193, 195, 196
Tucker, Sherrie, 111, 143, 186
Tupac, 195
Turan, Kenneth, 171
Turner, Ike, 143
Twine, France Winddance, 21, 24, 174
Tynan, John, 41
Tyson, Cicely, 142
Tzioumakis, Yannis, *American Independent Cinema: An Introduction*, 83

Ulanov, Barry, 34, 35, 134
underground hip-hop, 11
USA Today (newspaper), 171
US Film Festival, 91

Vanderbeek, Stan, 79, 81–82
Van Peebles, Melvin, *Sweet Sweetback's Baadasssss Song*, 12
Variety (magazine), 82
Velvet Underground, 9
Vestron, 91
videocassettes, 91
Vietnam War, 172
Village Voice (newspaper), 67, 74, 80, 82, 86, 144
violence: Davis and, 111, 117, 135–36, 140, 142–43; Hillary Clinton subject to threats of, 193; hypermasculinity linked to, 20; in Scorsese's films, 165–73, 187–88; women as target of, 19, 140, 142–43, 166, 170–72, 185

Wallace, George, 2
Wall Street Journal (newspaper), 117
Wan, James, *Saw*, 11
Warhol, Andy, 10

Warner Brothers, 123
Washington, Grover, Jr., 53, 57, 58–59; *Winelight*, 58
Washington, Kamasi, 179
Washington Post (newspaper), 75
Waters, Mary C., 149
Watts, Michael, 130–31
Weather Report, 52, 57, 58; *Heavy Weather*, 58; *Mr. Gone*, 58
Weinraub, Bernard, 72–73
Weinstein, Harvey, 195
West, Hollie I., 61
West, Kanye, 189–92, 195–97
Westhoff, Ben, 189–90
Weston, Randy, *Uhuru Africa*, 42
whiteness: and appropriation of jazz, 28, 40–41, 47, 111–12, 130, 141, 181–82; and claims of black racism, 112–13, 120, 126–27, 129–30, 183; Davis and, 37, 54–56, 113, 115, 120–30, 141; as ethnicity, 17–18, 147–49, 157–75, 184, 189, 193; in Heroic Age, 15; and hypermasculinity, 107; ideology of, 175; racial imagination associated with, 144–45; and racial resentment, 184; Scorsese and, 18, 106, 146–49, 151, 157–75, 183–84, 189

whiteness studies, 15
white privilege, 15, 120, 122, 125, 148–49, 165, 175, 182–84, 186, 188–89, 195
Whitney Museum of American Art, 77
Whodini, 68
The Wild One (film), 1
Williams, Bert, 109
Williams, Martin, 36, 134
Willis, Bruce, 93
Wilson, Cassandra, *Traveling Miles*, 183
Wilson, John S., 134
Winant, Howard, 13–14, 110
Wizard of Oz (film), 98
women: Davis and, 111, 137–40, 142–43; in Scorsese's films, 166–67, 170–72; socio-cultural marginalization of, 18, 19, 143; violence against, 19, 140, 142–44, 166, 170–72, 185
Wonder, Stevie, 131, 192

Young, Steve, 46, 49
Young Lions, 33, 62–63, 67

Zimmerman, Paul, 154
Zolberg, Vera L., 6
zoot suits, 110

A NOTE ON THE TYPE

This book has been composed in Adobe Text and Gotham. Adobe Text, designed by Robert Slimbach for Adobe, bridges the gap between fifteenth- and sixteenth-century calligraphic and eighteenth-century Modern styles. Gotham, inspired by New York street signs, was designed by Tobias Frere-Jones for Hoefler & Co.